A PRACTICAL GUIDE FOR PASTORS, COUNSELORS AND FRIENDS

CRISIS

counseling

UPDATED AND EXPANDED

A PRACTICAL GUIDE FOR PASTORS, COUNSELORS AND FRIENDS

CRISIS counseling

what to do and say during the first 72 hours

H. NORMAN WRIGHT

Regal Books

Published by Regal Books
A Division of Gospel Light
Ventura, California 93006
Printed in U.S.A.

Regal Books is a ministry of Gospel Light, an evangelical Christian publisher dedicated to serving the local church. We believe God's vision for Gospel Light is to provide church leaders with biblical, user-friendly materials that will help them evangelize, disciple and minister to children, youth and families.

It is our prayer that this Regal Book will help you discover biblical truth for your own life and help you meet the needs of others. May God richly bless you.

For a free catalog of resources from Regal Books/Gospel Light please contact your Christian supplier or call 1-800-4-GOSPEL.

This is a revised edition of H. Norman Wright's previously published book *Crisis Counseling,* by Here's Life Publishers, Inc., San Bernardino, California.

Any omission of credits is unintentional. The publisher requests documentation for future printings.

Library of Congress Cataloging-in-Publication Data
Wright, H. Norman.
    Crisis counseling: what to do during the first 72 hours / H. Norman Wright.
      p. cm.
    Includes bibliographical references.
    ISBN 0-8307-1611-4
    1. Pastoral counseling. 2. Crisis intervention (Psychiatry)
I. Title.
BV4012.2.W753   1993   93-10514
253.5- -dc20   CIP

1 2 3 4 5 6 7 8 9 10 11 12 13 14 / 02 01 00 99 98 97 96 95 94 93

Rights for publishing this book in other languages are contracted by Gospel Literature International (GLINT). GLINT also provides technical help for the adaptation, translation, and publishing of Bible study resources and books in scores of languages worldwide. For further information, contact GLINT, Post Office Box 4060, Ontario, California, 91761-1003, U.S.A., or the publisher.

CONTENTS

"Post-Traumatic Stress Disorder involves a crisis but the concern is the *response* to the crisis more than the event."

"As a counselor, it is vital that you be sensitive to the leading of the Holy Spirit concerning when to bring in Scripture and what Scriptures to discuss."

INTRODUCTION:

Anatomy of a Crisis

During the early 1960s I served on the staff of a large church as a minister of Christian education and youth. One Sunday evening we had a minister from another church as a guest speaker. His presentation had a dramatic effect upon every person in attendance. When it came time for the message, he stood up, walked to the pulpit, and without a note or opening a Bible proceeded to recite eight passages of Scripture from memory as the basis for his message.

The minister then said to the congregation, "Tonight I would like to share with you what to say and what not to say, what to do and what not to do at the time of bereavement." He paused, and I saw from my vantage point on the platform that every person in the congregation was searching for a piece of paper on which to record the principles the speaker was about to discuss. I, too, looked for some paper, and I still have those notes from that message. He gave all of us the help and guidance we needed, because we had not known what to say or do when someone has lost a loved one. (This is why people sometimes avoid a bereaved person or family.)

The practicality of that night is etched in my memory, and I have thought so often, *What would happen if pastors equipped their people for many of life's crises such as this one? We would have helping and caring congregations. We could do a much better job in reaching out to those in need.*

Life Is a Series of Crises

The journey through life is a series of crises—some are predictable and expected and some are total surprises. Some crises are developmental and some are situational. You as a minister or lay counselor probably have experienced many crises in your own life, and you know how it feels. Being alive means that we constantly have to resolve problems. Every new situation we encounter provides the opportunity to develop new ways of using our resources in order to gain control. Sometimes we have to try over and over again because our first efforts do not work. But by being persistent, we discover ways to overcome these problems. And when a similar problem confronts us in the future, we find it easier to resolve because of what we learned in the past.

One day, however, we encounter a change or problem that seems beyond our capacity to cope. When a problem is overwhelming, or when our support system, either within ourselves or from others, doesn't work, we are thrown off balance. This is called a *crisis*. And if anyone is ever called upon more than others to help during a time of crisis, it is the minister. Crises are a part of life. They should be anticipated and expected to occur. They are inevitable.

Helping Role of Ministry

Helping those in crisis can be a very important phase of one's ministry. Two of the tasks of the church's ministry are to equip all members to better handle their own crises and to equip them to help other people in crisis. The principles of understanding a crisis and helping others in crisis can be taught in sermons and classes. The reason people hesitate to become involved in the lives of others is that they feel inadequate—they don't know what to do or say. Even as a trained minister, you may have struggled with those same feelings and perhaps have even hesitated in getting involved in some crisis situations. This is a normal response.

All of us in ministry or professional counseling have felt the pangs of inadequacy at one time or another and will continue to feel them the rest of our lives. There is always more to learn, and our skills can always stand refining.

I will share with you some of my counseling experiences over the years. They are no different from what you will encounter as you minister in your church. As you read them, take the time to visualize the situation and the people involved as if you are the one they have come to for help. Consider two important questions: How would you feel? What would you do? Too many people bypass the first question and focus only upon resolving the problem. But our feelings affect what we do.

Crisis Examples

A woman from your congregation comes into the church office without an appointment and asks to see you. She is visibly shaken, and you ask her to come in and sit down. She says, "The police just left our house. They came to the door this morning and asked to see my husband. When he came into the room, they told us that he had been accused by three of the neighborhood children of sexually molesting them. He says that he did not. But the neighbors filed the complaint. What are we going to do? He wouldn't talk to me about it, and he has left. I don't know where he went. What should I do?" How would you feel, and what would you do?

You have been called to the hospital by the members of a man's family. You don't know much about the situation, and when you walk in you are met by the wife and the man's doctor. The doctor says the man is terminally ill and in such an upset emotional state that they have not told him of his condition. The husband is calling for a minister to talk with, but the doctor advises you to be careful what you say about his condition. You enter the room and immediately the man says to you, "I want to ask you something. Am I going to die? Do you know? Can you tell me? Am I going to die?" How would you feel, and what would you say and do?

A man walks into your office and you recognize him as one of the leading elders of your church. He is crying and with a pained expression on his face cries out, "She left me! I came home today and she was gone! Why? Where is she? Why did she leave? I didn't know there was any problem in our marriage! But she left! She said she didn't love me anymore and she is moving in with another man! Why? Why? Why?" How would you feel, and what would you say or do?

You are sitting in your office at church and the phone rings. You answer and a man on the other end of the line states that he wants to talk with you. He will not give his name or any information that would identify him. He says he is recently divorced from his wife. He explains that he is a Christian and wants to do the Lord's will. His wife is living with another man and has the children with her. He begins to talk with you about what the Bible says about suicide. He states that the only thing keeping him from taking his life is that he feels he would go to hell if he did it. He also feels, however, that it would be better to be out of this life, and he doesn't want his children to be with his wife, who is "wicked." He does not want his children to go through what he has gone through in this life. He also states indirectly that it would be nice to have them with him wherever he goes. How would you feel, and what would you say?

A woman makes an appointment to see you. You realize this is the person you heard about from another church member. She recently lost her fifteen-year-old son in a tragic accident. He fell out of the back of a pickup truck and landed on his head on the pavement. For eight days he lingered in a coma at the hospital. During that time the mother never left his side. The rest of the family would come and go, but she was there all the time, fasting and praying for the son's recovery. On the seventh day he began to respond, and then all of a sudden, after their hopes had been raised, he died. As she sits in your office, she looks at you and says, "Where was God during this time? Why did He punish me in this way? He took my son after He gave me hope that he would recover. I will...never...recover! I will live a living death until I can go to be with my son." How do you feel, and what would you say or do?

Bizarre Crisis

I will describe one last situation that was bizarre. It happened years ago when I was on the staff of my church. On several occasions I have asked myself what I would have done and said if I had actually met this person I am going to describe.

I arrived at church about 6:00 on Wednesday evening. As I went into my office, I checked the mailbox that had an opening on the outside of the building. In the box was a Bible. I did not think too much about it, assuming one of the high school students probably left it there. After the youth meeting, I glanced at the inside of the Bible. I was a bit surprised to find a color photograph of a man in a camouflage army suit with a bandolier of shells over his shoulder and a rifle in his hand. In the background were two other guns propped up against the wall. And then I noticed that there were several pages of what appeared to be a diary in the first part of the Bible. I began to read.

Lord Jesus, I believe you died for my sins on the cross. I receive you as my personal Savior and Lord. I invite you into my heart and life as best I know how. I turn over my life to you. Take me and run my life for your glory.

The love of Jesus has not captured the hearts of the little world around me. All who betray me in how ever small a matter also betray their Creator. I know that I am an authentic Christian artist. I trust that this truth is ringing through on my tapes. Soon I will be recording again and will send these tapes to everyone in the business. But I am under electronic surveillance and by minority manipulation I am kept from my rightful place in society.

All the women they brainwash or manipulate in my environment will never change me. They simply cannot control me no more than they can make me a tree. It is a strong weapon, their ability to influence women in this way.

That is the whole story: God created me to live as a singer, actor and a strong man, and the profane humanitarians have mocked God.

When they burn and destroy the Federal in-justice building, and burn the bill of rights, the U.S. constitution and all our so-called heritage documents, the whole world, the hypocrisy—then I will pay my taxes.

Robert Kennedy's brother was assassinated; so is mine. Only my brother still lives; his mind was assassinated against me.

Too many so-called Christians bear false witness.

I see no reason to continue this hypocrisy! Dear World, I'm not so much worried nor concerned with eternal life. I'd just like to know or have just a little of life right now. I am not living; merely existing. Psalm 19:13; 54:3; 55:17; 59:2,4; Jeremiah 23:1.

(Written to Police, State of California)

Many strange things happened at this house. The owner has proven himself an evil man.

If I die as the actor-singer that I am, then it is God's doing. If I die running these guns, fighting for self-determination and refusing to have my life nullified as it is being. So if my guns speak, the great society is the cause; I am only the effect. Remember world how many years and how many days this infamous crime of nullifying my life I held out alone against impossible odds. So I apologize for the blood I spill for I have been assassinated countless times. I, when I ever become a danger to society at large, find the causes for I have convicted them for many years. There are evil forces at work now in this world.

I'm going to meet God long, long before my time. Those who pursue me, and there is much evidence that they do, are the cause of my dying and lack of my progress here in California or anywhere. Whose influence is it?

This is a religious conspiracy as well as political or by the police. Both Christians and Jews are part of this conspiracy but it is truly a conspiracy and America has not been America to me. Love, Tom.

All the Masons I've known are without a doubt, Godless men. They play a heavy part of the influence behind this conspiracy. Washington and Jefferson, were they aware of today's Masons, would disassociate themselves and say _____ on them for they are evil.

My food has been drugged here. In defense of Masons, I'd like to say Charles, the husband of my landlady_____, is a fine man and certainly not like those I've written of who were conditioned against me. Her deceased husband was also a Mason, and I'm certain he was a fine man or a good woman.

God's word will keep you from sin or sin will keep you from God's word—Navigators.

It's a shame in this so-called society that some of us must die in order to be understood or believed in. I guess it was ever thus but certainly I'm not saying I'm one of the great men in this *book*

Especially the crime of those who pursue me, the profane humanitarians are trying to make a common man out of us. All the help they claim they are doing is to destroy me, make me ridiculous in society. All they do is destroy me because they do not know the mind God has given me, and not a mind they think I should have. I realize now that I should be in show biz as an actor-singer. All they are doing to prevent my taking my rightful place in society, proves to me that they mock God here in this once proud land. I repeat, I can only be the man God created. I cannot live the way they want me to. Right now I just exist, and I'm not living. I have God-given creative talents being denied and stopped by my enemies. I am aware that each society and religion for that matter, have created their own devils. I guess that is what their purpose is, those who pursue me. I'm obviously their devil. I see it so well in my own brother's psychological makeup. To him I'm his devil, but it's only in his mind not in my heart, certainly not my mind.

At the bottom of one page was the owner's name. I took the Bible with me and went home. It was past 10:00 P.M., but when I arrived my wife was concerned. Her mother had called from an adjacent city and told her about a police hunt and gunfight that had just occurred. It appeared that a man had entered a pharmacy and abducted one of the customers. He took the woman in his car to a hillside area with the police in pursuit, and after some shooting the man was apprehended and the hostage was released. There had been a statewide search for the man during the day.

It seems that this man was distraught and suicidal. He had sought out a pastor of a church that morning about five miles from our church. For three hours the minister talked with him. When the man left, he was still determined to take his life and decided to arrange a situation in which he would be killed by a police officer. He drove onto one of the freeways and raced at speeds in excess of 100 miles per hour until he attracted the attention of a state patrolman. Once he was stopped, he got out of his car and took out a rifle. As he began to point it at the patrolman, he was hoping the officer would respond by drawing his own gun and shooting him. For some reason, however, the officer was either slow in responding or did not see what was occurring, and this man shot and killed him. Later he entered the store previously mentioned and kidnapped a person.

After hearing all of this story, I decided to listen to the 11:00 P.M. news to see if there was any further information. There was. The story was told again in detail, and the newscaster mentioned the name of the suspect. When I heard it, I realized that I had just seen that name. I went back to the Bible I had discovered at church and read the man's name. The suspect and the owner of this Bible were one and the same! I called the highway patrol and told them what I had in my possession. They were very eager to have the Bible and the letters.

At some point during that tragic day, that man came by our church hoping to talk to someone. Not finding anyone available, he left his Bible in my mailbox. In his own way this was a cry for help, a cry that said, "Help me! Save me! Stop me!" What would I have said or done had I been there? How would I have felt? How would you have felt? What would you have done or said had you been there?

I'm sure you could add to this list many experiences and stories of your own.

Potential Crisis Situations

There is no limit to the number of crisis experiences that occur in life. Think of the possibilities.

The loss of a job, the loss of a friend or supporting person, or of a position of status and respect; an incapacitating illness, operation or accident; the death of a parent, friend, spouse, or child; the news that you are terminally ill; discovering a child is on drugs or is a homosexual; discovering a handicap in yourself or another family member; an abortion or an unwanted pregnancy; a hurricane, earthquake or tornado occurring; a suicidal attempt; separation or divorce; a child custody battle; being drafted or discharged.

A sudden spiritual experience that affects other family members; discovering your child is a member of a cult; miscarriage or premature birth; a lawsuit; parents having to be put into a home for the aged; one spouse experiencing a mid-life crisis; living with a chronically depressed person; discovering you or a spouse has Alzheimer's disease or Huntington's corea; having a heart attack and bypass operation with ensuing loss of memory for your newly married spouse; the list never ends.

None of these crisis situations is fictitious. They are all real. And you and I may be called to minister to real people in such situations.

This book is for pastors and lay counselors in the church setting. It will provide biblical principles, general instruction in crisis counseling and detailed advice for dealing with specific kinds of crisis situations. Finally, we will conclude with a matter almost as important as knowing how to counsel, and that is knowing when to refer a person to someone with more expertise than yourself.

WHAT IS a CRISIS?

1

The Word of God describes many people in a state of crisis. Paul was one of them.

> Now Saul, still breathing threats and murder against the disciples of the Lord, went to the high priest, and asked for letters from him to the synagogues at Damascus, so that if he found any belonging to the Way, both men and women, he might bring them bound to Jerusalem. And it came about that as he journeyed, he was approaching Damascus, and suddenly a light from heaven flashed around him; and he fell to the ground, and heard a voice saying to him, "Saul, Saul, why are you persecuting Me?" And he said, "Who art Thou, Lord?" And He said, "I am Jesus whom you are persecuting, but rise, and enter the city, and it shall be told you what you must do." And the men who traveled with him stood speechless, hearing the voice, but seeing no one. And Saul got up from the ground, and though his eyes were open, he could see nothing; and leading him by the hand, they brought him into Damascus. And he was three days without sight, and neither ate nor drank (Acts 9:1-9).

This is one of the most famous accounts of a sudden religious conversion, and frequently such a conversion can precipitate a crisis. It is an excel-

lent example of some of the characteristics of a crisis. This experience affected Paul in many ways. It affected him physically, for he could not see and
had to be led by the hand into the city. He was changed spiritually, for he
became a believer and reversed his whole pattern of responding to Christians.
He was affected mentally and emotionally, for he didn't eat or drink for three
days. His conversion caused a crisis, or turning point, and in his case for the
better.

We have talked about the word "crisis," but to properly minister to
others we need to become expert in understanding its meaning. Webster
defines crisis as a "crucial time" and "a turning point in the course of anything." This term is often used for a person's internal reaction to an external
hazard. A crisis usually involves a temporary loss of coping abilities, and the
assumption is that the emotional dysfunction is reversible. If a person effectively copes with the threat, he then returns to prior levels of functioning.

The Chinese character for crisis is made up of two symbols: one is for
despair and the other for opportunity. When doctors talk about a crisis, they
are talking about the moment in the course of a disease when a change for
the worse or better occurs. When some counselors talk about a marital crisis,
they are talking about turning points when the marriage can go in either
direction: it can move toward growth, enrichment and improvement; or it
could move toward dissatisfaction, pain, and, in some cases, dissolution.

When people are thrown off balance by the ensuing event, they are
then experiencing a crisis. The term is frequently misused. It is applied incorrectly to even everyday annoyances. The terms "stress" and "crisis" are used
interchangeably but incorrectly, as we will see later on.

A crisis can be the result of one or more factors. It can be a problem
that is too great or overwhelming, such as the death of a child. It could be a
problem that to most people is not serious but for a given person has special
significance and so becomes overwhelming for that individual. It could be a
problem that comes at a time of special vulnerability or when the person is
unprepared. Ordinarily people handle a stopped-up sink with no problem. But
if it happens when they are sick, they may feel overwhelmed. It could occur
when the person's normal coping mechanisms are not functioning well or
when the person does not have support from others whom he or she needs.

Crisis is not always bad. Rather, it represents a pivotal point in a person's life. Therefore, it can bring opportunity as well as danger. As people
search for their methods of coping, they may choose paths of destruction—

but they may also discover new and better methods than they previously had available.

Four Common Elements of a Crisis

First Element: A Hazardous Event

A hazardous event is some occurrence that starts a chain reaction of events culminating in a crisis. A young wife who prepared for her career for seven years now discovers she is pregnant. A college senior who gave himself to football all during school in order to be selected by the pros shatters an ankle while hiking. A widower raising five preadolescent children loses his job in a very specialized profession. All of these people have much in common. It is important for the person in crisis and for the helpers to identify the precipitating events.

Second Element: The Vulnerable State

The person must be vulnerable for the crisis to occur. Even going without sleep for two nights can make a person vulnerable to a situation that he or she would usually handle with no difficulty. Being ill or depressed lowers coping mechanisms. Recently I talked with a woman who wanted to give up her foster child, cancel an important fund-raising event and quit her business. She was depressed over the threat of another loss in her life. I asked her not to make any decision during her time of depression, because such decisions are often regretted later.

Third Element: The Precipitating Factor

The precipitating factor is the "straw that broke the camel's back." Some people seem to hold together very well during a time of extreme loss or heartache and then fall apart over a broken dish or a dropped glass. These were the last straw, but the reaction and tears are in response to the serious loss.

Fourth Element: The State of Active Crisis

When a person can no longer handle the situation, the active crisis develops.

Here are four indications of this state.

1. *Symptoms of stress—psychological, physiological, or both.* This could include depression, headaches, anxiety, bleeding ulcers. Some type of extreme discomfort is always present.

2. *An attitude of panic or defeat.* The person may feel that he has tried everything and nothing works. Therefore, he feels like a failure—defeated, overwhelmed and helpless. There is no hope. He has two ways of responding at this time: one is becoming agitated with behavior that is unproductive. This could include pacing, drinking, taking drugs, fast driving or getting into a fight. The second way of responding is to become apathetic. An example is excessive sleeping.

3. *The focus is on relief.* "Get me out of this situation!" is the concern and cry. The person wants relief from the pain of the stress. He is not in a condition to deal with the problem in a rational way. Sometimes people in crisis may appear to be in a daze or even respond in bizarre ways. They are somewhat frantic in their efforts and will look to others for help. They may become overly dependent upon others to help them out of their dilemma

4. *A time of lowered efficiency.* People in active crisis may continue to function normally, but instead of responding at 100 percent, their response may be at about 60 percent. The greater the threat from the person's appraisal of the situation, the less effective the coping resources will likely be. They may be aware of this, which further discourages them.

The appraisal aspect of any situation is an important part of the crisis sequence. The appraisal is what people "make" of an event. Every person has his or her own way of perceiving an event. The person's beliefs, ideas, expectations and perceptions all come together at this time to evaluate a situation as crisis or noncrisis. And it is important in helping people to try to see the event through their eyes and not your own. The death of a close friend is appraised from several points: how close the relationship was, how often they were in touch with one another, how the person has responded to other losses and how many losses there have been recently. A widow deeply involved in her husband's life perceives her loss differently from a close friend, a business associate or the uncle her husband saw once every five years.

Most people experiencing a crisis perceive the loss or threatened loss of something that is important to them. Even a job promotion can bring a sense of loss that precipitates a crisis.

John enjoyed the camaraderie with the other salesmen in the car agency. Then he was promoted to sales manager. This gave him status, more money and changes in the relationships. He was not on the same level as the salesmen anymore and in fact now had to push and urge them to make their sales quotas. John did not like this, and he became so dissatisfied that he began to call in sick to avoid the conflicts.

Balancing Factors

Some people feel that a problem will not lead to a crisis unless there are deficiencies in one or more of the balancing factors of a person's life.

Adequate perception is one of these factors—the way a problem is viewed and the meaning it has for the person. If their daughter gets a divorce, the parents could feel this is the greatest possible tragedy and a negative commentary on their ability to raise a daughter. Other parents, however, would not feel this way at all.

An adequate network is a second balancing factor. This involves having a group of friends, relatives or agencies that can give support during a problem. This is where the Body of Christ has the potential of being one of the greatest support groups ever available if they know how to respond to the person in need.

The coping mechanisms most of us lean upon is the third balancing factor. If these do not function well or break down, a crisis can be experienced. These mechanisms could involve rationalization, denial, finding new information in a book, praying, reading Scripture and so on. The greater the number and diversity of coping methods, the less likely the possibility of a person's experiencing a crisis.

Limited duration is the final factor. People cannot exist in a crisis state for an extended period of time. Something must be done and there must be some resolution. Experience and research shows that a crisis ends and balance is restored within a maximum of six weeks. The equilibrium may be different from before, but at least there is some balance.

It is sometimes easier to help the person who is in the state of active crisis, for those who are hurting the most are often motivated to make significant changes in their lives.

Transition as a Source of Crisis

Not all crises are unexpected. Another type of crisis is the predictable event. An event that is part of the planned, expected or normal process of life can actually lead to a crisis. Life is full of many transitions. A *transition* is a "period of moving from one state of certainty to another, with an interval of uncertainty and change in between."[1]

Many transitions occur throughout life that have the potential for becoming a crisis: the transition from being single to being married; the transition from the twenties to the thirties and the thirties to the forties; from being a couple to being parents; from being parents to the empty nest; from the empty nest to becoming grandparents; from being employed to retirement.

Many of these events we can see looming closer to the horizon. And a person can prepare for them and even rehearse mentally what he or she will do when they arrive. New information can be gathered to assist in the transition process.

One teacher who realized he would be having to retire in 10 years began to expand his interests. He started to take courses at the local college in subjects he thought he might have an interest in, took up photography, and began reading in areas he had never considered before. He began developing a list of projects he would like to tackle, health and finances permitting, upon retirement. As there would be a significant loss in his life—his job and livelihood—he planned in advance for a variety of replacements and worked through some of those feelings of loss. He developed hobbies and interests that could be enjoyed whether his health was good or poor. Through anticipation he eliminated the possibility of seeing this transition become a crisis.

Changing Roles

If moving through the various stages of life occurred smoothly and everything was predictable, life would be fairly easy for most mature people. But two factors must be considered. First, many people are not mature or able to take responsibility because of being stuck in their development at an earlier stage. Second, many changes are not so predictable or do not occur at the time we have planned.

Consider for a moment the additional changes that can occur as we move through life. We may take on some new roles such as becoming a part-time student while continuing as a homemaker or full-time employee. We may become foster parents while still parenting our own children. Or we may exchange one significant role for another. We might become divorced and so give up a spouse. We may graduate from school and become a full-time employee.

We give up some roles and do not replace them with others. These include retiring from work without finding a fulfilling role in retirement, losing a spouse without remarrying, or giving up being a parent (the empty nest) without taking on an outside job or becoming a grandparent.

We can also experience geographical changes such as moving from one country to another, from the rural south to the urban east coast, or from mid-city to the suburbs.

Socioeconomic shifts include shifting from the lower to the middle class or from the upper to the lower.

Physical changes include going from a hearing person to a nonhearing, from being confined to a wheelchair for years to regaining the ability to walk, and from being obese to becoming trim.

Transitions may be swift or gradual and may have a positive or devastating impact upon the person's life. All transitions, however, have the potential for being a crisis experience depending upon the person involved. Even the experience of a spouse's becoming a Christian has been the catalyst for a crisis in some families. Dr. Lloyd Ahlem discusses this experience in depth in his book *Living with Stress*. (For additional information, please see the listing of books at the conclusion of this chapter.)

The ministry of churches, if we are going to lessen some of life's crises, is to prepare our congregations in advance for the changes they will experience. This involves educating them to these stages of life and the actual transition they will go through, and helping them apply God's Word so they are better able to handle life's sudden changes as well as the predictable.

Mid-life Changes

Mid-life! Much has been said and written about this stage of life. The mid-life years can be a time of reminiscence, growth, challenge and delight, or a time of pain, frustration, frantic searching and anger. We see book after book written about the male mid-life crisis until we come to believe that a crisis is inevitable for every man. The fact is, it is not. Only a minority of men experience a mid-life crisis, whereas all men go through a mid-life transition, which is a normal process.

The term "male mid-life crisis" literally means changes in a man's personality. These changes usually occur rapidly and are substantial, thus appearing both dramatic and traumatic. At this time a man becomes aware of how he is changing physically and mentally, and even his values change. He reacts to these changes with other changes. For some, the changes are threatening. For a Christian, they present an opportunity to apply his faith and develop further toward maturity. It is not a bum-out time of life, but a time of both harvest and new beginning, a time of enrichment and stability. Our interpretation of life and its events can change. The dismay and despair of confronting disappointments and unreached expectations can be shifted to realistic acceptance. As we learn from the past, the future can be different.

David C. Morley puts it this way:

> To the Christian these middle-life changes have a different meaning. The change that is so threatening to the nonbeliever is an opportunity for the Christian to exercise his faith and to experience the process of true Christian maturity. The mature Christian is a person who can deal with change. He can accept all of the vicissitudes of life and not deny nor complain about them. He sees them all as the manifestation of God's love. If God loves me, then He is going to provide an experience that makes life richer and more in line with His will. To the Christian, "All things work together for good to them that love God..." (Romans 8:28). How often we hear that Scripture quoted. How little we see it applied to real-life experiences. What God is really saying is that we should comfort ourselves with the thought that what happens in our lives, victory or defeat, wealth or poverty, sickness or death, all are indications of God's love and His interest in the design of our lives. If He brings sickness to us, we should be joyful for the opportunity to turn to Him more completely. So often in the bloom of health, we forget to remember the God who has provided that health. When we are in a position of weakness, we are more likely to acknowledge His strength, we are more likely to ask His guidance every step of the way.[2]

The ideal is that a Christian be able to respond positively to the changes at mid-life. But unfortunately this does not always happen. Why? In most cases it is because too many of those in our churches are not aware of the various transitions of life, especially mid-life. And they have not been prepared for these transitions in order to prevent a crisis. It is possible for a man to avoid the crisis by preparing for mid-life in the following ways:

1. Building his sense of identity upon a solid basis and not upon his occupation and how well he does there.
2. Becoming more complete in his humanity by experiencing, accepting and expressing his feelings.
3. Developing strong and close friendships with other men.
4. Preparing for life's changes and crises by incorporating God's Word into his life.

At this point I would suggest you read two specific books and consider using a curriculum that covers these transitions of life. The books are *Seasons of a Marriage*, by this author—see especially chapters 4 and 5 on the mid-life crisis—and *Men Without Friends* by David Smith (Thomas Nelson Publishers).

People's Needs in Crisis

What are people likely to want from you when they seek you out at a time of crisis? People's needs vary. Do not be surprised by the wide range of requests you hear. In many cases, people will expect you to be the miracle worker. You are their last hope, and their expectations are excessive, unrealistic or both. And when you cannot produce what they want, don't be surprised if they become disappointed or angry. Yet you will be able to help in other ways that will meet some of their needs.

What are some of the types of people who will seek you out for counseling? Aaron Lazare and his associates conducted a survey of the types of patients who visited a psychiatric walk-in clinic. They were able to isolate 14 different categories that represent the wide variety of types of counselees who need crisis intervention work. Their categories appear here in adapted form.

1. Counselees who want a strong person to protect and control them. "Please take over for me."

2. Those who need someone who will help them maintain contact with reality. "Help me know that I am real."
3. Those who feel exceedingly empty and need loving. "Care for me."
4. Those who need a counselor to be available for a feeling of security. "Always be there."
5. Those ridden with obsessive guilt who seek to confess. "Take away my guilt."
6. Those who urgently need to talk things out. "Let me get it off my chest."
7. Those who desire advice on pressing issues. "Tell me what to do."
8. Those who seek to sort out their conflicting ideas. "Help me to put things into perspective."
9. Those who truly have a desire for self-understanding and insight into their problems. "I want counseling."
10. Those who see their discomfort as a medical problem that needs the ministrations of a physician. "I need a doctor."
11. Those who seek some practical help such as economic assistance or a place to stay. "I need some specific assistance."
12. Those who credit their difficulty to ongoing current relationships and want the counselor to intercede. "Do it for me."
13. Those who want information about where to get help to satisfy various needs, actually seeking some community resource. "Tell me where I can get what I need."
14. Nonmotivated or psychotic persons who are brought to the counselor against their own will. "I want nothing."[3]

Characteristics of Troubled People

Of the various people who seek your help some will cope quite well with their crises, and others quite poorly. It is possible to predict which will be which.

Overwhelmed. The first characteristic of those who cope poorly is that they are nearly overwhelmed in a crisis. Prior to the crisis they are emotionally weak. They respond in a way that makes matters worse, but from their perspective they are doing the most efficient thing possible. This is because they were already hurting emotionally.

Poor physical condition. The second characteristic of those who cope poorly in a crisis is a poor physical condition. Those who have some type of physical ailment or illness have less resources to draw on during a crisis. If you notice poor coping skills during difficult times, recommending a physical examination is important.

Hard time coping. Third, those who deny reality have a hard time coping with a crisis. Denying reality is their attempt to avoid their pain and anger. They may deny that they are seriously ill or financially ruined, or that their children are on drugs or terminally ill. Even well-educated, professional people sometimes respond in this manner.

"Magic of the mouth." A Harvard psychiatrist, Dr. Ralph Hirschowitz, has created a term for the fourth characteristic. He calls it "magic of the mouth," the tendency to eat, drink, smoke and talk excessively. When difficulty enters these people's lives, they seem to regress to infantile forms of behavior, and their mouths take over in one way or another. They are uncomfortable unless they are doing something with their mouths most of the time. This attempt to not face the real problem can continue after the crisis is over. The person is actually helping to create an additional crisis for himself.

Unrealistic approach to time. A fifth characteristic is an unrealistic approach to time. People who cope this way crowd the time dimensions of a problem, or they extend the time factors way into the future. In other words, they want the problem to be "fixed" right away, or else they delay and delay. Delaying avoids the discomfort of reality but enlarges the problem.

Excessive guilt. Sixth, people who struggle with excessive guilt have difficulty coping with a crisis. They tend to blame themselves for the difficulty and by feeling worse immobilize themselves even more.

Blamers. Seventh, blamers have a difficult time coping with a crisis. They do not focus on what the problem is but turn to "who caused the problem." The approach is to find some enemies, either real or imagined, and project the blame upon them.

Excessive dependence or independence. An eighth characteristic of those who do not cope well is the tendency to be either very dependent or very independent. They either turn away from offers to help or become a clinging vine. Those who cling tend to suffocate you if you are involved in helping them. Overly independent people, on the other hand, shun offers to help, and even if they are sliding down the hill toward disaster, they do not cry out for assistance. When the disaster hits, they either continue to deny it or blame others for it.

One other characteristic must be cited that has a bearing upon the others. A person's theology will affect how he or she copes with a crisis. Our lives are based upon our theology, and yet so many people are frightened by that word. Our belief in God and how we perceive God is a reflection of our theology. Those who believe in the sovereignty and caring nature of God have a better basis from which to approach life.

A book that has spoken to me repeatedly is Lewis Smedes's *How Can It Be All Right When Everything Is All Wrong?* His insights and sensitivity to life's crises and God's presence and involvement in our lives can answer many of our questions. One of his own experiences describes how our theology helps us move through life's changes.

> The other night, trying to sleep, I amused myself by trying to recall the most happy moments of my life. I let my mind skip and dance where it was led. I thought of leaping down from a rafter in a barn, down into a deep loft of sweet, newly mown hay. That was a superbly happy moment. But somehow my mind was also seduced to a scene some years ago that, as I recall it, must have been the most painful of my life. Our first-born child was torn from our hands by what felt to me like a capricious deity I did not want to call God. I felt ripped off by a cosmic con-artist. And for a little while, I thought I might not easily ever smile again.
>
> But then, I do not know how, in some miraculous shift in my perspective, a strange and inexpressible sense came to me that my life, our lives, were still good, that life is good because it is given, and that its possibilities were still incalculable. Down into the gaps of feeling left over from the pain came a sense of givenness that nothing explains. It can only be felt as a gift of grace. An irrepressible impulse of blessing came from my heart to God for his sweet gift. And that was joy...in spite of pain. Looking back, it seems to me now that I have never again known so sharp, so severe, so saving a sense of gratitude and so deep a joy, or so honest.[4]

Chuck Swindoll always talks so realistically and helpfully about life's crises:

Crisis crushes. And in crushing, it often refines and purifies. You may be discouraged today because the crushing has not yet led to a surrender. I've stood beside too many of the dying, ministered to too many of the broken and bruised to believe that crushing is an end in itself. Unfortunately, however, it usually takes the brutal blows of affliction to soften and penetrate hard hearts. Even though such blows often seem unfair.

Remember Alexander Solzhenitsyn's admission:

It was only when I lay there on rotting prison straw that I sensed within myself the first stirring of good. Gradually, it was disclosed to me that the line separating good and evil passes, not through states, nor between classes, nor between political parties either, but right through all human hearts. So, bless you, prison, for having been in my life.[5]

Those words provide a perfect illustration of the psalmist's instruction:

Before I was afflicted I went astray, but now I obey your word....It was good for me to be afflicted so that I might learn your decrees. (Ps. 119:67,71, *NIV*)
After crises crush sufficiently, God steps in to comfort and teach.[6]

We will look now at the typical pattern that occurs in a person's life as he or she goes through the change and crisis sequence. As you can see from the chart, there are four phases in any life-changing event or crisis.

The Impact Phase

The impact phase is usually very brief. You know immediately that you have been confronted with a major happening. For some people it is like being hit with a two-by-four. The impact phase involves becoming aware of the crisis and experiencing the effect of being stunned. This period lasts from a few hours to a few days depending upon the event and the person involved. In a severe loss, tears can occur immediately or a few days later. The more severe the crisis or loss, obviously, the greater the impact and the greater the amount of incapacitation and numbness.

It is possible for the impact phase to linger on and on, as in the case of a divorce proceeding. During this phase, the person has to make a decision

Change and Crisis Sequence

	Phase I IMPACT	Phase II WITHDRAWAL CONFUSION	Phase III ADJUSTMENT	Phase IV RECONSTRUCTION- RECONCILIATION

Emotional Level

Time	HOURS	DAYS	WEEKS	MONTHS
Response	Fight-Flight	Anger-Fear- Guilt-Rage	Positive Thoughts Begin	Hope
Thought	Numbness- Disorientation	Ambiguity Uncertainty	Problem Solving	Consolidation of Problem Solving
Direction	Search for Lost Object	Bargaining- Detachment	Search for New Object	Reattachment
Search Behavior	Reminiscence	Perplexed Scanning	Focused Exploration	Reality Testing
Guidance Needed	Acceptance of Feeling	Task-Oriented Direction	Support- Spiritual Insight	Breakthrough- Reinforce Hope[7]

whether to stay and fight the problem through to resolution or run and ignore the problem. Psychologists call this the fight or flight pattern. During this impact stage we are usually less competent than normal, and our usual tendency of handling life's problems will probably emerge. If our tendency in the past has been to face problems, we will probably face the problem now. But if our tendency has been to avoid problems, we will probably run from this one.

Fighting and attempting to take charge again in the midst of crisis seems to be the healthier response. Running away only prolongs the crisis. And as each of the succeeding phases is dependent upon the adjustments made in the previous one, avoiding reality does not make for good judgment. Pain is prolonged instead of resolved.

Thinking capability is lessened. During the impact stage, our thinking capability is lessened. We are somewhat numb and disoriented. It is even possible for some to feel as though they cannot think or feel at all. It is as though their entire system shuts down. Insight is lessened and should not be expected at this time. The factual information you give these people may not fully register at this time and may have to be repeated later on. You may explain something to them, and they in turn ask a question that indicates they never heard one word. Because they are numb and stunned, they may make unwise decisions. But, unfortunately, important decisions may be necessary; postponing them may not be an option. This is where they need the help of other people.

Searches for the lost object. During the impact phase, a person actually and symbolically searches for the lost object. His thought process is directed toward the loss. For example, it is common for a person who loses a loved one in death to take out photographs and other items that remind him or her of the person who died. When something is lost that means a great deal to us, we hold on to our emotional attachments for a while. It is very normal to search for the lost object or a replacement, and the searching is greater when we are not aware of what is happening to us.

Reminiscing about the loss is in proportion to the value of the object or person. A person needs to be listened to and have his feelings accepted at this point of the crisis. Feelings rejected delay the resolution of the problem. Feelings should not be buried or denied at this point. The person may even feel strange about the feelings and thoughts he is experiencing, and negative comments from others do not help. If you are feeling discomfort when you counsel a person in crisis, instead of having him shut down his feelings, take time to discover the source of your own discomfort, for in doing this you will become better able to respond to life yourself and to help others.

Has an emotion of guilt. The emotion of guilt frequently accompanies change and crisis. People feel guilty for so many reasons, from having failed to having achieved. Many people have difficulty handling success. They wonder if they deserve it, or they see others who do not succeed and in their empathy for them experience guilt over their own success. Children of parents who divorce sometimes feel guilty as though they were responsible for the destruction of the marriage. Those who witness accidents or catastrophes often experience guilt. "Why was I spared?" "Why did my young child die and not me? He had so many more years left than I did!" are common reactions.

The person experiencing guilt has several choices available to him to alleviate the guilt. He can rationalize his way out of the guilt. He can project blame onto others. He can attempt to pay penance and work off the guilt. Or he can apply the forgiveness available where there has been genuine sin and violation of God's principles. God can and does remove true guilt. But there will be other feelings of guilt that have no basis. The person who lives on his emotions most of the time will be more guilt-prone during a crisis than others. Those who have negative patterns of thinking or self-talk will exhibit guilt more than others. Forgiveness from God is not usually needed for false guilt. What is needed is help in changing their perspective or self-talk. But this will take time and will probably not be accomplished during the impact phase.

Before we go on to the next stage, I will explain how the use of the chart has been helpful in counseling people in crisis. Often the person in crisis feels overwhelmed and wonders if his response is normal. On many occasions I have shown people the complete chart, described the various stages, and asked them to indicate where they were on the chart. They respond by first identifying which stage they are in and then stating, "You mean, my response is normal?" By discovering the normalcy of their response, they feel relieved. Then they are able to see where they will be heading, which further alleviates their anxiety.

The Withdrawal-Confusion Phase

Decline in the emotional level. One of the key factors in the withdrawal-confusion phase is the decline in the emotional level. When this occurs, there is usually a worn-out feeling or depression. The person has no more feeling to experience. If you look back at the chart, you will note that each phase becomes progressively longer. This phase can last days and even weeks.

Denies feelings. During this phase, the tendency to deny one's feelings is probably stronger than at any other phase. Feelings now can become ugliest. Intense anger can occur toward whatever happened, which in some cases brings on guilt for having such feelings. Shame can then result, and the pain of all the various feelings can bring the tendency and desire to suppress all feelings. Christians and non-Christians alike refuse to let the process of grief occur. This denial leads to emotional, physical and interpersonal difficulties in time.

How do people actually FEEL when confronted by a crisis? What goes on in their emotional spectrum when they find they are unable to adjust to life's major difficulties? Dr. D. J. Swartz, a Christian psychologist, has pinpointed these emotions as follows:

Distinctives of a Crisis

1. A sense of *bewilderment:* "I never felt this way before."
2. A sense of *danger:* "I feel so scared—something terrible is going to happen."
3. A sense of *confusion:* "I can't think clearly—my mind doesn't seem to work."
4. A sense of *impasse:* "I'm stuck—nothing I do seems to help."
5. A sense of *desperation:* "I've got to do something, but I don't know what to do."
6. A sense of *apathy:* "Nothing can help me—what's the use of trying."
7. A sense of *helplessness:* "I can't cope by myself—please help me."
8. A sense of *urgency:* "I need help now."
9. A sense of *discomfort:* "I feel so miserable and unhappy."

Knowing this can assist you in relating to the person as you might make statements such as:

"Could it be that you just can't think clearly? Like your mind isn't working?" "Could it be that you feel stuck, like 'Nothing I do seems to help?'"

"Perhaps you feel immobilized like, 'Why try? Nothing I do seems to help.'"

If our shared feelings begin to shock and alarm our friends, we tend to repress them. But they are never repressed from God. He both understands and accepts our emotional state. Feelings need to be expressed, which means that friends, relatives or some other type of social support system needs to be available. Unfortunately, the availability of friends and relatives might not coincide with when a person needs help. Meals, gifts, cards, time and prayers come during the impact phase and the beginning of the withdrawal-confusion state. But usually in a few weeks, the support system diminishes, and that is when it may be needed most.

Over the years I have come in contact with more and more churches who have developed an ongoing ministry for those who have experienced the loss of a loved one. The church arranges for families to minister to the bereaved person in some way each week for a period of two years. This not only involves many from the congregation in this ministry but also supports the person over an extended period.

A minister who attended one of my crisis seminars shared that following a funeral or memorial service he writes the name of the family on his desk calendar every three months for the next two years to remind him to continue to reach out and minister to them over that period of time.

During this phase, the person does not need or benefit from spiritual and psychological insights. His emotional state, whether it be anger or depression, interferes with the information. We can only hope he will be able to draw on what he has already learned, since he will find it difficult to incorporate anything new.

One of the best ways to aid people during this phase is to give them some help organizing their lives. They need assistance in arranging appointments, keeping the house in order and other such routine responsibilities. They need this help because they may be suffering from some paralysis of the will.

Above all, when you work with a person in phase one or two, use sustainment techniques. These are basic and simple—listening, reassurance, encouragement and reflection. These approaches will help to lower their anxiety, guilt and tension, and provide emotional support. Your task is to assist in helping the counselee restore equilibrium. These techniques will be discussed in greater depth in chapter 4.

Self-pity. Another tendency at this phase is self-pity. It is not uncommon for the person to appear confused. This may be evident because he will begin some task or start to approach people and then retreat. He may approach new people and situations as a type of replacement for what was lost, but then retreat to reminiscence. Making a decision during this phase to replace what was lost—such as finding and marrying a new spouse—is not a good idea. The person is not ready, for whatever or whoever was lost has not yet been fully released.

The Adjustment Phase

Notice the length of time the adjustment phase takes—longer than the others. The emotional responses during this time are hopeful. Some depression may remain or come and go, but positive attitudes have started. Things are looking up. People talk with hope about such future possibilities as enjoying a new job or a new location, rebuilding a fire-destroyed home or considering a remarriage. The person has just about completed his detachment from what was lost and is now looking for something new to which he can become attached.

Climbing out. What is occurring in his world begins to take on new importance to him. He has been through the depths of the valley and is now climbing out. What he begins to attach to holds special significance for him. The outsider may not see the same significance and may feel that the person is making a mistake by choosing this new job, new home or a new partner. The person does not need us as critics, for he is responding from a perspective different from ours. We do need to see life through his eyes and not our own.

The one area in which we do need to caution the person is selecting a new partner. At this phase it is usually too soon. I encourage those who are going through a divorce to wait at least a year following the divorce to begin dating. Recovery needs to occur first or they select a new partner from a position of weakness and the baggage they bring from their previous relationship interferes with this new one.

Hopeful. Remember that the person at this time is hopeful, but it is not a consistent sense of hope. He fluctuates and will have down times. He still needs someone to be close or available. Because insight is returning, he can be objective about what has occurred and now can process new information and suggestions. He can gain new insights spiritually at this point, and his values, goals and beliefs may be different and have a greater depth.[8]

The Reconstruction-Reconciliation Phase

The final phase is reconstruction and reconciliation.

A spontaneous expression of hope. At this phase a characteristic is spontaneous expression of hope. There is a sense of confidence, and plans are made out of this sense of confidence. Doubts and self-pity are gone because the person has made a logical decision at this point not to engage in them anymore. He takes the initiative for progress, and reattachments are occurring. New people, new places, new activities, new jobs and new spiritual responses and depths are now in existence. If there has been anger and blame toward others or if relationships were broken, this is now the time for reconciliation. Helpful gestures, notes, meals shared together and doing a helpful act for others may be the forms of reconciliation.

Reflection of newness. The final resolution of a crisis is a reflection of the newness of a person. A crisis is an opportunity for the person to gain new strengths, new perspectives on life, new appreciations, new values and a new way to approach life. I have experienced the four phases of crisis in my life. Sometimes it is possible to work your way through the four phases in less time than indicated. And sometimes one or two of the phases may take less time because of the experienced or threatened loss.

Several years ago I experienced some strange physical symptoms. These included vertigo, pressure experienced in the back of the head and headaches. These symptoms persisted for about seven weeks, during which time the doctors had some theories but nothing concrete. There was a real uncertainty, and my own concerns and worries about what this might be added to some of the feelings I experienced.

Finally, after going through further examination including a CAT scan, the symptoms disappeared. As we pieced together what had occurred, we felt the physical symptoms were brought on by too many strenuous seminars with no recuperation time in between, coupled with a cold and some altitude changes. Physical exhaustion was one of the greatest culprits. But this experience, especially at the age of 47, caused me to think, reevaluate and consider some changes. I did not necessarily like what I went through, but I grew because of it and felt it was necessary.

Crises and trials can become the means of exciting growth. I have always been impressed with William Pruitt and his response to a physical problem he conquered. In many ways his crisis did not go away but was with him for the rest of his life. In his book *Run from the Pale Pony*, Pruitt uses an analogy to describe what happened in his life. In the foreword of the book he writes:

> About thirty years ago, one of my joys as a boy was to ride a white horse named Prince. That proud, spirited stallion carried me where I wanted to go, wherever I bid him to and at the pace which I chose. I don't have to explain to horsemen the feeling of strength, even authority, which comes from controlling such a powerful animal. Nor need I expand upon the excitement I felt when I galloped him at full speed, or about the quiet pride that came when I twisted him

through the corkscrew turns of a rodeo exercise. After all, he was mine and I trained him. Those experiences are a part of my heritage.

My cherished white horse was gone and seldom remembered about fifteen years later. It was then that I encountered a completely different kind of horse. When I first became aware of the specter, its shape was too dim to discern. I know only that I had never seen anything like it before. Too, I know that I had not sought any such creature, yet something different was with me wherever I went and that shadow would not go away. I told myself, "Really, now, you're much too busy to bother with something that seems determined to disturb you, get rid of it." And I tried to will it away. No matter what I did though, the specter followed my every move. Furthermore, the harder I tried to lose it, the clearer the creature's form became to me.

My uneasiness hanged to anxiety when I realized that this unwanted shadow had a will of its own. The chill of fear came when I understood that it had no intention to leave me alone. Without further warning, it began to communicate with me openly one day, and in a harsh voice which was almost rigid with animosity, it spat out, "You can no longer go where you want to go when you choose at the speed you pick. That's true because I will give you weakness instead of strength. Excitement and pride? Never again will you have them like before. I plan only confinement and disability for you. And I will be your constant companion. My name is Chronic Illness."

At the time I heard it speak, I shrank back from actually seeing it face to face. It spoke harshly of miseries which were inverse to joys with my white horse named Health and the bitter irony was reflected in the form of a malicious creature. Chronic Illness took the shape of a stunted misshapen pony. Its shaggy coat was pale in color, streaked with ages old accumulation of dark despair. But, unquestionably, the most frightening feature of the animal was its overwhelming glare—its glare-eyed stare which held me helpless. The pony's wild eyes stared restlessly from side to side, yet strangely were unblinding. This book is written first of all for those people who have met the pale pony face to face.[9]

The "pale pony" might come in many possible forms—serious physical or mental illness, accident, war or other injuries to name a few. Whatever shape the pony takes, the results can be quite similar. William Pruitt's pale pony was multiple sclerosis. He sensed that the disease was increasingly affecting his life, but his story is the story of hope. He realized that he had a number of years before he would be completely disabled, and realizing that he wouldn't be able to carry on the type of work he was in, he went back to college in a wheelchair. He earned a Ph.D. in economics and began to teach on a college level.

Pruitt's book is not a book about giving up but rather about fighting back and winning. It is a very honest book, telling of the pain and the hurt and the turmoil. But its emphasis is on faith and hope.

What causes a major crisis to become a restrictive, crippling, eternal tragedy rather than a growth-producing experience in spite of the pain? *Our attitude.*

Many people who work through their crisis find that they can then minister in a much better way to others. Out of our difficulties, we can feel with others and walk through their trials with them in a new manner.

Recommended Resources:

For additional information on the Transitions of the Family Life Cycle see the following:

Golan, Naomi. *Passing Through Transitions: A Guide for Practitioners.* New York: The Free Press, 1981.

Singer, Laura J., and Sten, Barbara Long. *Stages.* New York: Grosset and Dunlap, 1980.

Wright, H. Norman. *Seasons of a Marriage.* Ventura, CA: Regal, 1983.

Notes

1. Naomi Golan, *Passing Through Transitions* (New York: The Free Press, 1981), p. 12.
2. David C. Morley, *Halfway Up the Mountain* (Old Tappan, NJ: Revell, 1979), p. 26.
3. Aaron Lazare, F. Cohen, O. Jacobsen, et. al., "The Walk-in Patient as a 'Customer': A Key Dimension in Evaluation and Treatment," *American Journal of Orthopsychiatry,* 42 (1979):872-883, as quoted in *Counseling Teenagers,* Dr. G. Keith Olson (Loveland, CO: Group Books, 1984), pp. 283,284.
4. Lewis B. Smedes, *How Can It Be All Right When Everything Is All Wrong?* (New York: Harper and Row, 1982), pp. 16,17.
5. Alexander Solzhenitsyn, *The Gulag Archipelago,* quoted in Philip Yancey, *Where Is God When It Hurts?* (Grand Rapids: Zondervan, 1977), p. 51.
6. Charles R. Swindoll, *Growing Strong in the Seasons of Life* (Portland, OR: Multnomah, 1983), pp. 274,275.
7. Based on a similar chart from Ralph Hirschowitz in "Addendum," a special feature of the *Levinson Letter* (Cambridge: The Levinson Institute, n.d.), p. 4.
8. "Phases of a Crisis," adapted from Lloyd Ahlem, *Living with Stress* (Ventura, CA: Regal, 1978), pp. 31-64.
9. William Pruitt, *Run from the Pale Pony* (Grand Rapids: Baker, 1976), pp. 9,10, as quoted in *More Communication Keys for Your Marriage,* H. Norman Wright (Ventura, CA: Regal, 1983), pp. 19,20.

CRISIS COUNSELING from a BIBLICAL PERSPECTIVE

2

In any type of Christian crisis counseling—whether it be individual, marital or family—knowledge of the biblical approach is essential. One way to develop a biblical approach is to study the life of Jesus and His relationships with others. The way He ministered to others is a model for all of us who seek to help others.

As we look at the characteristics of Jesus' approach in counseling, we must remember that techniques alone are not effective. Jesus' relationship with the person to whom He was ministering was the foundation of His approach.

An individual, couple or family coming for counseling needs to know the minister cares about them, and the minister demonstrates that by his warmth, understanding, acceptance and belief in their ability to change and mature.

How Jesus Responded to People

One important observation we can make about Jesus' approach to counseling is that His work with people was a process. He did not see them for just a few minutes during an appointment. He spent time helping them work through life's difficulties in an in-depth manner. He saw people with their problems, as well as their potential and hopes.

Jesus had compassion. A basic characteristic of Jesus' approach was His compassion for others. We see His compassion expressed in Mark 8:2: "I feel compassion for the multitude because they have remained with Me now three days, and have nothing to eat." Another passage showing His compassion is Mark 6:34: "And when He went ashore, He saw a great multitude, and He felt compassion for them because they were like sheep without a shepherd; and He began to teach them many things." His concern was to alleviate suffering and meet the needs of the people.

Jesus accepted people. When Jesus first met people, He accepted them as they were. In other words, He believed in them and what they would become. The characteristic of acceptance is seen in John 4, John 8 and Luke 19. When Jesus met the woman at the well, He accepted her as she was without condemning her. He accepted the woman caught in adultery and Zacchaeus, the dishonest tax collector, as well.

Jesus gave people worth. People were Jesus' top priority. He established this priority and gave them worth by putting their needs before the rules and regulations the religious leaders had constructed. He involved Himself in the lives of people who were considered the worst of sinners, and He met them where they had a need. In so doing, He helped them elevate their sense of self-worth. This is an important step in crisis counseling.

One of the ways Jesus gave worth to people was by showing them their value in God's eyes, by comparing God's care for other creatures with God's care for them: "Are not two sparrows sold for a cent? And yet not one of them will fall to the ground apart from your Father" (Matt. 10:29). At the heart of many people's problems is a low self-concept or feeling of lack of worth. Helping a person discover his personal worth because of who God is and what He has done for us helps to stabilize the person.

Jesus met people's needs. Another characteristic of Jesus' ministry was His ability to see the needs of people and speak directly to them, regardless of what they might have brought to His attention. We see discernment in the example of Nicodemus's coming to Jesus during the night. Whatever might have been his reason for wanting to talk with Jesus at that time, Jesus discerned Nicodemus's real problem and confronted him with the need to be born again.

In meeting the immediate needs of people, Jesus did not use the same approach with everyone. Gary Collins explains this well in his book *How to Be a People Helper:*

Jesus not only dealt with people in different ways, but He also related to individuals at different levels of depth or closeness. John was the disciple whom Jesus loved, perhaps the Master's nearest friend, while Peter, James, and John together appear to have comprised an inner circle with whom the Lord had a special relationship. Although they were not as close as the inner three, the other apostles were Christ's companions, a band of twelve men who had been handpicked to carry on the work after Christ's departure. In Luke 10 we read of a group of seventy men to whom Jesus gave special training. Following the resurrection He appeared to a larger group of five hundred people, and then there were crowds, sometimes numbering in the thousands, many of whom may have seen Christ only once and from a distance.[1]

Each one who comes to you in crisis has a desperate need.

Jesus used the right words. Sometimes Jesus spoke directly, even harshly. Other times He was soft-spoken. Sometimes He conveyed His feelings nonverbally, as in Mark 3:5: "And after looking around at them with anger, grieved at their hardness of heart, He said to the man, 'Stretch out your hand.' And he stretched it out, and his hand was restored."

Jesus emphasized right behavior. Jesus said to the woman caught in adultery, "Go, and sin no more" (John 8:11, *KJV*). "Everyone who comes to Me, and hears My words, and acts upon them" Jesus compared to the wise man who built his house upon a foundation of rock (Luke 6:47).

Jesus sought to have people accept responsibility. In John 5, Jesus responded to the man at the pool of Bethesda by saying, "Wilt thou be made whole?" (v. 6, *KJV*). In other words, "Do you really want to get well? Do you want to be healed? Do you want to change?" By asking this question, Jesus sought to have the man accept responsibility for remaining sick or being made well. In another instance He asked a blind man, "What do you want Me to do for you?" (Mark 10:51).

In crisis counseling, the person, couple or family must see that they need to make a choice to remain the same or to change and grow, and they must make that choice before much progress will be seen. A goal of crisis counseling, as you will see, is helping the person in need to accept and take responsibility.

To other people, Jesus gave *hope:* "And they were even more astonished and said to Him, 'Then who can be saved?' Looking upon them, Jesus said, 'With men it is impossible, but not with God; for all things are possible with God'" (Mark 10:26,27).

Jesus encouraged people. "Come to Me, all who are weary and heavy-laden, and I will give you rest. Take My yoke upon you, and learn from Me, for I am gentle and humble in heart; and you shall find rest for your souls. For My yoke is easy, and My load is light" (Matt. 11:28-30). How important is encouragement in crisis counseling? Should it be used sparingly in any phase of the crisis sequence? Encouragement provides the counselee with hope and with the desire to change.

Jesus emphasized peace of mind. "Peace I leave with you; My peace I give to you; not as the world gives, do I give to you. Let not your heart be troubled, nor let it be fearful" (John 14:27). If there is one thing a person in crisis usually does not have it is peace of mind. Jesus offered that hope.

Jesus helped reshape or refashion people's thinking. Jesus helped people redirect their attention from the unimportant things of life to the important (see Luke 5:22-25; 12:22-27).

Jesus taught. Teaching is a definite part of counseling, and we see over and over again how Jesus taught. Often He used direct statements in His teaching. At other times He used questions:

> And it came about when He went into the house of one of the leaders of the Pharisees on the Sabbath to eat bread, that they were watching Him closely. And there, in front of Him was a certain man suffering from dropsy. And Jesus answered and spoke to the lawyers and Pharisees, saying, "Is it lawful to heal on the Sabbath, or not?" But they kept silent. And He took hold of him, and healed him, and sent him away. And He said to them, "Which one of you shall have a son or an ox fall into a well, and will not immediately pull him out on a Sabbath day?" And they could make no reply to this (Luke 14:1-6; see also Luke 6:39,42).

Jesus spoke with authority. Another characteristic of Jesus' approach was that He spoke with authority. He was not hesitant, backward or bashful, but authoritative: "For He was teaching them as one having authority, and not as their scribes" (Matt. 7:29). How might your authority as a minister be used properly or misused in counseling with a person in crisis?

Jesus admonished and confronted. Notice how Jesus, when necessary, admonished and confronted people. "And He said to them, 'Why are you timid, you men of little faith?' Then He arose, and rebuked the winds and the sea; and it became perfectly calm" (Matt. 8:26). "And if your brother sins, go and reprove him in private; if he listens to you, you have won your brother" (Matt. 18:15).

Another example of how Jesus admonished and confronted is in John 8:3-9:

> And the scribes and the Pharisees brought a woman caught in adultery, and having set her in the midst, they said to Him, "Teacher, this woman has been caught in adultery, in the very act. Now in the Law Moses commanded us to stone such women; what then do You say?" And they were saying this, testing Him, in order that they might have grounds for accusing Him. But Jesus stooped down, and with His finger wrote on the ground. But when they persisted in asking Him, He straightened up, and said to them, "He who is without sin among you, let him be the first to throw a stone at her." And again He stooped down, and wrote on the ground. And when they heard it, they began to go out one by one, beginning with the older ones, and He was left alone, and the woman, where she had been, in the midst.

Sometimes it is necessary to confront the counselee directly about his problem.

Factors in the Effectiveness of Jesus' Ministry

Jesus' ministry was that of helping people achieve fullness of life, assisting them in developing their ability to deal with the problems, conflicts and burdens of life. Perhaps what is really important for the counselor—whether professional or layman—is to consider why Jesus was so effective in His ministry. As we look at His personal life, the answer is evident.

Jesus was obedient to God. Foremost in Jesus' personal life was obedience to God. There was a definite relationship between Him and His Father, and obedience was the mainstay of His life. Two verses from the book of John emphasize this point: "For I did not speak on My own initiative, but the Father Himself who sent Me has given Me commandment, what to say, and what to speak" (John 12:49). "I glorified Thee on the earth, having accomplished the work which Thou hast given Me to do" (John 17:4).

Jesus lived a life of faith. Another reason Jesus' ministry was effective was that He lived a life of faith and therefore was able to put things in proper perspective, seeing life through God's eyes. The example of the synagogue official's daughter in Mark 5 and Jesus' response to his statement that his daughter was dead shows this faith.

Jesus lived a life of prayer. A third reason for Jesus' effectiveness was the power of His prayer life. His example indicates that prayer is a very important element in one's ministry: "But the news about Him was spreading even farther, and great multitudes were gathering to hear Him and to be healed of their sicknesses. But He Himself would often slip away to the wilderness and pray" (Luke 5:15-16). "And it was at this time that He went off to the mountain to pray, and He spent the whole night in prayer to God. And when day came, He called His disciples to Him; and chose twelve of them, whom He also named as apostles" (Luke 6:12,13).

Some counselors find it helpful to pray either at the beginning or the end of their counseling sessions. Others do not, but prayer is still an important part of their counseling ministry. Some counselors pray specifically for each counselee each day and let the counselee know they are doing this. Some have also asked their counselees to pray for them that God would give them wisdom and insight as they minister.

One pastor says that it is his practice, when he is completely stymied in a counseling session and does not know what to do next, to admit this fact openly to the counselee. He states that he would like to pause for a moment and ask God to reveal to him what should be done next, what should be said and the direction he should take. This pastor said that on many occasions, as soon as he had finished praying, what needed to be done or said next was very clear to him.

Jesus spoke with authority. A fourth reason for Jesus' effectiveness was the authority by which He spoke. "For He was teaching them as one having authority, and not as their scribes" (Matt. 7:29). Jesus was very conscious of

His authority. Those who know Christ and are called to a ministry of helping in counseling have the authority of God's Word behind them.

There is a distinction, however, between using the authority of the Scriptures and being authoritarian. Some counselors pull out a scriptural passage and apply it to any problem without hearing the full extent of the difficulty and without knowing whether Scripture is necessary at that particular time. Some people who are unwilling or fail to examine the problems in their own lives but who nevertheless attempt to counsel and use scriptural authority might misapply Scripture or distort it because of their own difficulties.

Jesus was personally involved. A fifth reason for the effectiveness of Jesus' ministry was His personal involvement *with* the disciples and with others. He was not aloof; He was personal, sensitive and caring.

Jesus had the power of the Holy Spirit. The power of the Holy Spirit enabled Jesus to be effective. Some have called this power an anointing of the Spirit. We see how His ministry began when Jesus received the power of the Holy Spirit in Luke 3:21,22: "Now it came about when all the people were baptized, that Jesus also was baptized, and while He was praying, heaven was opened, and the Holy Spirit descended upon Him in bodily form like a dove, and a voice came out of heaven, 'Thou art My beloved Son, in Thee I am well-pleased.'" The next chapter of Luke indicates that Jesus was full of the Holy Spirit and led by the Spirit, and the Spirit of the Lord was upon Him.

Luke 5:17 states that the power of the Lord was with Him to heal: "And it came about one day that He was teaching; and there were some Pharisees and teachers of the law sitting there, who had come from every village of Galilee and Judea and from Jerusalem; and the power of the Lord was present for Him to perform healing."

William Crane, in his book *Where God Comes In: The Divine Plus in Counseling,* talks about the ministry of the Holy Spirit in the lives of the counselor and counselee:

> The Holy Spirit has access to all the materials that other psychotherapists know and use. In addition, He has direct access to the inner thoughts and feelings of the counselor. When the counselor becomes counselee in the presence of the Wonderful Counselor and sincerely seeks the honest

reproval, correction and training in righteousness which the Holy Spirit promises, then he may find it. Many have.[2]

Establishing a Biblical Counseling Process

We have looked at the ways Jesus responded to people and factors that made His ministry effective. What we need to do now is apply them to the counseling process.

Girard Egan, a leading therapist, suggests four stages in the counseling process: (1) attending to the counselee and building rapport; (2) responding to the counselee and helping him to explore his feelings, experiences and behavior; (3) building understanding in both counselor and counselee; and (4) stimulating action that subsequently is evaluated by counselor and counselee together.

Lawrence Brammer, a psychologist, has a longer but similar list: opening the interview and stating the problem(s); (1) clarifying the problem and goals for counseling; (2) structuring the counseling relationship and procedures; (3) building a deeper relationship; (4) exploring feelings, behavior or thoughts; (5) deciding on some plans of action, trying these out and evaluating them; and (6) terminating the relationship.

To a large extent, what we do in counseling will depend on the type of problem involved, the personalities of the helper and the helpee, and the nature of their relationship. Building on the suggestions of Egan and Brammer, I would suggest that the counseling process has at least five steps, most of which are clearly illustrated in the Bible.

1. Building a relationship between helper and helpee (see John 16:7-13).
2. Exploring the problem, trying to clarify issues and determine what has been done in the past to tackle the problem.
3. Deciding on a course of action. There may be several possible alternatives that could be tried one at a time (see John 14:26; 1 Cor. 2:13).
4. Stimulating action that helper and helpee evaluate together. When something doesn't work, try again (see John 16:13; Acts 10:19,20; 16:6).
5. Terminating the counseling relationship and encouraging the helpee

to apply what he has learned as he launches out on his own (see Rom. 8:14).

Much of this process is beautifully illustrated in Luke 24, where Jesus met two men on the road to Emmaus. When He met the men, He used a variety of techniques to help them through their crisis and period of discouragement.

First, Jesus came alongside the men and began traveling with them. Here was rapport-building. As they walked, Jesus asked some very nondirective questions. He spent a lot of time listening. He surely didn't agree with what the men were saying, but He listened, gave them opportunity to express their frustrations, and showed them the love that sent Him to die for sinners in the first place.

After a while, Jesus confronted these men with their logical misunderstandings and failure to interpret the Scriptures correctly. The confrontation was gentle but firm, and it must have begun the process of stimulating the men to change their thinking and behavior.

At the end of the journey, Jesus got close by accepting an invitation from the two men to eat a meal together.

Then an interesting thing happened. It is something that every helper dreams of doing with some of his helpees—especially the more difficult ones. Jesus "vanished from their sight" (v. 31). In so doing, Jesus left them on their own and spurred them to action. This is the ultimate goal of all helping—to move the helpee to a point of independence where there is no longer any need to rely on assistance from the helper.[3]

Remember this last point, for it is the crux of crisis counseling.[4]

Notes

1. Gary Collins, *How to Be a People Helper* (Ventura, CA: Vision House/Regal Books, 1976), p. 37.
2. William Crane, *Where God Comes In: The Divine Plus in Counseling* (Dallas, TX: WORD Incorporated, 1970), p. 28.
3. Collins, *How to Be a People Helper,* pp. 51-53.
4. H. Norman Wright, *Marital Counseling* (Santa Ana, CA: Christian Marriage Enrichment, 1981), adapted.

APPLICATIONS of BIBLICAL PRINCIPLES

~~~~~~~~~~~~~~~~~~~~~~~~~~

3

In spite of many years of training and experience, on many occasions every week ministers and counselors wonder what they should do or say in a counseling situation. These occasions force the Christian counselor to go back to the Lord and ask, "Lord, what should I do now? What does this person need?" If we begin to help people out of our own strength, we will make mistakes. We need to *rely upon the power and wisdom of God.*

In Proverbs 3:5,6 we are instructed to "lean on, trust and be confident in the Lord with all your heart and mind, and do not rely on your own insight or understanding. In all your ways know, recognize and acknowledge Him, and He will direct and make straight and plain your paths" *(AMP)*. A similar thought is expressed in Proverbs 15:28: "The mind of the [uncompromisingly] righteous studies how to answer, but the mouth of the wicked pours out evil things" *(AMP)*.

Learning to Listen

One problem counselors suffer from more than any other, is not knowing when to listen and keep quiet. Most ministers in counseling want to talk and offer advice or exhort from the Scriptures. There is a time for advising and exhorting, but how will one know what to say unless he has first listened? *Listening* is a crucial part of counseling.

As we look into the Scriptures, we see God as our model for listening (see Ps. 34:15-18; 116:1,2; Jer. 33:3). The Scriptures have much to say about the importance of listening. James 1:19 says that each of us is to be "a ready listener" *(AMP)*. (See also Prov. 15:31; 18:13,15; 21:28.)

Factors That Influence Listening

It is important as a minister or lay counselor for you to be aware of some personal factors that influence the way you listen and interpret what you hear. Peter Buntman and Eleanor Saris, instructors in parenting courses, have identified seven things that determine how and how well a person listens.

Age. People in different age groups tend to hear and react to things differently.

Sex. Men and women have been trained by the socialization process to hear and respond differently. (For additional information on this point, see *More Communication Keys to Your Marriage* by this author.)

Education. A psychologist well trained in a Ph.D. program that specializes in the psychodynamic orientation will likely hear something differently from the pastor who graduated from an evangelical seminary.

Past experiences. The variety of experiences and relative degree of pain and difficulty a counselor has lived through will affect his or her level of understanding and capacity for empathetic response.

Perception of future expectations and goals. Counselors who tend to be either optimistic or pessimistic about their own future will usually hold the same attitude toward their clients' expectations and goals. If you have ever taken the Taylor Johnson Temperament Analysis, what was your score on the Subjective-Objective trait? Your listening will be greatly affected by your score. If you are very subjective in your approach to life, you will tend to read into the comments and interpret much of what you hear through your own filters. (For more information about this personality test, write to me at Christian Marriage Enrichment, 17821 17th St., Suite 290, Tustin, CA 92680.)

Personal feelings about the counselee. Counselors are attentive, open and positively responsive to counselees whom they like, whereas they tend to be less attentive, closed and negatively responsive to counselees whom they dislike. If you are threatened by the counselee or are afraid of being dominated by the person, you will listen differently from a person who is not.

Current emotional and physical feelings. If you feel depressed, have a headache, or had very little sleep the night before, you will tend to hear more negative statements from the counselee, while the happy, energetic counselor may hear more positive statements.[1]

Listening is a skill that can be learned. Are you aware that people can listen to human speech at three times the speed normally spoken without any significant loss of comprehension? Try listening to people who speak at different rates and determine which ones you tend to respond to the best.

There is a difference between hearing and listening. Hearing is the gaining of information for oneself. Listening is caring for and being empathetic toward others. In listening we are trying to understand the feelings of the other person, and we are listening for his sake. Hearing is determined by what goes on inside of me, what effect the conversation has on me. Listening is determined by what is going on inside the other person, what my attentiveness is doing for him.

In listening we interpret and try to understand what we have heard. Paul Wilczak says:

> It is the "heart," however, that is our total emotional response, that integrates these various perceptions into full, personal contact, and this is what is needed today. We can listen with our heads. We can comprehend the thought content of a person's messages and systematically analyze what is communicated. This is cognitive empathy and can be readily learned. But cognitive empathy has severe limitations.
>
> It misses the dimension of meaning that goes beyond what is explicitly said. It overlooks the feelings and experiences usually conveyed without words. These other messages come from the heart, the center of a person's experience.[2]

Listening is one of the most loving gifts you can give to another person whether it be counselee, friend or family member.

When to Speak—and When to Be Quiet

Ecclesiastes 3 emphasizes the next principle of biblical counseling—*knowing when to speak and when to be quiet*, when enough has been said. Proverbs 10:19 further emphasizes it: "In a multitude of words transgression is not lacking, but he who restrains his lips is prudent" *(AMP)*. *The Living Bible* is very graphic: "Don't talk so much. You keep putting your foot in your mouth. Be sensible and turn off the flow!"

The counselor who understands the counselee's problems chooses his words well: "He who has knowledge spares his words, and a man of understanding has a cool spirit. Even a fool when he holds his peace is considered wise; when he closes his lips he is esteemed a man of understanding" (Prov. 17:27,28, *AMP*).

Proverbs 29:20 is another passage applicable to the principle of knowing when to speak and when to be quiet: "Do you see a man who is hasty in his words? There is more hope of a [self-confident] fool than of him" *(AMP)*. Being hasty means blurting out what you are thinking without considering the effect it will have upon others. When you are ministering to a person who says something that shocks you, do not feel you have to respond immediately. Take a few seconds to think and ask God to give you the words. Then formulate what you want to say.

If you do not know what to say, one of the best things to do is ask for more information: "Tell me some more about it" or "Give me some more background." This gives you time to think. You do not have to say something right away. There may be times when you say to a person, "I need a few seconds to go through what you said and decide how to respond at this time." This takes the pressure off you and also off the counselee.

Show genuine interest and love. You can listen to the person, you can rely upon the power of God for knowing how to counsel, but little will be accomplished without being truly interested in the other person and loving him. Sometimes a counselor or minister will give an off-the-cuff, superficial answer that does not meet the counselee's need and does not deal with the problem. All of us must ask ourselves, "How do I really feel about this person who is coming to me? Am I genuinely concerned?"

Timing is important. "A man has joy in making an apt answer, and a word spoken at the right moment, how good it is!" (Prov. 15:23, *AMP*). The right answer, the correct answer, is the word spoken at the right moment.

Keep confidences. Keeping confidences builds trust. It is a trait of a trustworthy person. "He who goes about as a talebearer reveals secrets, but he who is trustworthy and faithful in spirit keeps the matter hidden" (Prov. 11:13, *AMP*). Nothing that is told to you in a counseling situation should ever escape your lips. "He who guards his mouth and his tongue keeps himself from troubles" (Prov. 21:23, *AMP*). (Legal exceptions to this will be discussed later. Regarding the examples cited in this book, the people involved have given me permission to use them, and sufficient information has been changed to ensure privacy.)

Say the right words in the right manner. Proverbs 25:20 says: "He who sings songs to a heavy heart is like him who lays off a garment in cold weather and as vinegar upon soda" (*AMP*). Being jovial around a person who is deeply hurting is not appropriate. "Oh, you really don't feel that way, come on out of it; let me tell you this story I heard—" can cause the person to hurt even more. On some occasions, casual or off-the-subject conversation can help lift a person, but it is usually not appropriate for the person who is hurting deeply.

Teaching and giving advice. Sometimes you will need to give directions, advice and help on impending decisions or problems that need to be resolved. Sometimes you will give guidance on handling conflicts. Teaching should not be overdone and must be used only when there is a receptivity. A principle to follow is this: Use the teaching technique when, and only when, the counselee needs new information that would be difficult for him to acquire on his own. Find out if the person already has this information or has access to it. Invite the counselee to describe what he knows. Be sure the person is ready to hear what you have to say.

Giving advice is a form of teaching, but it is often overused and not especially effective. Often we leave our role as a counselor when we give advice and become more of a friend or parent who may be trying to help the counselee. However, given in the proper manner, advice is a part of counseling. When you give suggestions in counseling, try to draw them from the person or give them as options: "What if you did...?" "Have you considered...?" "What possibilities have you come up with?"

Do not say to a person, "This is exactly what you need to do." If you do, you are assuming the responsibility for the solution. If your suggestion does not work, he may come back and say, "You really gave me a stupid idea. It didn't work. It's your fault." Instead, give several tentative suggestions, which is safer for you and also will help the person think through the alternatives. Most people have the ability to resolve their problems but need encouragement to do so.

But what if the counselee wants advice? What is the reason for this request? It may be he is looking for reassurance that you care, or he may want you to live his anxiety. He may be looking to you as the great miracle worker, or he may just want the hope that there is a solution.

It could be that other responses besides handing out advice would be more beneficial in a given situation. Think back to the characteristics of a crisis and the chart describing the four phases of a crisis. At what point do you think teaching would be most helpful in the sequence of a crisis?

Teaching is an effective tool if it helps the counselee become more independent and move toward maturity. Teaching can be most helpful during the adjustment phase of the crisis. It will not be heard during the impact phases, and during the last phase it is not usually needed.

The Art of Asking Questions

One of the most frequently used techniques in counseling is questioning. We have seen how Jesus used questions. In my work with interns and ministers, I have asked them to tape their counseling sessions and then tabulate the number of questions asked compared with the number of statements. Many have found that every response was a question. The counselee is then able to predict the responses from the minister and may begin to perceive him as nothing but a question box. Some counselees said, "I go in to see the pastor, he asks me a question, I answer and then wait for the next question to be asked."

Questioning is a greatly overused technique, especially by those just starting out in counseling. You feel comfortable because it helps you gather information and you are not as involved, nor do you have to work as hard as you do with other responses. It is safe and easy to use. I usually ask the interns or ministers to go back through their taped interviews, write down each question asked, and then rewrite it into a statement rather than a question. By doing this they will learn a greater variety of ways to respond and will become more conscious of their responses.

Know why you are asking a question. What is the purpose, and was the question necessary. Using this technique can indicate that you assume you know better than the counselee what needs to be discussed.

When you ask questions, use open-ended ones that give the person the greatest amount of latitude and freedom to respond. Asking questions calling for a yes or no response will not be helpful for either of you. Be careful that your questions do not convey, through tone, nonverbal messages or inflection, a sense of judgment or suspicion. Asking questions can be helpful through the various stages of counseling and the phases of a crisis, but if the person is already giving information, the need for questions drops. They are not as necessary during the last phase of a crisis.

Sometimes it is beneficial during a time of crisis to do a little probing when you think the person would benefit from further discussion about the situation or issue. But this should be done in a low-key, unobtrusive manner, and the counselee should carry the responsibility for what is discussed.

Edifying and Helping

Galatians 6:2 teaches the principle of edifying and helping by bearing one another's burdens: "Bear (endure, carry) one another's burdens and troublesome moral faults, and in this way fulfill and observe perfectly the law of Christ, the Messiah, and complete what is lacking [in your obedience to it]" (AMP). Romans 14:19 reads: "So let us then definitely aim for and eagerly pursue what makes for harmony and for mutual upbuilding (edification and development) of one another" (AMP).

The word "edify," which is part of helping, means to hold up or to promote growth in Christian wisdom, grace, virtue and holiness. Our counseling should include edification.

Helping means assisting a person to do something for his betterment. We have to ask ourselves, "Is what I am accomplishing with this person going to cause him to grow in the Christian life and help him to be strong?" A person might come to you and say, "I want you to help me," but what he really means is that he wants you to agree with his point of view. If it is a marital dispute, he will probably want you to take sides. This is where the counselor gets into difficulty—taking sides.

Another way of helping others is to encourage them. "Anxiety in a man's heart weighs it down, but an encouraging word makes it glad" (Prov. 12:25, *AMP)*. "Therefore encourage (admonish, exhort) one another and edify—strengthen and build up—one another, just as you are doing" (1 Thess. 5:11, *AMP)*.

Encouraging, along with listening, is one of the most important techniques in helping a person in crisis (see 1 Thess. 5:14). Encouraging means urging forward, stimulating a person to do what he should be doing. It is saying to the person, "I believe in you as an individual. I believe you have the ability and the potential to follow through in doing this. Now, can we talk about this together so that you would feel more competence in yourself?" Encouraging a person helps him to believe in his own personal worth, which is one of the goals of counseling.

Because counseling can be painful as well as helpful for the counselee, reassurance all through the various stages of counseling is important. I don't mean statements such as "It will be okay" or "Everything is going to turn out for the best." We don't know the outcome, and as people in ministry we must be careful when and how we offer assurances from the Word of God. The counselee first needs to be honest with his feelings and to make sure he is being heard by you in order for him to be receptive to the support and comfort of God's Word.

Eight types of reassurance that can be given to a person in crisis are listed below.

1. The counselee might be reassured by knowing that his or her problem is really quite common.
2. Reassurance can be given that the problem has a known cause and that something can be done about it.
3. Reassurance can be given that though the symptoms are annoying, they are not dangerous.
4. Counselees can often be reassured that specific treatment methods are available.
5. Reassurance can be given that a resolution of the problem is possible.
6. The counselee may need reassurance that he or she is not going insane.

7. Reassurance may be needed to the effect that relapses might occur and that their appearance does not imply the condition is worsening.

8. When appropriate, counselees should be reassured that their problems are not the result of sinful action.[3]

As you counsel people in crisis, remember that to help them become more self-sufficient, they need to be weaned gradually from your insights, help and counsel. Your task is to work yourself out of a job and to rejoice with the person when that occurs.

Showing Empathy

Empathy is one of the most important commodities for effective counseling. But, unfortunately, the word "empathy," as with other words, has many meanings to many people. What does empathy mean in the counseling relationship? The word comes from the German word *einfühlung,* which means "to feel unto" or "to feel with." It is as though we are in the driver's seat with the other person and feeling and sensing with him. It is viewing the situation through his eyes, feeling as he feels, Galatians 6:2 and Romans 12:15 admonish us to bear one another's burdens, to rejoice with those who rejoice and to weep with those who weep. To do that is to have empathy.

Girard Egan has said that empathy involves discrimination—being able to get inside the other person, looking at the world through his perspective and getting a feeling for what his world is like. It is the ability to discriminate, and being able to communicate this understanding to the other person in such a manner that he realizes we have picked up both his feelings and his behavior. It is being able to see another person's joy, to understand what underlies that joy and to communicate that understanding to the person.[4]

Joshua Liebman describes the function of empathy:

It serves us in two ways. First, it helps us to understand the other person from within. We communicate on a deeper level and apprehend the other person more completely. With this kind of communication we often find ourselves accepting that person and emerging into a relationship of appreciation and sympathy. In another sense, empathy becomes for us a source of personal reassurance. We are reassured when we feel that someone has succeeded in feeling himself into our own state of mind. We enjoy the satisfaction of being understood and accepted as persons. It is important for us to sense that the other person not only understands our words but appreciates the person behind the message as well. We then know that we are recognized and accepted for the particular person we are. When friends fail to empathize, we feel disappointed and rejected. When empathy is lacking, our self-awareness and self-respect are diminished. We then experience ourselves more as objects and less as persons.[5]

Empathy is an understanding *with* the counselee rather than a diagnostic understanding *of* the client.

Empathy requires the ability to go beyond factual knowledge and become involved in the counselee's world of feelings. But it also involves doing this without personally going through what the other person does. You cannot experience the identical emotions of a person; that would be overinvolvement. Empathetic responding focuses exclusively on the feelings expressed by the other person. Sympathetic responding focuses on the expression of your care and compassion in order to comfort the other individual.

Donald Houts writes of empathy in terms of involvement in the lives of others:

Love is the capacity to involve oneself, unselfconsciously, in the lives of other men—without using these relationships primarily to minister to oneself. To understand their weaknesses, to suffer with them, to hate the things that hurt them, to grieve over their hard-heartedness—these are manifestations of the kind of relationships which contribute to new life in those whose lives have been so touched.[6]

William Crane describes the importance of agape love as the basis of empathy:

For a better understanding of the meaning of this "larger love" in empathy, let me quote from J. B. Phillips' translation of 1 Corinthians 13:4-8: "This love of which I speak is slow to lose patience—it looks for a way of being constructive. It is not possessive; it is neither anxious to impress nor does it cherish inflated ideas of its own importance.

"Love has good manners and does not pursue selfish advantage. It is not touchy. It does not keep account of evil or gloat over the wickedness of other people. On the contrary, it is glad with all good men when truth prevails.

"Love knows no limit to its endurance, no end to its trust, no fading of its hope; it can outlast anything. It is, in fact, the one thing that still stands when all else has fallen."

First of all, there can be no empathy when one loses patience quickly with a troubled person. This can happen when one is more concerned about his own affairs than about his counselee's interests or needs. Lack of patience may destroy any possibility of empathy; it can easily be detected by the counselee whether through words or through actions and attitudes.

Sometimes the counselor shows his impatience by "pushing" the counselee too fast to get on with his problems, so that, presumably, the counselor may begin his "important work."

The basic love from which empathy springs "is not touchy." "Touchy" implies a degree of oversensitivity on the part of the counselor, which really means that he is more concerned about receiving the counselee's praise and approval than he is of giving his attention to the counselee's needs. Here is an area where lack of insight and failure to be aware of the counselor's own emotional blocks may cause trouble and destroy empathy or make it impossible to establish empathy in the first place.

A touchy counselor is one who listens primarily for things that might reflect upon his own character or worth rather than seeking for constructive ways to be helpful to the counselee. A neurotic counselor is inclined to become extremely touchy and to be thrown on the defensive by any slight word or act on the part of the counselee which would insinuate that the counselor is not as important as the counselee.

Love also refuses "to keep an account of evil or gloat over the wickedness of other people."

Rather than having a judgmental attitude, the counselor is glad with all good men when truth prevails. This is to say that the counselor is responsive to the counselee wherever he sees in him potential for good and evidence of truth. The counselor's joy is a contributing factor in the deepening and strengthening of empathy.

There is an ongoingness in love which "knows no limit to its endurance." The counselor must learn to endure all sorts of things in his counselees.

But the next factor is even more difficult at times. Love knows "no end to its trust."

Every counselor, especially every pastoral counselor, has people who come to him clothed in hypocrisy, insincerity, and falsehood. Their neurotic problem makes them need to test the sincerity of the pastoral counselor by their very insincerity.

The smiling face, smooth words, and overly pious attitude which some counselees bring to their counseling relationship with their pastors may be deceptive for a while. Eventually the real nature is discovered—and then the counselor has a real problem. He needs to trust his counselee, but how can he trust one who is so false, deceptive, and insincere?

Actually he cannot. Nevertheless he must learn to trust his belief in and knowledge of his counselee's need for help. Above this he must have an unfailing trust in the presence and power of the Wonderful Counselor, the Holy Spirit, who is ready and willing to change the counselee from an untrustworthy person to a person of integrity and honor, through the instrument of the counselor. This basic personality change is impossible without the work of the Holy Spirit within the heart, but the pastoral counselor need never doubt it as an unfailing possibility and desirable result in the counseling relationship.[7]

Test your ability to empathize with people in the following hypothetical situations. A counselee comes to you quite upset over the possibility of losing her job. "I have really been trying hard at work to please my supervisor," she says. "But I just can't seem to make him happy. He's cross and blunt when I make a mistake. Just yesterday I made a mistake on a letter. He gave me this hard look and said he would like to have someone who uses better grammar and style than he does." Which of the following responses would you use?

1. Minister: "He sounds very unreasonable. Why don't you tell him you're doing your best and no one is perfect." This is an *advice giving* type of response and shows no awareness of the person's feelings. The counselee could feel misunderstood and may not be willing to divulge too many of her feelings.
2. Minister: "It sounds as though you have a hard person to work for." There is an *indirect reference* to her *feelings* in this statement, but it actually focuses mainly on the supervisor.
3. Minister: "I sense that you're feeling overwhelmed and lost concerning how to please your supervisor, and you wonder if the situation isn't hopeless. You're afraid your job might be threatened, and you may be wondering 'What do I do now?'" This type of response seems to *reflect the counselee's feelings* of distress and possible hopelessness in her situation. The last phrase includes an *action* statement, which may help her explore some possible alternatives.

For you to be seen as a person who cares and is sensitive and empathetic, you need to use language that conveys that feeling. Repeating the same phrases over and over borders on redundancy. What you need is a repertoire of appropriate introductory phrases. Below is a list of possible empathetic response leads. If you will read this list out loud once a day for a month you will be amazed at how these phrases will just come to mind as you counsel others.

Empathetic Response Leads

"Kind of feeling..."
"Sort of feeling..."
"As I get it, you felt that..."
"I'm picking up that you..."
"Sort of a feeling that..."
"If I'm hearing you correctly..."
"To me it's almost like you are saying, 'I...'"
"Sort of hear you saying that maybe you..."
"Kind of made (makes) you feel..."
"The thing you feel most right now is sort of like..."
"So, you feel..."

"What I hear you saying is..."
"So, as you see it..."
"As I get it, you're saying..."
"What I guess I'm hearing is..."
"I'm not sure I'm with you, but..."
"I somehow sense that maybe you feel..."
"You feel..."
"I really hear you saying that..."
"I wonder if you're expressing a concern that..."
"It sounds as if you're indicating you..."
"I wonder if you're saying..."
"You place a high value on..."
"It seems to you..."
"Like right now..."
"You often feel..."
"You feel, perhaps..."
"You appear to be feeling..."
"It appears to you..."
"As I hear it, you..."
"So, from where you sit..."
"Your feeling now is that..."
"I read you as..."
"Sometimes you..."
"You must have felt..."
"I sense that you're feeling..."
"Very much feeling..."
"Your message seems to be, 'I...'"
"You appear..."
"Listening to you, it seems as if..."
"I gather..."
"So your world is a place where you..."
"You communicate (convey) a sense of..."[8]

Empathetic statements respond to the counselee's surface feelings, and also focus on those deeper feelings the person may not be expressing or may not be fully aware of at the time. Often, when a person is expressing his anger, he is also feeling hurt. You can respond to both those feelings. These phrases are sometimes called "additive empathetic" responses because they attempt to help the counselee put deeper feelings into words. They do require the counselor to make an inference. Statements such as these are not stated as definite fact but in a very *tentative* manner. This allows the counselee to accept or reject the possibility of the statement. It allows him to say that part of your response was accurate and part inaccurate. Some phrases might be:

"It sounds as if..."

"I'm wondering if you're saying..."

"Perhaps..."

"Maybe..."

"Is it possible that..."

"Would this fit..."

"Do you suppose..."

Confrontation

The word "confrontation" is used frequently in discussions of counseling techniques. What is confrontation? When should it be used? A counseling confrontation has been defined as an act by which a counselor points out to the counselee a discrepancy between his own and the counselee's manner of viewing reality. Confrontation is really part of everyday life, and it can be used effectively when we are involved in helping another person. Confrontation is not an attack on another person "for his own good." Such a negative and punitive attack would be detrimental to the counselee. As William Crane puts it:

> A judging confrontation, unprepared for, may end any relationship which would make counseling possible. The person already feels guilty and ashamed, and to be judged and condemned rather than understood and accepted is nothing less than absolute rejection. A person laden with guilt already feels cut off and rejected by all that stands for rightness and justice; he surely does not need to be condemned by the one to whom he goes seeking help.[9]

Girard Egan suggests that confrontation at its best is an extension of advanced, accurate empathy. That is, it is a response to a counselee based on a deep understanding of his feelings, experiences and behavior. Such a response involves some unmasking of distortion and the client's understanding of himself, and it includes a challenge to action.[10]

William Crane says, "Only when empathy is established is the climate ready for confrontation; until then it is neither wise nor helpful."[11] The relationship between confrontation and empathy is very important, yet many counselors fail to see it.

Act of grace. Confrontations have also been called acts of grace. Egan defines confrontation as "a responsible unmasking of the discrepancies, distortions, games and smoke screens the counselee uses to hide both from self-understanding and from constructive behavioral change."[12]

Challenging the counselee. Confrontation also involves challenging the undeveloped, the underdeveloped, the unused and the misused potentials, skills and resources of the counselee with a view to examining and understanding those resources and putting them to use in action programs. Confrontation is an invitation by the helper to the counselee to explore his defenses, those that keep him from understanding and those that keep him from action.

Our purpose in confronting a person is to help him make better decisions for himself, to become more accepting of himself, and to be more productive and less destructive in his life. There are times when professional and nonprofessional alike hesitate to confront because it involves a commitment. There is also the possibility that the counselor could be wrong or the person might misunderstand and feel rejected. We also need to be careful that the confrontation does not work against what we are trying to accomplish in the counselee's life, even though it is given with proper intentions.

When is confrontation appropriate? Earlier it was mentioned that empathy must be a part of the relationship. The quality of the relationship between counselor and counselee is very important. Generally speaking, the stronger the relationship, the more powerful and intense the confrontation can be. A confrontation must come about because the counselor cares about the counselee. If we do not care about him or his improvement, confrontation can be harmful.

Confrontation is the constructive act of "bringing close together for comparison or examination." It is the minister's or counselor's opportunity to explore growth-defeating discrepancies in the counselee's perceptions, feelings, behavior, value and attitudes in order to compare and examine them. This helps the counselee view his life and behavior in a different light. Challenging some of the counselee's thinking or behavior can be a bit threatening to the person unless the counselee senses your concern and goodwill for him.

Confrontation is not used during the early phases of counseling. At what point during the various phases of a crisis do you think the person would be able to handle a confrontation?

Another factor involved in confrontation is the ability of the counselee to understand and see what you are saying. Is he able to accept the confrontation? Can he follow through with what you are suggesting?

At the appropriate time, confrontations can be made in a tentative manner with statements such as "I wonder if..." "Could he be..." "Is it possible..." "Does this make sense to you?" and "How do you react to this perception?"

How might a counselee respond when confronted? Egan suggests several possible responses. The counselee might try to discredit the counselor. He could do this by attacking the counselor, showing that he knows better than anyone else. If this occurs, it could mean that the counselor has been wrong in the confrontation and has not been perceptive. A counselee might attempt to persuade the counselor to change his views. He might employ reasoning. He might try to show the counselor that he is really not that bad or that he is being misinterpreted. He might also try to minimize the importance of the topic being discussed by rationalizing it. As often happens in pastoral counseling, the counselee might seek support for his own views from others.

Often a counselee will agree with the counselor. His agreement could be valid or it could be a game. He might agree in order to get the counselor to back off. If the agreement does not lead to behavioral change, the sincerity of the counselee should be questioned. The goal in confrontation is not necessarily to have the person agree, but to have him reexamine his behavior so that he can understand himself better and act in a much more effective manner.

One example of a direct confrontation in Scripture is in 2 Samuel 12:7-14. Nathan confronted David with his sin against Uriah and Uriah's wife, Bathsheba. David openly admitted his sin, and Nathan responded by saying, "The Lord also has taken away your sin; you shall not die. However, because by this deed you have given occasion to the enemies of the Lord to blaspheme, the child also that is born to you shall surely die" (vv. 13,14). Because of the wrong David committed—against Uriah, against his position as king of Israel, against Bathsheba, and against the unborn child—David had to be confronted with the total picture.

William Crane notes:

> The judgment placed upon David for his sin was not without an expression of the love and mercy of God in providing pardon and forgiveness. When Nathan was able to say, "The Lord has also put away your sin; you shall not die," he was giving reassurance to David of his acceptance by God and his pardon as a result of his true repentance. Had David not been confronted by Nathan in this way it is doubtful that he would have come to recognize or admit the fact of his sinfulness and need for forgiveness.[13]

Adaptability. When you work with people, you cannot use the same approach every time. You must be sensitive to their needs. The need for adaptability is stated in 1 Thessalonians 5:14: "We earnestly beseech you, brethren, admonish (warn and seriously advise) those who are out of line— the loafers, the disorderly and the unruly; encourage the timid and fainthearted, help and give your support to the weak souls [and] be very patient with everybody—always keeping your temper" *(AMP)*.

How do you confront a person when he is doing something wrong? In John 5, Jesus asked the man at the pool, "Do you really want to be healed? Do you really want to change?" When I work with people, I ask those questions in one way or another. In John 8, Jesus responded to the woman caught in adultery by saying, "Go, and sin no more."

Honesty and acceptance. Important principles to follow in all our counseling are honesty and acceptance. Proverbs 28:23 states: "In the end, people appreciate frankness more than flattery" *(TLB)*. In Proverbs 27:5 we read: "Open rebuke is better than hidden love" *(TLB)*. "Brethren, even if a man is caught in any trespass, you who are spiritual, restore such a one in a spirit of gentleness; each one looking to yourself, lest you too be tempted" (Gal. 6:1). "But when they persisted in asking Him, He straightened up, and said to them, 'He who is without sin among you, let him be the first to throw a stone at her'" (John 8:7).

Barriers to Helping the Person in Crisis

Even when we attempt to follow all the principles of effective counseling, there is always the possibility that our counseling could affect a person in an adverse manner. This occurs when destructive elements enter into the counseling process. We will identify a number of these in the hope of preventing them from taking place.

Passivity. Passivity on the part of the minister can be very frustrating to the counselee. Listening and responding with nonverbal encouragement is important, but if there is little or no verbal activity, the counselor's responses will be questioned, and he may appear ambiguous. If the person is insecure or dependent, he may interpret a passive response as not caring, criticism or even rejection. Naturally, your verbal activity will vary from counselee to counselee, and this is a judgment you will need to make. The timing of when you are silent as well as when you speak is important but can be determined by sensitive listening on your part.

Counselor dominance. Counselor dominance is a contrast to passivity. Unfortunately, it occurs all too frequently among those in ministry. Why? Perhaps some ministers are frustrated, would-be counselors, and this is their opportunity to show the person what they can do. It could be out of their own insecurity that they feel the need to dominate. Or they may simply desire power, and this is a place where it can be obtained.

A dominating counselor or minister, however, does not enter into the world of the counselee's experience and thinking. Instead, he jumps in with advice and erroneous conclusions and makes dogmatic pronouncements or interpretations. Because he responds from an external frame of reference and not within the life of the counselee, he is prone to act all-knowing and infallible. The question then is: Whose needs are being met by this counseling? Certainly not the counselee's. Rather, the needs of the person doing the counseling are being met at the counselee's expense.

How can we tell if we are becoming dominant? Symptoms include frequent interruptions, impatience, changes of subject, attempts at persuading the person and lectures. Some dependent people may welcome this approach, but it does not help them in the growth process.

Self-disclosure. Another ineffective approach is inappropriate self-disclosure. Talking too much about yourself and your own struggles, feelings, family, success or failures causes the counselee to wonder how your "ego-trip" relates to his problem. Again, his needs are not being met. There are occasions when describing your own experiences can benefit the counselee, but do it sparingly.

Interrogation. Improper use of questions falls into the category of interrogation or grilling. We need to do more than use questions to gain access to the counselee's feelings or to gain information. Statements, being encouraging, and listening well will bring you the information and feelings. The counselee's level of comfort built from your responses will assist him in being open with you. Do not overload the early stages of counseling with questions.

Inappropriate patterns of response. Inappropriate patterns of response create a distance between the minister and the counselee. Because they keep the counselee at a distance, genuine caring, trust and openness cannot develop. These patterns protect the counselor from his or her own discomfort, fears or anxieties that are associated with deep involvement in the client's life.

One way to promote distance is to prohibit the counselee from crying in one way or another. By doing this, the counselee begins to feel that crying is either wrong or a sign of weakness. The counselee needs the beneficial release that tears provide. Denying their expression can be harmful.

Limiting discussion to safe topics only, topics that do not involve emotions or self-disclosure, also creates distance. By doing this the minister avoids the risk of becoming involved in highly personal, painful or emotionally laden topics. Weather, sports, news and so on all serve as a buffer but accomplish nothing.

False reassurance. False reassurance is dangerous to the counselee, too. Giving the reassurance prematurely or without justification helps the minister avoid exploring significant feelings of the counselee that could include anger, despair, depression, anxiety or hopelessness, or subjects that may be uncomfortable such as abuse and incest. When there is a genuine basis for reassurance, then it becomes appropriate. Too much usage, however, promotes dependency and raises the question of whether the minister knows what he is talking about. Sometimes it can eliminate anxiety and conflict that need to remain a while so the person is motivated to continue seeking counsel.

Emotional detachment. Emotional detachment creates some of the same problems as passivity but is manifested by taking the role of a technical expert who is aloof. Intellectualizing is a form of detachment that again keeps the minister from real involvement. Theorizing about issues may be interesting, but is it productive? Debating or lecturing on theology may be interesting, but is the counseling setting the proper place? If the counselee has the tendency to use intellectualization as a defense, be careful not to respond in like manner.

Passing judgment. Moralizing, admonishing, or passing judgment may actually be expected by some who seek out a minister. In fact, they may have a need for this. But responding in this manner does not bring about genuine change on the part of the counselee. Many counselees are fully aware of the way they are living, and it is best to take the time for them to make their own value judgments. And for people in crisis, such responses do not help them move through the crisis phases but may keep them stuck at a specific point.

Patronizing behavior. Patronizing or condescending behavior is also ineffective because it does not reflect respect. Counselees can feel demeaned by this and inferior to the counselor, which may produce resentment. Flattery, insincere praise, catering to win favor and giving excessive advice fall under this category. Such actions by the counselor do not motivate the person to take responsibility.

Inappropriate confrontations must be mentioned even though we have already said much about confrontation. Ministers who use confrontation excessively are betraying a belief that the problem must be fixed as soon as possible. A confrontation should never be used until a caring relationship has been established and there is emotional involvement.

Pressure tactics. Pressure tactics can create distance. Pressuring counselees to accelerate their progress by prodding, assigning too much outside work, browbeating, predicting negative consequences if they do not respond, and questioning the sincerity of their motivation all fall into this category. These tactics usually ignore the feelings of the person and are perceived as punishment.

We need to realize that for some people, change will be very slow. But they need our encouragement and our faith to move them along. Because some lack faith and hope, they need our sense of hope and faith in the Lord and the future to carry them until their own hope and faith builds and they can rely upon their own inner strength. All of these are just a few of the unproductive patterns that can occur. Becoming familiar with them may help us help others

Notes

1. Peter Buntman and Eleanor Sais, *How to Live with Your Teenager* (Pasadena, CA: Birch Tree Press, 1979).
2. Paul F. Wilczak, "Listening as Ministry," *Marriage and Family Living*, LXII, 3 (March 1980), p. 4.
3. Frederick C. Thorne, *Principles of Personality Counseling* (Brandon, VT: Journal of Clinical Counseling, 1950), as quoted in *Counseling Teenagers*, by Dr. G. Keith Olson.
4. Girard Egan, *The Skilled Helper* (Monterey, CA; Brooks/Cole, 1975), p. 76.
5. Joshua Loth Liebman, *Peace of Mind* (New York: Simon and Schuster, 1946), pp. 7,8.
6. Donald C. Houts, "Sensitivity, Theology and Change: Pastoral Care in the Corinthian Letters," *Pastoral Psychology*, XX, 193 (April 1969), p. 25.
7. William Crane, *Where God Comes In: The Divine Plus in Counseling* (Dallas, TX: WORD Incorporated, 1970), pp. 31,36.
8. D. Corydon Hammond, Dean H. Hepworth, and Veon G. Smith, *Improving Therapeutic Communication* (San Francisco, CA: Jossey-Bass, 1977), pp. 114,115.
9. Crane, *Where God Comes In*, p. 57.
10. Egan, *The Skilled Helper*, p. 158.
11. Crane, *Where God Comes In*, p. 60.
12. Egan, *The Skilled Helper*, p. 158.
13. Crane, *Where God Comes In*, p. 56.

THE PROCESS of CRISIS INTERVENTION

4

Eight basic steps are needed to help a person in crisis. These steps are applicable to various types of crises, but you will need to be sensitive and flexible in their application. Each client and each specific concern is different, and you need to adapt to the person.

Immediate Intervention

The first step is *immediate intervention*.[1] Crises are perceived as a danger. They are threatening to the person involved, and there is a time limit to the opportunity for intervention. This is a time of turmoil with a high level of distress.

The vulnerable or disturbed state of the person is his or her reaction to the initial impact. Each person will respond to the problem in a different way. Some see it as a threat to their needs, their security, or to their being in control of their own lives. Others may see it as a loss. Still others see it as a challenge to growth, mastery, survival or self-expression.[2]

Every minister has his or her own schedule. Many ministers have set aside specific times for counseling. When a call comes into the church, either you or the church secretary will need to determine if this is a crisis that requires immediate attention or an issue that could wait until later in the day or for your next opening.

Some people handle an accident, discovery of child abuse or sexual molestation, an affair or a job loss quite well. Others fall apart. The waiting list, however, has no place in crisis counseling. The preparation of a message, a committee meeting, luncheon engagement or golf game must be interrupted. Crisis experiences do not check your calendar to see when it would be convenient. People in crisis may be hesitant to reach out if they see you as exceptionally busy. They may hesitate to interrupt and will need your reassurance that they did the right thing by contacting you. They need to know you are glad they did. Let them know that their issue takes priority.

Create a State of Equilibrium

Remember that people cannot tolerate the stress of a crisis for long. In one way or another they will resolve it within a period of six weeks. A state of equilibrium must be achieved. If they must wait to see you, it shouldn't be for more than one night. And if there is a wait, at least talk with them briefly over the telephone.

The way people in crisis achieve equilibrium may or may not be healthy. They may be so overwhelmed that they become self-destructive if they do not receive immediate help. You need to act quickly because your assistance can make the crisis less severe and may help protect the person from inflicting harm upon himself.

In a crisis there is tension, a sense of urgency, misperceptions and lowered efficiency. Therefore, many attempts for quick relief that the person makes will not be well thought out. They could even be counterproductive by worsening the problem or crisis.

Use Sustainment Techniques

During the beginning phase of helping a person in crisis, sustainment techniques are used. The purpose is to lower anxiety, guilt, and tension and to provide emotional support. All of these are efforts to restore equilibrium.

Reassurance is used in the beginning phase to help the person who is worried about cracking up. But remember that too much reassurance may eliminate all the anxiety when some is needed for positive change to occur. Encouragement helps the counselee overcome his feelings of helplessness and hopelessness.

Procedures of direct influence are used to promote desired changes in a counselee. These are used more often in crisis counseling than other types of counseling. These can include encouraging new behaviors as well as reinforcing what the person is already doing.

When a person is depressed, confused or bewildered, he may need more forceful techniques. You might advocate a definite course of action or warn the person of specific consequences if he acts a certain way. A suicidal person needs direct intervention.[3]

Some of the most severe outcomes of a crisis are suicide, homicide, running away, physical harm, psychosis or a family breaking apart. Cutting oneself off from acknowledged emotional ties of a family is a disaster for both the person and the family members.

Avoid a Disastrous Outcome

Therefore, one of our goals in crisis counseling is to *help avert a disastrous outcome*.

During crisis times, you have a tremendous opportunity to help and minister. The unsettled state of a crisis is also a time of change and flexibility. The person is never more open to growth, more accessible and less defensive. Because he is unsuccessful in his typical ways of responding and coping, he is open to trying something new. If you are going to have an effect upon the life of a person or family, it will be at this time. That is one reason crisis counseling is so important for those in ministry.

As I mentioned earlier, you may need to talk with the person on the phone first. Ask some questions to help you determine the urgency of the situation and if it really is a crisis. I have had some people call and say there was an emergency or crisis and then discover the problem had been in existence for months. While on the phone, arrange for the first meeting and determine who is to be present. Try to gain enough information to formulate a tentative idea about the problem and make some simple plans if needed for the first meeting. By doing this you are not totally unprepared for your first meeting, but you do need to be flexible. Some crises would necessitate having several people come to the counseling session if they are affected or if they could be a support group.

Be sure you maintain control of the conversation over the phone. You may need to limit it. It is all right to let the person know you have a few minutes to talk in order to arrange for the first meeting. If you get too involved, the counselee will want you to solve the dilemma over the phone. If you hear too much of the story at this time, the person may be hesitant to discuss it again. You are expected to remember the details. This conversation is simply to make contact and establish the beginning of a relationship. This can, by itself, be a support to the person.

If for some reason you are unable to see the person immediately, arrange for him to be seen by someone else. This may mean a minister or worker from another church if you do not have anyone else available. Church or denominational loyalties are unimportant during a person's crisis.

Taking Action

The second step of crisis counseling is *action*. Something needs to start happening right away. People in crisis tend to flounder, and we need to move them toward meaningful, purposeful, and goal-directed behavior. They need to know that something is being done by them and for them. They need to feel this right from the first session. This is not the time to have them fill out questionnaires, take a personality test, explore their history or just establish rapport. You, as a minister, need to be very active. You will need to participate in, contribute to and direct this first session. Listening is an important part of gathering information.

During this time, help the person understand the crisis. Usually the crisis is related to some event, but he is not able to bridge the two. He needs to bring his feelings of despair together with the event. Encourage the person to express his feelings.

Probe into the Past

Even though crisis counseling does not focus too much upon the past, it is important to determine how the person was functioning prior to the crisis. It is not necessary to do a structured investigative inquiry, but listen for significant information through the interaction process. You are looking for indications of the previous emotional state, behavioral patterns, thought processes, relationships with other people and any physical problems. In a sense you are endeavoring to discover what happened, who is involved, when it happened and so on. The questions who, what, when, where and how will be your guide. This is usually accomplished by having the person tell his story.

Significant issues need to be discovered and considered such as: What are the person's strengths? What are the weaknesses or deficiencies? (Low paying job, low self-image, few friends and so on.) Why did their problem solving ability break down at this time? Has anything similar to this ever occurred before? These questions are necessary because in crisis theory there is a basic premise. Most people involved in a crisis have experienced some type of precipitating event and it needs to be identified. The person also experiences an inability to cope, which leads to the crisis. And the reason for this inability needs to be determined. As the person tells his story, listen to how he feels. What impact has this crisis had on his work, friendships, family life and physical health? Is his daily routine the same, or has it been altered? What are his thought processes like? Is his thinking intact and clear? Are there excessive fantasies? Dreams?

Explore the Person's Strengths and Weaknesses

As you work with a person, give attention to both his strengths and his weaknesses. Many people in crisis have aspects of their lives that are not affected. Look for these as well as the weak areas. As you discover some strengths or abilities that are part of the person's life-style, you can encourage the person in that direction.

One counselee was involved in a physical exercise program. He was encouraged to continue this regularly because it served as a basis for breeding self-confidence, distraction from his problem and energy. Family members and friends can be a strength. Are they available? Is there an indication of dangerous behavior to the person or someone else? (Suicidal difficulties will be discussed in a later chapter.)

Look at any potential future difficulties for the person or his family. Some might need help in telling parents or children what has occurred. An abused spouse may need a safe place to stay.

Determine Immediate Needs

As you are gathering this information from his story and your questions, you are seeking to discover the following: (1) Which issues in the person's life need to be attended to immediately; and (2) which issues can be postponed until later? Help the person make this determination, for so often people in crisis are not aware of what can wait and what must be handled now. As you work more and more in crisis situations, you will discover that you seldom have to conduct a question-by-question approach to derive this information. The person will volunteer most of it. But as you discuss the situation with the person, *be sure to keep all these questions and issues in mind.*[4]

Be aware of the person's level of alertness and his communication capabilities. Attempt to identify the cause of the crisis with questions such as, "Tell me what has happened to make you so upset," or "Can you tell me the reason you're so upset? I would like to hear what you have to say." Those in a crisis state sometimes have difficulty stating clearly what they want to say. When this occurs, you will need to be very patient. Any verbal or nonverbal indications of impatience, discomfort or urging the person to hurry will be detrimental. Allow for pauses, and remain calm. Remember that, especially during the impact phase of the crisis, there is a stage of confusion and disorientation, and the mental processes are not functioning as they normally would. Some of the pain is so extreme that the words will not come easily.

As you listen to the person, notice if any important themes are being expressed. You can detect this either through statements being repeated or through their being stated with great intensity. These are clues to the person's point of distress.

On occasion you will need to channel the direction of the conversation. Some crisis situations need *immediate* action rather than tomorrow or next week. You can reinforce statements that are related to the crisis and avoid responding to unrelated topics, such as rambling statements that deal with the past or peripheral events. You might say, "What you have just said sounds important to you, and in the future we can talk about it. But right now, it doesn't seem directly related to your real concern. Let's come back to that." This process of focusing helps filter out any material that is irrelevant to the crisis but that the person may not realize is meaningless.

Seek Clarification

If you are confused by what is said, don't hesitate to ask for clarification. When the person is able to express himself fairly well, help him to explore the alternatives available to deal with the situation. Questions such as, "What else might be done at this time?" are helpful. Discover what type of support system the person has—spouse, parents, friends, fellow workers, or even people in your congregation whom you have trained to be a support for an isolated person. It could be the person is new in town with no contacts or roots in your area. You will need to help create a new support system in addition to whatever help you can personally give.

A person in a crisis will interpret his environment as something that is difficult to manage. He sees confusion and perhaps even chaos. Try to determine if you might be able to bring a greater sense of order to the person's environment. If you can assist in bringing a sense of calm and stability, you will help the person a great deal. Perhaps the person needs to stay at a different location for a while. He may need some space and quiet, or even to be away from others who are attempting to help but actually add to the confusion by their inappropriate attempts.

As the person is talking with you, assess what he is telling you and compare it to the problem as you see it. A crisis is triggered by the person's perception of what has occurred. You may have times when you feel the counselee is overreacting, but remember that what he is reacting to might not be the main problem. Some people fall apart over an insignificant occurrence that is really only a trigger mechanism. They may have blocked or delayed a response to a crucial problem.

For example, a mother seemed to be functioning quite well after a major accident that killed one person and critically injured her son. But while doing dishes in her kitchen, she dropped a plate and immediately fell apart. She alternated between hysterical weeping and intense anger. A relative visiting in the home could not understand this reaction to the simple breaking of a plate. The minister who worked with her later in the day, however, was able to bring all the factors together.

Ministers and lay counselors alike often ask, "How do I know how much action to take?" A rule of thumb is this: only if circumstances severely limit the counselee's ability do you take extensive action. And when you do, you want to move the person to an independent role as soon as possible.

Facilitative or Directive Roles?

It has been suggested that you will take either a facilitative or a directive role in helping the person deal with the crisis.

If the crisis is high in danger to the person, or to others, if the person is so emotionally overwhelmed that he has no capability to function or take care of himself, if he is on drugs or alcohol, or if he has been injured, then you would take a *directive role*.

When the person is not a danger to others or himself, when he is capable of making phone calls, running errands, driving and caring for himself or others, your role is *facilitative*. The counselee and you make the plans together, but the counselee carries out the plan. You may even want to work out a contract with the person detailing how the plans are to be carried out.

If your action is directive, the two of you need to work out the plan together, but the action involves both of you. The agreement or contract agreed upon could involve others such as a friend, spouse, parent, child, agency or church deacon. You need to be involved to the extent that the next step will be carried out by the person and the support people.

Whether you are taking directive action or facilitative, *listening* and *encouraging* are primary tools.

Advice falls under facilitative. You might say, "You know, I am concerned about what's happening to you at this time. Let's do this for now..."

Consider New Alternatives

You can advise new approaches and actions. You can also advise a new way of thinking or looking at the situation. Often I have people come in with statements such as, "I'm cracking up," "I think I'm going crazy," "I must be the only person to feel this way," "Other people don't have this much pain, do they?" "I am really a crummy Christian, aren't I?" "If I had more faith, I wouldn't be responding this way." What are these people really saying? What are they really feeling? They're saying "I'm out of control. I'm afraid." They are trying to figure out what is happening to them, and this is their attempt to understand their predicament.

Here is your opportunity to offer realistic reassurance with statements such as, "It is very common to feel this way, but in reality it's doubtful that you are going crazy. Your reaction and feelings are normal considering all that you have been experiencing." Or you might say, "With all you've been through, I'd be a bit concerned if you weren't reacting in some way." Helping them realize their feelings and reactions are normal can be a source of relief.

Often I show counselees the crisis sequence chart described in chapter 1; this helps to relieve pressure. Consider the implications of thinking you are going crazy or cracking up. Would that pattern of thinking help you recover or hinder the progress? Subtly and perhaps unconsciously, it becomes a blockage. Relabeling what is occurring is a part of the process of building hope.

When you are involved in helping a person with direct action, keep in mind the specific laws and legal procedures of your state and community. For example, do you as a minister, professional counselor or lay counselor have the status of privileged information or confidentiality when you counsel? What does the law state if the person talks specifically about suicidal or homicidal intent? Can someone in your county be involuntarily confined in a hospital for observation if the person appears emotionally distraught or suicidal? What if a parent tells you that he or she physically abused his or her child four years ago? What if an adolescent tells you she has been sexually abused? You need to know the law and any recent changes. (See Appendix 1 for additional information on laws and answers to some of these questions for the state of California. Resource books on counseling and the law that need to be read by every minister, counselor, lay counselor and church board member are also listed.)

Many ministers, because of time constraints, their own personality, or lack of available training tend to take direct action too often. Before you take action, ask yourself questions such as:

"Is this something the person could do for himself?"

"What will this accomplish in the long run?"

"How long will I need to be involved in this way?"

"Are there any risks in doing this? If so, what are they?"

"How could this person be helped in a different manner?"

Because the feeling of helplessness is so strong during a crisis, you can counter this feeling by encouraging the person to create alternatives and take action. It will also help the person operate from a position of strength rather than weakness. One way of doing this is to ask how the person has handled previous difficulties. Once again, remember to have the counselee do as much work as possible in order to build his self-esteem.

Coach the person to consider the possibility that there are other alternatives. Some statements can be structured in this way: "Let's consider this possibility. What if you were to..." "What might happen if you would..." "What do you think someone else might try at this time?" "Let's think of a person you feel is a real problem solver. What might that person do?" Be sure to help the person anticipate any obstacles to implementing the plan. We cannot assume that the person will follow through without first considering the obstacles.[5]

Avert a Catastrophe

The third step is to start achieving the *limited goal* of crisis counseling, *to avert catastrophe and to restore the person to a state of balance.* This is not a time to attempt personality changes. You must first help the person achieve some type of limited goal. There should be a bit of challenge to it, but it must also be attainable. A person who just lost his job may be able, with your help, to make a list of his qualifications, abilities and job experiences. Just the simple task of completing some action can provide a sense of relief.

Foster Hope and Positive Expectations

Fourth, since people in crisis feel hopeless, it is important to *foster hope and positive expectations.* Do not give them false promises, but encourage them to solve their problems. Your belief in their capabilities will be important. This is a time when they need to borrow your hope and faith until theirs returns. You expect the crisis to be resolved in some way at some time, and you expect them to work and be able to solve problems. It is your approach and interaction with them that usually conveys this rather than making blanket statements to them.

The problem-solving approach, rather than giving false reassurances, is a positive step. On occasion it is helpful to ask about past crises and upsets to discover how these were handled. This helps the person see that he has been able to work through past problems, which can help in instilling hope for his current problem. Begin to help him set goals for his future if he is at that phase of the crisis sequence.

As the anxiety level of the person drops, he will see the situation in a more objective manner. When this occurs, he can reflect on what has happened and what is now occurring.

Here are several important ways to help a person restore balance.

Information

First, look at the information the person is giving you about the situation. Does he see the complete picture or only selected aspects? Does he have all the facts? Is he distorting the situation because of his emotions or his own biases? Does he understand that certain responses and feelings are normal during times of crisis?

Asking pertinent questions and prodding for informational answers can help the person in two ways: (1) you can help to fill in some of his informational gaps; and (2) his fears and overconcerns can be diminished as he receives accurate information. Both steps help to restore equilibrium.

Interaction

In addition to considering the information the person in crisis is dealing with, note how he is interacting with the objective situation. How does the person grasp the choice of action open to him in light of the recent changes in his life (such as the loss of a job or a spouse)? What options are open to this person (such as caring for the children if a spouse has died or left)? Help the person consider the choices and the consequences of any decisions to himself and others who may be involved. Examining choices and consequences and then selecting a path enables a person to cope both now and in future situations.

As the counselee gains greater strength and capability, he will be able to examine his own part in the situation and how he is responding with feelings and behavior.

Provide Support

The fifth step in counseling a person in crisis is *to provide support*. One of the reasons for a problem's developing into a crisis is the lack of an adequate social support system. Intervention in a crisis involves giving support, and initially you may be the only one giving it. Just being available to talk by phone is a source of support.

The knowledge that you are praying for the person each day and are available to pray with the person over the phone is a source of support. Do not be surprised by a number of "urgent" calls during the early stages of a crisis. These need to be returned promptly and often. The purpose is to gain support just through simple contact with you.

Return Phone Calls

It is important to return calls promptly, but that is not the same as immediately. If you drop everything you are doing to call back within a few minutes, a dependency relationship could be encouraged. If, however, a half hour goes by, the person has the opportunity to do some thinking on his own. He may calm down, and by the time you do talk to him, the problem or issue is no longer as critical. This is important, because it takes you out of the role as the magical miracle worker. If the person is highly suicidal, of course, then you do need to call immediately. You also need to provide him with the phone numbers of other agencies and ask for his commitment to call them if you are not available.[6]

People in crisis need the assurance that they can call you at any time and you will be willing to talk to them for a few minutes. Even if you offer, they will still struggle with whether or not to call. If you do not let them know they can call, however, their struggle is intensified and could add to the crisis condition. Their self-esteem lessens even more with these struggles.

At some point you may need to set some limits on the phone calls as a person becomes better able to handle his life. In fact, that is how to express the limits! Because you can tell the person is better able to handle what is occurring, you want him to exercise his capabilities a bit more. You want him to call only during your office hours. Set a time limit on the calls, and perhaps suggest that he begin trying to let a day go by between phone calls. If you know he will probably call, suggest a time when it would be more convenient for you to respond. Sometimes I have suggested to clients that they give me a call at, for example, 2:00 P.M. on Tuesday. I have a brief break in my schedule at the time, I say, and I would just like to know how the person is getting along.

Expand the Support System

The best way of supporting the person is to expand his support system as soon as possible. This reduces demands on you. It helps the person through the crisis now, and it can also help to prevent a crisis in the future. More and more churches are training and equipping lay people to become involved in counseling. And since crisis counseling is short term, this is one of the best types of counseling to prepare them for.

A large church in southern California has selected about 70 couples from the church to be involved in their premarital counseling ministry. These couples have been given instruction in how to help engaged couples. They are available to meet with an engaged couple to help them in their preparation for marriage. A similar training program could be developed for crisis counseling.

When you see the person in crisis, try to determine what type of support system he has. Does he have any relatives or friends in the area? Who has he told about his difficulty? Be aware of the helping agencies in your area so you can direct him toward such help when needed. Neighbors and friends can provide baby-sitting or transportation. People from the church can provide cooked meals over a period of time. Try to determine who you can draw in and what they can do to reduce the pressures upon this person during his time of crisis.

Be sure you give some specific guidance to the support people. They are not to give a lot of verbal advice, which may be well intended but unnecessary and not beneficial at this point. Note how the person is stabilizing with this support, and as soon as possible gradually withdraw the support. We do not want counselees to expect and depend upon others living their lives for them over an extended period of time.

Be in Charge

In any type of crisis counseling, be sure you take charge of the sessions. You need to control the direction of the meeting, control the level and expression of anger, protect the counselees from too much pressure or trauma, and control both the person and the general level of anxiety.

If you have a crisis counseling session that involves either a couple or a family, here are some other principles to follow. When the couple or family come to your office, take the initiative to go out, greet them and invite them into your office. Indicate where they are to sit. By greeting them I mean introduce yourself to them and be courteous. Speak to each one and show an equal interest and friendliness. Let them know your purpose for the session and how much time you will be spending together.

You will be the most important element involved in setting the atmosphere for the joint or family sessions. Tell them you want to help them and they have the freedom to tell you how they perceive their current situation. Everyone will have the opportunity to talk, and you will help them look at the problem as it now exists, assist them in coming up with some new solutions and work with them in choosing a better way of handling the issues. It is also important to create a healthy atmosphere of communication. This may involve setting some specific guidelines such as the following:

1. Only one person at a time should speak. Each one is listened to for the purpose of understanding his perception of the issue and how he is feeling. It's okay to ask questions.

2. Each one needs to speak for himself and not for others. Any assumptions about another person's thoughts or feelings need to be checked out and verified.

3. A definite distinction will be made between thoughts and feelings and between facts and opinions.

4. Anything expressed that may be vague will be clarified so that all those present understand the specifics.

5. There will be differences in opinions, which is all right. The points will be clarified rather than argued. Some issues will be resolved, and others may not be. Some issues raised may be dropped because they cannot be resolved.

6. When a person is speaking, he may do so without being interrupted, but monologues will not be acceptable. A monologue causes others to lose interest, and the person talking gains control. Further, as the person continues to talk, it may cause his own feelings to escalate or may bother the others. You can interrupt the monologue to clarify a point, ask another person what he is hearing, comment upon someone else's nonverbal responses, or even say, "You know, you've brought up so many good points that I want to stop and clarify some of them."[7]

There may be occasions when it is difficult to stop the person. Lean forward, raise your hand a bit, and say, "Let's stop for a minute" in a definite, firm voice, which should keep you in control. I remember a very volatile family conference with five adults. The anger had escalated and people were rudely interrupting, each trying to outtalk the others. I listened a bit to see if they would gain control and then in a loud, definite, firm voice said, "All right, hold it!" They stopped and looked at me in shock. I went on to say, "None of you is listening, and you are getting nowhere. Now, this is what we are going to do if we are going to get anywhere." And I proceeded to again establish the guidelines and also stated that if there were a violation, I would interrupt the person to keep him on track. This does not happen too often, but you may need to be firm if it does.

If you are involved in ministering to married couples, here is a suggested resource to assist you in learning how to counsel. It is from the Counselor Training Video Series and is titled *Dr. H. Norman Wright on Marriage Counseling.* The three hours of instruction is designed to train ministers and lay counselors and covers crisis counseling principles as well as regular marriage counseling procedures. Half of the series is actual live footage of marriage counseling with several couples. It is available from either Christian Marriage Enrichment or Gospel Light. I would also encourage you to read the helpful book on affairs, *Broken Promises,* by Dr. Henry A. Virkler, published by WORD, Inc.

Focused Problem Solving

Step number six, *focused problem solving,* has been called the backbone of crisis counseling. You and the counselee try to determine the main problem that led to the crisis, and then you help the person plan and implement ways to resolve it. You may discover other side issues and problems along the way, but you need to stay focused on this one problem until it is resolved.

Think of yourself and the counselee as a team. You will work together. Dr. William Glasser, author of *Reality Therapy,* uses the word "we" in his counseling: "What can we do?" "How can we figure this out?" or "Let's see what we can develop as we spend this time together." Involving the counselee in the plan accomplishes two things: it increases his chances of following through, and it helps to develop self-reliance.

During the problem solving, the focus is on setting goals, looking at the resources available to use in solving the problem and brainstorming alternatives. Make a list of the alternatives that could be used. If the person is running dry on ideas, which often occurs, you can suggest some alternatives. You are not giving advice or telling him what to do; rather, you are offering other possibilities from which he can choose.

Help the person look at the consequences of each action, both negative and positive. A major question is: Will this alternative in any way go counter to the person's sense of values? For example, a husband who is having financial difficulties but highly values his time with his family and having his weekends free for church involvement may struggle with taking a second job that requires him to be out four nights a week and work three weekends a month.

Look for conflicts of values by asking for both the possible consequences and the person's feelings about each possibility. Let the counselee give his perception of the consequences first, and then (if you have additional valid information) you may want to offer some other possible suggestions.

Offer Tangible Steps

This week I talked with a woman whose divorce was to be final soon. She experienced a crisis time during the Christmas holidays that she did not expect to be so severe. As we talked, she indicated her tendency of wanting to return to her husband because of the emptiness of being alone. Through some simple questions, she was able to evaluate what had occurred in the marriage and whether her husband was willing to change if they got back together.

I also discovered that the woman had not clearly and in writing expressed to her husband the changes she needed to consider stopping the divorce. This was posed to her as a possible course of action, along with reading the book *Growing Through Divorce,* (Harvest House Publishers) by Jim Smoke, and seeking out a divorce recovery group to assist her. When she left the 45-minute appointment, she seemed to be in better control. Since she now had some tangible steps to follow, she was no longer immobilized.

After you evaluate the various alternatives, help the counselee select a course of action. You may need to encourage and even urge him to do so. Ask him for a commitment covering what he will do, how he will do it and when he will do it. Go through the process step-by-step in detail, and try to anticipate any roadblocks or ways the person may inadvertently sabotage himself.

You may become frustrated if the person says, "Oh, I've tried all of these things that we've talked about and they've never worked before" or "Oh, yes, I know what to do. I've had these plans before, but somehow I never get around to completing them." Your patience, your belief in his capabilities and your help to construct a workable plan may make the difference. It could help to ask for a commitment in writing, spelling out the details of the plan for both of you to remember.

Again, this past week, I talked with a woman who had three specific alternatives to use for her difficulty, all of which she had used before. And when these were used, her difficulties began to subside. This was a case where she said, "Oh, I know what to do, but I don't know why I don't follow through." I suggested, "Let's put those three steps into action this week. Will you take the medication your physician prescribed, follow the reading and exercises recommended by your treatment program each day for this next week, and then evaluate how you are feeling?" She agreed to do so, and I was confident she would follow through.

Any of the plans that have been developed may need to be refined through a reviewing process. You may need to help the person redefine the problem. A man may say his problem is that he "lost his job." Your interpretation of that could be that he has not yet adjusted to the loss of his job or started to consider a new source of employment. An older person may be shattered by the loss of a 17-year-old dog who was a constant companion. The problem seems to be the "dog died," but you would interpret it as "she has not yet adjusted to this loss in her life."

Focus on Reality

Be sure you do not make either the problems or the solutions appear overly simple. Information may resolve the problem, but not always. Remember that you need to be an expert, not in solving the person's problem for him, but in the process of problem solving and helping the person solve the problem himself. This will be noted by your attitude and approach. As you begin working with the person, first focus on the problem so it is properly defined and identified, and then turn to the problem solving.

Some people tend to avoid the reality of the problem and thus hope to avoid pain. Part of our task is to help them face the pain, but this must be done gradually so they are not overwhelmed. We can create an environment in which they feel safe and comfortable enough to face their situation fully.

One of the best ways to respond to emotions is to use active listening. This type of listening involves being alert for the underlying or latent message and then checking it out to see if you have heard correctly.

Counselee: "I just don't think it's worth the time and effort."

Pastor: "You're feeling kind of hopeless about it and doubt if it's worth trying."

In a sense, we sometimes guess about their feelings to help them clarify them. We are guessing at the meaning of what they are saying. Even if we are wrong, our listening will help counselees clarify their problems. When you are listening in this way, you are making statements rather than asking many questions. This approach keeps the problem within the counselee's responsibility, but he feels your support with him as he seeks to discover a solution. It conveys respect and acceptance as well as your expectation that the person will be able to solve the problem. This approach is useful when talking with someone who has a problem, but it should not be used in other circumstances.

Develop Listening Techniques

When I taught counseling courses in seminary, the other professors could always tell when we were covering active listening techniques. The students would begin using this approach in all their conversations. Not only was it difficult to get an answer to a direct question, but they would drive you up the wall with their listening responses. If guests came in and asked, "Where is the bathroom?" he might hear, "You're concerned about finding the bathroom." Or if a professor asked a student, "What do you think about this passage of Scripture in light of this commentary?" he might receive a response such as, "You're wondering about my understanding and perception of this passage." There are proper times and places to be an active listener, and there are times to be a proper and active responder!

Check Counselee's Anxiety Level

Monitor the anxiety level in each person, and attempt to regulate that level. There will always be some amount of anxiety, and some is necessary for the person to be motivated to face his problems. But we want to keep it from overwhelming the person. One way to accomplish this is to regulate the amount of emotion expressed and how it is expressed. When you work with couples or families, anger is the most common emotion. Your tone and example can be helpful in regulating the level. Note how each person may be responding by his posture and the intensity of his verbal responses.

Explore Counselee's Feelings

Within the process of problem solving, feelings of the counselee are important. If these are short-circuited, they will tend to short-circuit the problem solving later on. There are no shortcuts to helping a person in crisis. In many crises there is a grief over loss. It is common to equate grief with the loss incurred in the death of a loved one. But the loss of a job, a home, a valued object, a friendship, a family member through divorce or separation, an opportunity, hope, or ambition, as well as impending bad news, all bring grief. Encourage the person and help him work through the feeling of loss. It is necessary that the grief work be accomplished. If you become upset or overwhelmed by an upset person, however, you will not be able to help. And your tendency may be to try to stop him from being upset as soon as possible.

Counselees will express many feelings. You can help them sort out their feelings and identify those that are most acute. You can respond to the verbal and nonverbal expression of their feelings. Listen to them with your eyes and ears. Hear their tone and see their body posture.

As counselees share their hurt, you may feel it to an extreme degree and even feel like crying with them. But perhaps they need your strength at that point and just want you to be a good listener. I remember a woman who made an appointment for counseling some time back. When she came in she said that her husband had been killed in a steam shovel accident two weeks before while working on a job.

All of a sudden, I knew what the woman was talking about, for I remembered seeing the newscast showing the accident. She went on to describe, through tears, her feelings for her husband and what each of the children said about him after his death. She relived their hard times and their good times. She mentioned that the night before his death he had attended church with her and given his life to the Lord. As she expressed the feelings and gave me all this information, I had to fight back my own tears and struggle to maintain composure. She could sense my feelings with her, but she did not need to handle the intensity of my emotion at that time.

On another occasion a young husband described his feelings of being stuck in life with no where to go and no hope. I could feel his hurt and despair and I said to him, with tears in my eyes, "I can feel your hurt and wish there was more that I could say or do." He said, "I know and I thank you."

Take note of the person who is not experiencing or showing grief when grief should be the normal response. I have seen several people who appeared quite composed and seemingly in control. They even expressed the fact that they "are handling everything quite well." You might say something like, "I guess if I were in your situation, I would be hurting and feeling the loss like an empty spot in my life. I wonder what you might be feeling." Or you might say, "There will be a time when you feel the hurt and loss and you will probably weep. Maybe this is not yet the time to weep, but it will come."

With this last statement I have seen the composure break and the tears flow as the pain is experienced. This was not hard-hearted but a loving gesture on my part. It was an invitation to feel the hurt and share it with another person who would be there during the time of grief.

Think about feelings in crisis counseling in this way: They are an obstacle that must be dealt with before the real work of problem solving can occur. These can be handled by good listening procedures. In time, move from relating the feelings to the problem-solving process. This means moving from the ventilation of feelings to rational evaluation and resolution. This occurs whether the crisis situation involves a family or one person. If you see a family in crisis, there may be blaming, anger and attacks. Sometimes feelings can escalate and get out of hand if you do not help them make the connection between feelings and solutions. Encourage the person or people to begin the thinking process as soon as possible. At this time you may be functioning like a guide bringing the person or persons to their destination.

Building Self-esteem

It may sound strange to bring in the subject of self-concept within the context of crisis counseling, but this seventh step is one of the most important. It involves (1) assessing and understanding the person's self-image; and (2) discovering how the crisis is affecting it and how what you do also will affect it. This is a time to both protect and enhance the self-image. During crisis there is both anxiety and low self-esteem.

Here are some typical ways people respond to feelings of low self-esteem: (1) an anger at other people or even you; (2) a desperation that involves demanding help; and (3) a passivity that involves sitting back and waiting for help.

Sometimes the person who seeks your help is the one experiencing a crisis, or it may be someone who is trying to help a person in crisis and is not succeeding. Either one may have the same struggle with self-esteem. Be aware of the tendency to blame in order to protect the self-image. The blame will be coupled with anger. Anger sometimes gives a person a sense of control or of being in charge again. And even if it is irrational, it feels better than the state of hopelessness.

Some ministers and students have told me of their shock at the extent of the antagonism and belligerence that has been shown toward them as they tried to help. We don't have to be thrown by this if, in our own minds we can say, "It is all right for them to feel this way, and I do not have to take it personally. It is their protection against their feelings of failure and helplessness."

Expect negative feelings, and see them for what they are, camouflage against the pain of feeling bad about the situation and not too good about oneself either.

Be Consistent

Your task, then, is to be consistent in helping the person elevate feelings about himself. It also involves helping him to protect his self-image. Treat the person with respect and courtesy, and do not be condescending. It sometimes helps to show an interest in some nontroubled areas of his life.

If you are working with a family and this person is identified as the problem person, determine the effect of this labeling. Unfortunately, when families come in with a crisis and point the finger at one person, they fail to realize their own contribution to the problem and the ways they reinforce the behavior they do not like. You may need to divert attacks by family members by reinterpreting what they are saying, helping them to see the positive points or strengths in the person, and moving toward a solution rather than lingering on the blame. You can focus on the attacker and talk about his feelings and responses, or you can change the subject and begin asking, "What can we try at this time to change this situation? I would like a couple of suggestions from each of you, and I would like to know why you feel your suggestions would work?"

Believe in Counselee

Help them see how they have resolved difficulties before. When they say, "I can't handle anything; I can't even get through the day," respond with something such as, "I saw you come into my office by yourself, and you have been a big help by being able to provide so much information about your difficulty." If someone says he has difficulty expressing himself, you could say, "You're concerned that you are not communicating well, but you are very clear and doing very well in telling me the problem."

One of your goals is to help the counselee see your perception of him and belief in him and take that as his own. You need to believe that he or she has value, worth, and capabilities and at the present time is simply overwhelmed by the difficulty. Your assessment of the person may be more positive than his own, and eventually he may accept your assessment. An additional problem that besets Christians is the belief that they "should" be able to handle the difficulty, and that if they had more faith or a stronger relationship with the Lord, they would not be floundering. This produces more guilt, worse feelings about themselves and even less self-esteem. At some point later in the recovery phase, they may be able to recall that many of the people God used in Scripture went through their times of trouble as well.

As the counselee perceives that you believe in him (a reflection of 1 Corinthians 13:7: "Believe the best of every person" [AMP], which would mean giving that person the benefit of the doubt) and see him as a capable person, he will catch the fact that you have expectations for him. Again the idea of teamwork needs to be emphasized because you will brainstorm together, plan together, pray together and solve the problem together.

Instilling Self-reliance

Along with helping to strengthen the person's self-image, we work through this process to *instill self-reliance,* the eighth step in crisis counseling. Remember that a person in crisis is at the end of his rope. And because of this, his behavior may be regressive—he responds at an earlier level of functioning. He wants to be rescued and healed instantaneously by you. Do not respond to this need, however, for it will lower his self-esteem and create, in time, hostility toward you.

You may be surprised by the person's reaction if you have known him over a period of time. You may have seen him as alert, strong, and very capable. Now you cannot understand why he is falling apart. You may be shocked, threatened and overwhelmed yourself. You may be angry because you are seeing a strong person become so weak. His reaction may threaten your own sense of security, which may be solid or fragile. If he can fall apart, perhaps you, too, have that same capability under stressful conditions. And it can happen to any of us!

Build Team Effort

To keep a person from becoming too reliant on you, you need to make it clear you do not have all the answers. You expect effort from the counselee. Make sure the person is beginning to do things and doing them successfully. This means that small steps should be undertaken or the person becomes overwhelmed. This is especially true for anyone in depression, for any failure sends him two steps back down the ladder.

As stated before, you are developing a team effort in planning and evaluating the situation. Self-reliance comes from the counselee's being involved in the planning.

If you are working with someone who is basically a dependent person, it will be more difficult to get him to take responsibility. Others who know this person may alert you to this fact.

Encourage Self-help

One of the most basic principles to follow in crisis counseling is this: *Do nothing for the counselee that he or she can do successfully.* If there is a choice between you or the counselee making a phone call, if he has the capability of doing it, have him do it. As Douglas Puryear puts it:

> You are attempting to convey by your entire approach, your attitude that the client is a capable, decent person who has been temporarily overwhelmed by extreme stresses, and who will use your help to cope with these stresses and get back on the track.[8]

Let's dissect this sentence: "convey by your entire approach"—better than conveying it verbally; "is a capable, decent person"—supporting the self-image; "temporarily overwhelmed"—by the definition of crisis, it will be temporary, which provides hope and expectation; "who will use your help to cope"—defining your role (he will cope, with your help; you can't cope for him, but you can offer your support to his problem solving); "get back on track"—the goal of returning to equilibrium.

When people attempt to cope with their stress, their emotions run deep. They may have to cope with the threat to their source of past security and sense of competence and self-esteem. If these have been shattered, they have to deal with feelings of loss and longing.

In addition, new anxieties and frustrations will emerge now. Because of the upheaval of the crisis, the person has to make new decisions, devise new solutions or find new resources, and also may have to move into a new role of some sort.

And the new solution or role, once selected and implemented, may carry with it some stresses of its own. Adjustments to the new solution and role will occur because of shifts in position and status in the family and community. This involves acceptance of the new solution, the level of satisfaction with this solution, or even learning to live with less than being satisfied until the new solution or role level is stabilized.

Note: It is important that you read *Recovering From the Losses of Life*, by this author, for additional information on grieving and how to respond. In addition, a complete curriculum is available to accompany the book, which can be used for teaching or preaching in the local church. Both are available from Christian Marriage Enrichment.

You are the helper God has called to walk through these transitions with the person.

In Appendix 2, you will find a Crisis Assessment Summary that many have found helpful. Turn to the appendix at this time and read through the questionnaire. You may want to reproduce copies of this to have available. This can be given to the person in crisis, or you can use it as a guide as you talk with the person. This is an adaptation of the Crisis Questionnaire prepared by Karl A. Slaikeu and Ruth Striegel-Moore (1982) in *Crisis Intervention* (Boston: Allyn and Bacon, 1984), pp. 289-293.

Notes

1. Douglas A Puryear, *Helping People in Crisis* (San Francisco, CA: Jossey-Bass, 1979), eight steps adapted.
2. Lydia Rapoport, "Crisis Intervention as a Mode of Brief Treatment," in R. W. Roberts and R. H. Nee, eds., *Theories of Social Casework* (Chicago: University of Chicago, 1970), p. 277, adapted.
3. Naomi Golan, *Treatment in Crisis Situations* (New York: The Free Press, 1978), pp. 98,99, adapted.
4. Karl A. Slaikeu, *Crisis Intervention: A Handbook for Practice and Research*, (Boston: Allyn and Bacon, 1984), pp. 89,90, adapted.
5. Ibid., pp. 90,91, adapted.
6. Golan, *Treatment in Crisis Situations*, pp. 98-101, adapted.
7. Puryear, *Helping People in Crisis*, p. 62, adapted.
8. Ibid., p. 49.

THE CRISIS of DEPRESSION

~~~~~~~~~~~~~~~~~~~~~~~~~~~~~~~~

5

She sat there quietly, her eyes downcast. Now and then she would look up and sigh. "Every day seems longer than the day before," she said. "It's a chore, and I don't see things getting any better. Some days I don't even want to get out of bed, and when I do, I don't have any energy or interest in doing anything. And then I see the mess the house is in and that makes me feel worse. Sometimes I feel as though I were paralyzed. It's so hopeless. I can't do anything. I feel like I'm stuck in quicksand at the bottom of a pit."

Depression: a painful experience, a feeling of hopelessness. Whether it is the depression of a short-term crisis experience, a rejection, a child getting into trouble or the loss of a loved one, it all feels the same. It is one of the most common and oldest of all disorders.

Depression is no respecter of persons. It hits the 6-year-old as well as the 70-year-old, the rich and the poor, the black person and the white, the Christian as well as the non-Christian.

Have you any idea how many people in your own congregation are dealing with some degree of depression right now? What do you think the response would be if you were to ask your congregation next Sunday morning, "How many here today are experiencing some type of depression?" It could be 1 percent or 5 percent, but more likely it would be 10 to 20 percent. And if you were to ask, "How many have experienced depression in the last five years?" the percentage would probably be even higher.

Depression has been called "the common cold of the mind." It occurs in both crisis experiences and when there isn't a crisis. Mental health experts conservatively estimate that 1 in every 10 people in our country suffers from depression. Actually, the rate is probably much higher because in its milder forms it often goes unnoticed and undetected. One out of every 8 people can be expected to require treatment for this condition at some time during his or her life. We are now seeing more symptoms of depression occurring in childhood and adolescence. Each year it is estimated that between 4 and 8 million people are depressed to the extent that they cannot effectively function at their jobs or must seek some kind of treatment.

Neither you nor your congregation is immune. If you want a very attentive audience when you preach or teach, speak on depression. Present what it is, the causes, its purpose, what to do to lessen it, and how to come out of a depressed state and learn and grow from the experience.

Depression Is a Normal Emotion

Is it normal to be depressed? Many people are confused about depression and even question its existence in the life of a Christian. It is a normal and natural emotion, and we would be abnormal if we did not become depressed when the causes for depression are present.

In many cases depression is a healthy response to what is taking place in a person's life. Being depressed is not a sin. It is a normal reaction to what is happening to us psychologically and physically. Depression is a scream, a message telling us that we have neglected some area of our lives. We must listen to the depression, for it is telling us something we need to know.

Depression is a warning system that we are moving toward deep water. It is also a protective device that can remove us from stress and give us time to recover if we use it in that way.

This is not to say that we should choose to linger in our depression. Rather, we should discover its purpose and move on in life. The depression of grief over some type of loss may lift a bit and reoccur in various intensities again and again.

Depression Is a Family of Systems

What is depression? It is a family of systems, and under its umbrella we find everything from a mild feeling of gloom to an incapacitating state.

1. A person *feels hopelessness, despair, sadness and apathy.* It is a feeling of overall gloom. A move toward depression is a move toward deadness and emptiness. Feelings change, and there may appear an air of sadness about the person.

2. When a person is depressed he *loses perspective.* The way you perceive your life, your job and your family is discolored when you are depressed. Depression is like a set of camera filters that focus upon the darker portions of life and take away the warmth, action and joy from the scene. There's a distortion of ourselves, of life and of God.

As one man said, "There's a real difference between being unhappy and being depressed. When my wife and I have an occasional argument, I'm unhappy about it. I don't like it. But it's a part of living. We make up in a fairly short time. I may be concerned over it, but I can sleep all right, and I still feel in good spirits. But when I'm depressed, that is a different matter. It hurts all over; it's almost something physical. I can't get to sleep at night, and I can't sleep through the night. Even though there are still times when I'm in pretty good spirits, the mood comes over me nearly every day. It colors the way I look at everything. If my wife and I have a fight, our marriage seems hopeless. If I have a business problem, which I can normally react to with some tension and frustration but which I deal with promptly and appropriately, I feel as though I'm a lousy businessman and I battle with the problems of self-confidence instead of dealing with the issues in front of me."[1]

Depression produces a negative thinking pattern toward all of life. Aaron Beck describes this as a "cognitive triad."

False beliefs begin to invade the person's mind and are typically negative. It is also important to note the topics that do not enter the person's

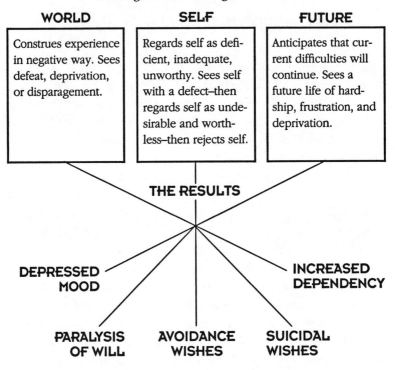

Depressive Triad
Thinking Patterns – A Negative View of

WORLD	SELF	FUTURE
Construes experience in negative way. Sees defeat, deprivation, or disparagement.	Regards self as deficient, inadequate, unworthy. Sees self with a defect–then regards self as undesirable and worthless–then rejects self.	Anticipates that current difficulties will continue. Sees a future life of hardship, frustration, and deprivation.

THE RESULTS

DEPRESSED MOOD **INCREASED DEPENDENCY**

PARALYSIS OF WILL **AVOIDANCE WISHES** **SUICIDAL WISHES**

mind, as they are just as important. No longer do positive memories produce appreciation for one's self and hope for the future.

3. The depressed person experiences *changes in physical activities*—eating, sleeping, sex. Sexual interest wanes, and some men find that they cannot perform. This reinforces their feelings of worthlessness. A lessening of sexual interest should always raise the question of depression. Some lose interest in food, while others attempt to set a world record at gorging themselves. Some sleep constantly; others cannot sleep. All types of physical aches and pains may occur when a person is depressed.

4. There is a general *loss of self-esteem*. The person feels less and less positive about himself and questions his value. Self-confidence is very low.

5. There is a *withdrawal from others* because of a groundless fear of being rejected. Unfortunately, the depressed person's behavior could bring on some rejection from others. The depressed person cancels favorite activities, fails to return phone calls and seeks ways to avoid talking with or seeing others. The more serious the depression is, the more unpleasant it may be to be around the person.

6. There is a *desire to escape from problems* and even from life itself. Thoughts of leaving the home or running away as well as the avoidance of others enter in. Suicidal thoughts and wishes arise because of the feeling that life is hopeless and worthless.

7. A depressed person is *oversensitive* to what others say and do. He may misinterpret actions and comments in a negative way and become irritable because of these mistaken perceptions. Often the person cries easily because of misinterpretations.

8. There is a *change in the activity and level of thinking*. A person may become agitated and experience a slowdown in his or her thinking ability. This may include an inability to concentrate or make decisions.

9. The person has *difficulty in handling most of his feelings, especially anger*. Anger can be misdirected toward oneself and others. The anger at oneself is based upon feelings of worthlessness and a lack of knowing how to deal with the situation; often this anger is directed outward.

10. *Guilt* is usually present at a time of depression. The basis for the guilt may be real or imagined. Frequently, guilt feelings arise from the assumption that the depressed person is in the wrong somehow or that he is responsible for making others miserable because of the depression.

11. Often depression leads to a *state of dependence* upon other people. This reinforces feelings of helplessness; then the person becomes angry at his own helplessness.

It is important to remember that once a person starts becoming depressed, he usually behaves in a way that reinforces the depression.

Depressive Episodes

There are various types of depressive episodes. Some are what we call acute reactions that have a sudden onset, have intense symptoms, last a brief period of time and often lift without treatment. The depression experienced during a crisis or loss is usually acute.

Chronic depressions take a longer period of time to occur and have symptoms that vary in intensity. They tend to last for years and are more difficult to treat.

Reactive depression is a response to some event in the person's life. This can include a reaction to any type of loss such as that of a loved one, a job, opportunities, or friendships. It can be a reaction to an injury or illness, or even to some type of success or positive event such as a new job or promotion, marriage or new home. The reaction makes sense even though the depression is really affecting the person's life.

Grieving depression is involved in the death of a loved one. This is a normal and healthy response to such a loss. It is a depression we need in order to resolve the loss and move on with life.

Whenever you work with a person who is depressed, whether it be a child, adolescent or adult, look for: (1) the causes of the depression; (2) how the person is functioning and if he or she has resources to give help and support; and (3) whether or not the person has had a complete and thorough physical exam recently.

Discovering the cause for depression can sometimes be complicated, for there are a number of them and several could be in operation at the same time. Inadequate food and rest, insufficient exercise, improper treatment of the body, a glandular imbalance, hypoglycemia, repressed anger, violating one's value system, sin, unrealistic expectations and negative thinking are all causes.

(A resource on depression to use with counselees: *Dark Clouds, Silver Lining* by Dr. Archibald Hart, Focus on the Family Publishing, 1993.)

Loss and Change

In order to really understand the depression experienced by people in crisis, it is important to consider in a bit more depth the concept of loss and change.

Loss is one of the major themes underlying depression, but it is often overlooked by those endeavoring to help the counselee. A real or perceived loss is often the cause for the depression. We must see the loss from the counselee's perspective, since from our own perspective we would probably not consider it a loss, or at least not a serious one. Explore the meaning of loss for the person. Losses become a trigger for depression. They threaten our security, our sense of stability and our well-being.

Our self-image may be affected, and we may feel out of control. If there is excessive attachment to another person, a loss may even mean the loss of life's purpose or meaning.

The more sudden a loss, the more out of control and floundering we feel. A sudden, unexpected death may disrupt our ability to activate the emotional resources needed to cope. At least a gradual loss, although painful, can be prepared for to some degree. Couples can plan for the time when their children will be grown and will move away. They can discuss their feelings and make plans. But if the separation occurs years earlier, with no plans and no forethought, the reaction is one of devastation.

Often the depression is heightened if what is lost was seen as necessary and irreplaceable for the person to function. Archibald Hart describes four different types of losses:

Abstract losses. Abstract losses are intangible, such as the loss of self-respect, love, hope or ambition. Our minds actually create these losses, and we feel we have experienced them. At times the loss may be real, but at other times it may not be as bad as we feel it is.

Concrete losses. Concrete losses involve tangible objects—the loss of a home, a car, an heirloom, a photograph or a pet. We can feel and see the loss.

Imagined losses. Imagined losses are created from our active imaginations. We think someone doesn't like us anymore. We think people are talking behind our backs. Here is where our self-talk is focusing on negatives and our perceptions may not be based on fact.

Threatened loss. The most difficult type of loss to handle is threatened loss. This loss has not yet occurred, but there is a real possibility that it will happen. Waiting for the results of a biopsy or a state bar exam, or waiting to hear from the admissions office of a college to which we've applied, carries the possibility of loss. Depression can occur because in this type of loss we are powerless to do anything about it. In a sense we are immobilized

When the attachment to whatever was lost is normal and balanced, the person quickly attempts to reorganize his life without the lost value or person.

Sometimes an experience of success triggers the depression. Those who reach their goals after extensive time and struggle may find that it was the struggle that gave meaning to life. Often, achieving sought-after goals does not produce the anticipated satisfactions.

Some success carries with it the threat of having to produce even more or feelings that perhaps we have overachieved and overextended ourselves and are setting ourselves up for failure. If a success produces tension and uneasiness instead of a comfortable feeling of satisfaction, it could produce depression.

Transitions of Adult Life

We are becoming increasingly aware that depression often accompanies the transitions of adult life. When roles change, a challenge may come to our beliefs, values and assumptions about how we have been living our lives. A number of changes can mean a loss of control over some phase of life. If control is a strong value, depression may follow. Some people have never learned to express dependency. They have a deficit in this area, and when control is taken away, they flounder. The balance they have lacked now results in depression.

For example, the "loss of youth" throws many as they realize their bodies have changed and they no longer have the years left to do what they may want to do. Depression may occur when a person in mid-life faces the fact that they too will die, and perhaps sooner than they think. It has been suggested that the age of the forties and fifties is a time of mourning, anger and disappointment about our inevitable death.

Depression occurs when a person recognizes the need to make the transition but has difficulty making the changes. He may feel he is failing in the new role, or he may not be satisfied with it. The transition to retirement is a very common problem. Depression also occurs when the person recognizes failure in the new role but is unable to change his behavior or his role. He feels stuck. There is a prevailing feeling of hopelessness.

If there is a problem in coping with a role transition, the following issues are usually involved:

1. The person has lost some familiar social supports and attachments.
2. He is struggling with managing his emotions over this, such as anger or fear.

3. He feels the demand for a new repertoire of social skills.
4. He experiences a diminishing of self-esteem.

The cause of depression over role transitions varies. A young adult may be depressed over problems in creating a satisfactory sense of role identity or forming close peer relationships. A middle-age person's depression may occur because of lack of success or decrease of satisfaction in career, marriage, social status, parenting roles and so on. Older-age depression occurs because of retirement or loss of health, friends or relatives.

Specific questions you ask the person can help both of you clarify the adjustment difficulty.

Look for evidence that the depression has followed changes related to life's transitions. Ask questions such as: "Tell me something about the change (move from a home to an apartment, retirement, divorce, empty nest and so on)." "How did your life change?" "What important people or places were left behind? Any important activities left behind?" "Who or what took their place?" "How do you feel in the new role?"

Simple questions such as, "Tell me about the old (home, job, spouse, friendship and so on). I'd like to hear the good things and the rough spots. What didn't you like? What did you like?"

As you encourage the person to express his emotions, attempt to elicit feelings about the change. Let him know it is all right to talk about them. Use questions such as: "How did it feel to change or give up or leave—I'd like to know the details of leaving. How did you feel when you first learned about the change? And when did the change actually occur? How did you feel in the new situation? What was it like at first and has that changed? What is it like now?"

The majority of transitions require learning new skills. Your task in counseling is to help the person look at and evaluate the meaning of the new role expectations. In doing this, you are trying to discover the beliefs and emotions that are hindering the person from utilizing potential coping skills. Help the counselee analyze the resources and skills he has for making the transition. Look for areas where there may be an under- or overestimation of resources.

Sometimes the counselee is struggling with performance anxiety. To overcome this, help him or her rehearse the difficult situation. Ask him to imagine in detail the worse thing that could happen. Is it likely to happen?

What would the results be? How would he recover from it? You may want to use some positive imagery techniques and have him visualize himself successfully handling the situation. Obviously, this assumes your ability to use this important approach.

Another transition problem may be stereotyped or incorrect assumptions about the new role. How do these occur? Usually by observation or identification with significant others from the past who were undesirable models. By evaluating these beliefs and bringing in reality, a shift in attitude can occur.

To handle the last problem of adequate support groups, you need to deal with the person's fear. New people and new relationships can be threatening. Will the new people and groups be as good as the old ones? Help the counselee evaluate the opportunities available for getting involved with other people and groups. What assistance does your church have to offer? People who are depressed tend to overlook the available opportunities. They tend to expect the worst, including rejection, and also behave in such a way as to perpetuate the belief.[2]

Counseling the Depressed Person

A minister or lay counselor can take the initiative in helping a depressed person. Commenting on someone's verbal or nonverbal expression or absence from meetings or involvement can create an opportunity for assisting the person. Even social contacts or pastoral calls may be the starting point for counseling. Or perhaps a neighbor, friend or relative will ask you to make a contact because of his or her concern.

Taking the initiative may be necessary, since the depressed person tends to isolate himself from others, though that is actually self-destructive. His self-imposed separation reinforces his negative assumptions. A depressed person needs others who are trustworthy to assist in bringing the facts of life into proper perspective. The depressed person, however, feels that no one cares. So he may reject the offer to help, which once again reinforces his feeling that "no one cares."

The depressed person needs to know that one of your main goals is to help relieve his depression. You want to help him discover and understand the cause of his depression and strengthen his defenses, which will help lift the depression.

Rapport

One of the first and most crucial steps is to establish rapport with the counselee. A depressed person may feel dependent upon the minister, but he may also feel unworthy of receiving help from him or incapable of responding to his suggestions. Thus, you may have to make a greater effort to establish rapport with the person. Some rapport may already have been established if the person is involved in part of the life of the church. If he seeks you out on his own because of previous contact, a basic trust has already been established.

If the person was a referral or you have to seek him out, he may have already attempted other means of coping with his depression. These include worry, alcohol, withdrawal, reading Scripture or books, praying and talking with friends. Because of his confusion, not even positive methods have worked. He has already experienced failures in trying to resolve his problem, which is difficult for him to understand. And the more failures he has had, the less hope he has now.

During the first contact, the person needs to be given hope that this new approach and effort is worth trying. Be sure he experiences a balance of warmth and understanding in the first session. He needs a person who cares and is willing to express his care and concern for him. You can establish rapport with a person by becoming involved in his life. This means talking with him about his family, business, friends, hobbies, and personal background. Rapport is best established by being quiet, warm, accepting, firm and objective. An assertive, aggressive, boisterous counselor is not always appreciated, nor is the passive, noncommittal, uninvolved person. "How can I help you?" you ask. The person may not know exactly how you can help, but he does know he wants to be rid of the depression.

It is important to be an active listener with a depressed person. If you listen well, the person will be willing to talk about the pain and hurt of the depression. Listening and responding can provide some release for the person.

But often the depressed person's thought processes are such that he cannot move beyond his focus upon his own mood. Yet you need to move his attention away from his feelings to the cause or trigger of the depression. With depressed people you must be more actively involved, more assertive, directive and interactive than with other problems. The depressed person's energy and motivational level for change are lower than with many other types of difficulties. You will have to work harder for progress in the counseling sessions. You must move strongly but not aggressively. You do this by conveying to the counselee that you and he are a search team working together to discover the cause, what may be the loss if there is one, and what to do now.

Relief

If a loss is at the heart of the depression, identifying and acknowledging the loss can bring a sense of relief. Simple questions are helpful at this stage.

"How long have you felt this way?"

"When do you remember this starting?"

"What happened at that time to change your mood?"

"Do you feel depressed all the time, or do you feel depressed only periodically?"

"If you do not feel depressed all the time, how frequently do you have episodes of depression? How long do the episodes last?"

"Have you ever experienced this mood before? When?"

"When does the depression tend to occur? Is it morning, afternoon, evening or night? Is it weekdays, weekends or holidays? What is happening when you feel depressed? Are you at a particular place doing a specific thing? Are you with someone? If so, who?"

"Did you seek help at that time? What did you do? What was the outcome?"

"Now that this has occurred, how do you think it will change your life?"

"What are the options you have to handle this change?"

"What is the worst thing you can imagine happening?"

Many ministers and counselors use the Holmes-Rahe Social Readjustment Rating Scale to help the counselee examine the recent remembered and forgotten events that may have caused the depression. Remember that each person varies in his or her reaction to each event. Here are the events with their point value and the explanation of the meaning. When I give this to a person, I eliminate the actual point value so it will not influence the person's response.

Holmes-Rahe Stress Test

In the past 12 months, which of these have happened to you?

EVENT	VALUE SCORE	EVENT	VALUE SCORE
Death of a spouse	100___	Son or daughter leaving home	29___
Divorce	73___	Trouble with in-laws	29___
Marital separation	65___	Outstanding personal achievement	28___
Jail term	63___	Spouse begins or starts work	26___
Death of a close family member	63___	Starting or finishing school	26___
Personal injury or illness	53___	Change in living conditions	25___
Marriage	50___	Revision of personal habits	24___
Fired from work	47___	Trouble with boss	23___
Marital reconciliation	45___	Change in work hours, conditions	20___
Retirement	45___	Change in residence	20___
Change in family member's health	44___	Change in schools	20___
Pregnancy	40___	Change in recreational habits	19___
Sex difficulties	39___	Change in church activities	19___
Addition to family	39___	Change in social activities	18___
Business readjustment	39___	Mortgage or loan under $10,000	18___
Change in financial status	38___	Change in sleeping habits	16___
Death of a close friend	37___	Change in number of family gatherings	15___
Change in number of marital arguments	35___	Change in eating habits	15___
Mortgage or loan over $10,000	31___	Vacation	13___
Foreclosure of mortgage or loan	30___	Christmas season	12___
Change in work responsibilities	29___	Minor violation of the law	11___

TOTAL _____

According to the two doctors, Holmes and Rahe, if your score is under 150 stress units, you have only a 37 percent chance of getting sick or becoming depressed within the next two years because of the amount of change in your life. If your score is between 150 and 300, the probability rises to 51 percent. And if your score is over 300, the odds are 4 to 5 (80 percent) that you could become ill or depressed during the next two years because of the amount of change in your life. This test is widely used, especially in the military, to predict whether one will be sick during the subsequent two years.[3]

Note: This test was recently revised for women and can be found in the book *The Female Stress Syndrome* by Georgia Witkin (Newmarket Press, 1991). Her research and new findings are worth reading. At the conclusion of the chapter on ministering to children in crisis you will find the Holmes-Rahe Stress Test adapted for use with children and teens.

Reassurance

A depressed person seems to have an insatiable need for verbal reassurance. Unfortunately, however, such a person is unable to gain any relief or satisfaction from it. Yet his need is genuine, and you need to be able to give reassurance again and again in a warm, calm and nonirritated manner. It can be helpful also to let the person know that you are aware of the difficulty he has in gaining comfort from the reassurance.

In some cases, a depressed person may have been told a hundred times that his mood will eventually return to normal, and he may even agree. But he may not feel a real emotional comfort from the prospect of eventually gaining some relief. Even times of former strength and happiness are covered over by the present gloom. The person may feel that he never was really happy or joyful.

Reassurance is needed early in your encounters with the depressed person. Reassurance is *not* "Pull yourself together," "Snap out of it," or offering a magical promise that "Everything will work out all right." You do not know exactly how things are going to work out or when. You need to be able to work through the suffering with the person. Attempting shortcuts only drives the person to bottle up his real feelings and pain.

Depressed people say that what gives them reassurance is a caring, patient, loving relationship; helping them search for the cause of their difficulty; and the counselor's belief in them. It is important to gently show them passages from the Word of God that can be of comfort and strength.

Scripture. Perhaps you already have some Scripture you use, but here are several verses that are helpful: Isaiah 40:28-31; 41:9; 42:3; 43:1-4; Philippians 4:4-9. I have used a paraphrase of 1 Corinthians 13 entitled "Because God Loves Me" for several years. (See the end of this chapter for a copy that you may reproduce.) Give the person a copy, and read it out loud together.

Ask the person to read it aloud morning and evening. In time, many depressed people have derived comfort from the thoughts expressed in it.

Activity. Make every effort possible to keep the depressed person active. This can be a task because of the tendency to be apathetic and listless. Personal encouragement, setting up a very specific, detailed plan with the person and physical exercise can be helpful.

Exercise is an active approach to life, whereas depression is a malady that creates passivity. Inactivity gradually becomes the style of life. Exercise can be partial inoculation against depression, and can also be part of the treatment. Active people or those who engage in regular exercise each week report a better sense of psychological well-being than those who do not exercise.

Dr. Otto Appenzeller of the University of New Mexico has found that the nervous system releases hormones called catecholamines during marathon running. In his research project, he discovered that the catecholamines in all marathon runners were increased to 600 percent above normal. It is also known that these hormones are low in people suffering from depression. Therefore, it would appear that the connection between running and the release of these hormones could be generalized to include moderate forms of exercise.[4]

In another experimental study, a number of depressed clients became involved in a gradual planned program of running. They reported reduced tension and sleep improvement, and depressive symptoms began to lift.[5]

Normal patterns. Another question you might ask the counselee is, "If you were not depressed, what would you do when you leave here today?" You may find the person saying, "Well the department store has a sale on, and I could stop by there. And when I get home I could do the dishes that have stacked up for two days. And a friend of mine called and wanted to have me help her with her sewing, so I could go over there for an hour. And I think I could fix my husband a better meal than he has been getting for the past few weeks." So it might go. When the person has finished listing these things, suggest that this is what you would like her to do when she leaves. There is probably very little that would keep her from doing these things. If she agrees, work out with her the specific details of how to proceed with these new tasks.

Ask questions such as, "How long will you spend at the department store? What will you look for? What are you interested in buying? What do you want to spend? What is the first thing you will do when you arrive home? How will you do the dishes? What will you wash first?" This may sound trite and overly detailed, but it is very necessary to help construct a detailed plan so the person will be successful in carrying out this new pattern of behavior.

Counseling a depressed person is a time when advice and persuasion can be useful. Timing and sensitivity can help the person avoid rash decisions and break through the apathy.

Say, "Let me make a suggestion and see what you think about it," and then make your suggestion. After the person responds, no matter what he says, you could respond, "Let's give it a try this week. We really don't have that much to lose, do we? What day could we start? What time?" and so on.

Revelation

Self-discovery, or personal revelation, is part of the process of counseling. Often the person you are counseling is learning more about himself than you realize. These revelations may be positive or negative. One must be aware that both can occur. It is important to assist the depressed person to look at all sides of these revelations, for he may have the tendency to put them into a negative state because of being depressed. Incorporate all these revelations into your overall strategy for helping the person recover.[6]

Reorganization

A depressed person will reorganize his life-style and in some way his personality. As his mood lifts, spend time reviewing what happened to him—the causes of his depression as well as what he might do the next time in a similar situation. Actually, the two most important features that can be covered at this time are a thorough understanding of what caused the depression and the construction of an even stronger self-concept than he had prior to his depression.

Here are some other specific suggestions you could make to help the person reorganize his life:

1. Try to keep up your daily routine. If you work outside the home, try to go to work each day. It is more beneficial for you to get up in the morning, get dressed, have breakfast, go to your place of work, and go through the motions of working than to remain home in bed with your discomforting thoughts.

2. If your work is in the home, the same procedure may be followed. Consider your daily chores important. You may feel that "it doesn't matter what I do." But it does.

3. Try to get out of the house, even for very short periods of time. You might go out for the paper in the morning after breakfast, to a shop or for a walk around the block. Try to go to a favorite place or store.

4. If you can push yourself to do it, try to see family members and friends as much as possible, but for *very short periods of time*. Don't try to entertain in your own home, but visit others informally and briefly. Try to do things spontaneously.

5. Deliberate physical activity is very important for overcoming depression. Involvement in any kind of physical activity you ordinarily might like is helpful. It is difficult to remain depressed when you are singing, swimming, bicycle riding, jogging, playing tennis and so on.

6. If it is difficult to talk to the people you live with, write a note. Explain briefly, for example, that it is of no use to you if they try to lift your spirits by kidding you, however well-intentioned they may be.

7. If your friends and family are the kind of people who think you will be strengthened by being scolded and criticized, tell them your counselor says they are mistaken. You need encouragement, support and firmness.

8. Let your partner know what you are feeling and that your performance is not as it usually is.

9. Remember that severe depressions usually end. Accept this whether you feel like it or not. It might be easier to get through each day.

10. In all depressions, have a person you can trust (a family member or a friend) to whom you can complain and express feelings of anger. Find one—and let out your feelings!

11. If your appetite is poor and you are losing weight, try very hard to eat small amounts of food frequently.[7]

These next suggestions are in no way exhaustive but are included to give you an idea of the various approaches to use. The first one is a behavioral approach used to activate the person at the start of the day. Because people suffering from depression have difficulty remembering what has been suggested and agreed to, reproduce your suggestions and send them home with the person. But be sure to read through the instructions with them while they are in your office.

Morning is the worst time for depressives. They awake feeling awful, often have slept fitfully, have a "heart of lead," may feel anxious and dread facing the day. Despite their activity list scheduled the night before, through their sleep and depression-fogged senses the day looks dreadful. A difficult awakening is to be expected but does not need to rule the day. Give specific morning homework such as the following example:

Homework Assignment No. 76
Arise Immediately. Awaken Your Body. Charge into Activity.

Upon awakening do not lie in bed—you will ruminate and become more depressed. Get up immediately no matter how hard it seems. Keep a radio or tape deck handy; turn it on and listen as you walk into the bathroom. Turn on the shower, adjust it to warm, and move in. Scrub yourself briskly and feel the pleasant strong stimulation. Make the water gradually cooler and scrub, slap, move faster. Cool the water as cold as you can stand, feel it, then jump out. Towel off vigorously and listen to the radio music or conversation. As you move into your room to dress, begin to think about your pleasant activities for the day. Refer to your activity list, which should be in the room on your dresser or table, and plan a rapid transition into the first activity after you are dressed. If you live with someone else, talk to them, draw them into conversation. The worst part of the day is now under your control—congratulate yourself and keep up the momentum. Now is a good time for a walk or other physical exercise.[8]

As stated before, the thinking pattern of a depressed person is basically negative and hopeless in its perspective. It is important to help the depressed person change both his behavior and his thought processes. Often changing behavior first gives the person the fuel he needs to alter his negative thinking. Here are three suggestions by Dr. Archibald Hart that are very helpful to offer depressed counselees. Again, after you discuss these with the person, send home the printed instructions.

I. Positive Thinking
   A. Take a card and write down five or six events you know will give you pleasure.
   B. Next to each pleasant event, write down two or three specific ideas or aspects of the event that interest or captivate you.
   C. Keep this card with you at all times. Every hour or two take out your card, select a pleasant event and deliberately begin to think about one of the specific ideas you have written down.

II. Thought Changing
   A. Set aside 20 minutes for contemplation at the beginning and end of each day. Get yourself a small notebook specifically for this exercise, and during these periods of contemplation, write down every worry, anxiety, concern, bothersome thought, event or person that comes into your mind.
   B. Review your list of bothersome ideas. Ask yourself, "Which of these can I take care of right now? Is there anything I can change?" Then take that action immediately and cross that concern off your list.
   C. Take a moment to pray about the rest of your list—those concerns you cannot take care of there and then. Commit to God any concern you cannot change. Then close your notebook and go about your business, trusting that God is in control of all you cannot control.
   D. If any concern continues to bother you, make a note of it once more in your notebook.
   E. Writing down thoughts and ideas helps to get them out of your memory where they will otherwise be kept alive by the memory-refreshing mechanisms of your brain. Your notebook, therefore, serves as an external memory. It can be taken with you everywhere.

III. Changing Self-Talk
Purpose: This helps you become aware of the conversations you have with yourself, especially those that are illogical and irrational.
   A. Set an alarm or use some device to signal you at least once every hour. You can use class breaks or any other natural break in your day to signal the time for the exercise.
   B. At the moment you are signaled, stop what you are doing and review very carefully the conversation you have been having with

yourself during the previous five minutes. Write it down as sentences. Try to recall as many ideas or self-statements as possible.

C. Take your list of self-talk sentences and review each one. Ask yourself the following questions about them:

    1. Is it true?

    2. How do I know it is true?

    3. Is it reality?

    4. Am I overreacting?

    5. Will it be different tomorrow?

    6. Am I being sensible and realistic?

    7. What's the real issue?

    8. Where will this idea take me?

D. Deliberately counter your negative self-talk with positive, realistic, reassuring sentences.

E. Find someone (a friend or spouse) to discuss your thoughts with. Irrational self-talk is best challenged in open conversation with another person.[9]

Another way to help in changing negative thoughts is to employ some type of action approach. Below is a written exercise that describes the process. Ask the counselee to keep a notebook. On the left side of the page list the negative thoughts, in the middle list his answer, and on the right list the action he will take to counter the negative thought.

Role of Action in Changing Beliefs

NEGATIVE THOUGHTS	ANSWERS	ACTION
I can't do anything about my depression.	If I try, I can beat it.	Write out answers to negative thoughts. (Strengthens belief you can control your emotions.)
I don't enjoy anything.	Maybe if I do something I used to do, I'll have fun.	Go to a movie. (Strengthens belief that thoughts aren't facts.)

NEGATIVE THOUGHTS	ANSWERS	ACTION
It's too hard for me to finish my term paper.	I'll try an experiment and work on it for 10 minutes.	Work on it 10 minutes. (Strengthens belief that it's best to test out negative predictions.)
I bet this lump is cancer.	I'd better see a doctor to check it out.	See doctor. (Strengthens belief that it's best to have good information.)
I can't think of the answers to this test. I'm going to fail.	Stop thinking about failure. Think about the question.	Focus thinking on test questions. (Strengthens belief that you can control thinking.)
I'm ashamed of how I talk.	Shame is self-created. If I don't think it is shameful, I won't feel it is.	Give a public speech. (Strengthens belief that you can control painful feelings.)
If I disagree, she'll think badly of me.	I have survived the disappointment of others quite well before.	Express your disagreement. (Strengthens belief that you are an adequate person.)
I made a terrible mistake. What if people find out?	It's a mistake to think I can never make a mistake. So what if they find out? It won't be the end of the world.	Tell someone about the mistake. (Strengthens belief that you don't have to be perfect.)

Depression will be one of the most common maladies you encounter. Equip yourself through additional study and reading so you can become proficient in recognizing depression, helping to your level of ability, and so you will know how and to whom to make a proper referral when necessary.

The following paraphrase of 1 Corinthians 13 has been used for years by those assisting depressed persons. Ask the person to read this paraphrase out loud twice a day and in time the truth of this Scripture passage will begin to seep into their thought life.

Because God Loves Me
1 Corinthians 13:4-8

Because God loves me He is slow to lose patience with me.

Because God loves me He takes the circumstances of my life and uses them in a constructive way for my growth.

Because God loves me He does not treat me as an object to be possessed and manipulated.

Because God loves me He has no need to impress me with how great and powerful He is because *He is God,* nor does He belittle me as His child in order to show me how important He is.

Because God loves me He is for me. He wants to see me mature and develop in His love.

Because God loves me He does not send down His wrath on every little mistake I make, of which there are many.

Because God loves me He does not keep score of all my sins and then beat me over the head with them whenever He gets the chance.

Because God loves me He is deeply grieved when I do not walk in the ways that please Him, because He sees this as evidence that I don't trust Him and love Him as I should.

Because God loves me He rejoices when I experience His power and strength and stand up under the pressures of life for His Name's sake.

Because God loves me He keeps on working patiently with me even when I feel like giving up and can't see why He doesn't give up with me, too.

Because God loves me He keeps on trusting me when at times I don't even trust myself.

Because God loves me He never says there is no hope for me; rather, He patiently works with me, loves me and disciplines me in such a way that it is hard for me to understand the depth of His concern for me.

Because God loves me He never forsakes me, even though many of my friends might.

Because God loves me He stands with me when I have reached the rock bottom of despair, when I see the real me and compare that with His righteousness, holiness, beauty, and love. It is at a moment like this that I can really believe that God loves me.

Yes, the greatest of all gifts is God's perfect love!

(Dick Dickinson, INTERFACE Psychological Services, Los Alamitos, CA)
This page may be reproduced for your personal use.

Notes

1. Frederic F. Flach, *The Secret Strength of Depression* (New York: Lippincott, 1974), p. 15.
2. Gerald L. Klerman, Myrna M. Weissman, Bruce J. Rounsaville, Eve S. Chevron, *Conducting Interpersonal Therapy of Depression* (New York: Basic Books, Inc., 1984), pp. 120-124, adapted.
3. T. H. Holmes and R. H. Rahe, "The Social Adjustment Rating Scales," *Journal of Psychosomatic Research*, 11 (1967), pp. 213-218.
4. Richard F. Berg and Cristine McCartney, *Depression and the Integrated Life* (New York: Alba House, 1981), p. 117, adapted.
5. John H. Geist, Margorie H. Klein, Roger R Eishens, John Faris, Alan S. Gurman and William P. Morgan, "Running as Treatment for Depression," *Comprehensive Psychiatry*, 20 (1979), pp. 44-54, adapted.
6. Fredric F. Flach and Suzanne C. Draghi, eds., *The Nature and Treatment of Depression* (New York: Wiley, 1975), pp. 47-50,170-173, adapted.
7. Helen D. Rosis and Victoria Pellegrima, *The Book of Hope: How Women Can Overcome Depression* (New York: Macmillan, 1976), pp. 17,18, adapted.
8. John L. Shelton and J. Mark Ackerman, *Homework in Counseling and Psychotherapy* (Springfield, IL: Charles C. Thomas, 1974), p. 96.
9. Archibald D. Hart, *The Success Factor* (Old Tappan, NJ: Revell, 1984), pp. 146-150, adapted.

THE CRISIS of SUICIDE

6

I arrived home late Monday afternoon after spending the day at the lake with my daughter and nephew. Everything seemed fine at home, and we ate our dinner. As we concluded, my wife, Joyce, said to me, "Let's go into the other room. There's something I need to discuss with you." We went to the living room and sat down. Joyce looked at me and said, "Norm, a tragedy happened to a couple at church yesterday, and there was nothing you could have done about it." She went on to tell me that a distraught husband who was separated from his wife and two children went to see his wife on Sunday morning and demanded that she give him custody of the children. When she refused he took out a revolver, killed her, and then turned the gun on himself and committed suicide.

I had seen the man three days before for the first session of counseling. He talked with our pastor on two occasions. The day before the tragedy, he called and talked to me awhile on the phone.

Prepare Yourself

We always feel stunned when someone we know of or have talked with takes his or her life. I appreciated the way Joyce informed me of the suicide incident, for she anticipated my reaction. I wonder how you will respond when it happens.

The above incident was not an isolated experience, although I wish it were. Most of us hope we will not have to handle suicidal situations. But we will. And those of you in ministry will see a number of people who are thinking about suicide or have already planned to take their own lives. Some give you no warning, whereas others do give indication as their way of crying out for help.

Prior to my appointment as minister of education and youth at a church where I used to serve, a young man from the church was attending college away from home. During his senior year, he failed to receive an *A* in a course for the first time in more than nine years. For some reason he could not handle that, so he jumped off of a 200-foot tower at the campus and died. Five years later, the boy's father put a gun to his head and ended his life. There were two other sons who were in our youth group. I always wondered what went through their minds as they thought about two loved family members who were no longer with them. Fortunately they seemed to be stable, and no more tragedies struck the members of that family.

On one occasion a few years ago I was asked to see the fiancee of a young man who had committed suicide. He had jumped off the main bridge in Long Beach, and his body was discovered after being in the water for two weeks. In talking with his fiancee, I soon discovered a high level of insecurity and low self-esteem in her. She had depended so much upon this young man, and now her world was shattered. She, too, was highly suicidal, to the extent that during the time I counseled her I was never sure that I would see her for the next session.

When she came to the second session of counseling, I noticed her hand was bandaged. I asked her what had happened, and she explained that three days before a man had broken into her apartment and tried to kill her. She fought him and cut her hand. He proceeded to rape her and then fled. As she described this to me, I was taken aback by the quiet, determined, controlled rage in her voice as she said, "I hope the police don't find him. I want to find him, and I know what I will do to him."

I continued to work with her for a few weeks, but because the suicidal risk in her case was so high, I referred her to a psychiatrist.

As you minister to those in a suicidal crisis, you need to be aware that the crisis involves not only the person with the suicidal intent, but also the family members or other loved ones who would be left behind.

Years ago I was conducting a teacher training course in a church and noticed a man who was there for the day-long session but was not very involved. At the afternoon break he came up to explain to me why he was there. He told me that a month earlier, his twenty-year-old son who was away at a state university took his life. His son was the most brilliant student to go through the school system in this large city and yet had nothing to live for. He planned for his death very carefully. He went to the beach near the university and drank a beaker of cyanide. In his 20-page suicide note, which I was allowed to read, he said he wanted to be sure to take enough so he would die, but not an excessive amount so he would be unable to experience the death process. What would you say to that father? This is what our ministry is all about, reaching out to the hurting and suffering.

Prepare Your Staff

I urge you to have every person in your church who has any kind of counseling responsibility read this chapter. Have your church secretaries and your spouse read it as well. They may have to be the one to handle a call or person who is suicidal when you are not around. They cannot put this person on hold and tell him to wait for your return.

I learned the importance of the entire staff's being prepared years ago. I had counseled several suicidal people, and one night at the start of the evening service, I was called to the phone. One of my counselees had slashed her wrists and turned on the gas at home. I had her turn off the gas and also determined that the cuts were superficial. But I did need to go over and help. I asked someone to have my wife summoned from the sanctuary, and when Joyce walked in I told her what had happened, handed her the phone, and said, "It will take me 20 minutes to get there. Keep her talking about anything, but keep her on the line. See you later." With that I rushed out the door. I stayed at the home for 2 hours until the husband got there. In spite of her protests, he needed to be informed and become part of the support team.

Later when I returned home, Joyce said, "Norm, you're teaching the seminary students how to counsel the suicidal. I would really appreciate some of this teaching for myself." I understood her need and invested the time to train her. There have been times when she has been the person to handle the call whether she wants to be or not. And that will occur with your church staff and your spouse as well. Let's help them feel comfortable about ministering to others.

Suicide is a deliberate act of self-destruction in which the chance of surviving is uncertain. It is a major problem. More than 34,000 people kill themselves in the United States each year. These are just the ones we know about, as so many suicides are not reported or go undetected. Estimates indicate that suicide is the tenth leading cause of death in our country. The death rate from suicide could be as high as 100,000 a year. And there are more than 5 million attempts each year. Between 10 and 20 percent of those who make a suicide attempt eventually kill themselves.[1] About one-half million people commit suicide each year worldwide.[2] In the 15- to 19-year-old group, suicide is surpassed as a cause of death by only 2 other factors—accidents and cancer. On some college campuses it is the leading cause of death.[3]

In the Scriptures we do not find any judgments on suicide, but we do find several instances of suicide recorded as historical facts. In the Old Testament the following suicides are mentioned: Abimelech (Judg. 9:54), Samson (Judg. 16:28-31), Saul (1 Sam. 31:1-6), Saul's armor bearer (1 Chron. 10:5), Ahithophel (2 Sam. 17:23) and Zimri (1 Kings 16:18). In the New Testament we have the account of Judas Iscariot (Matt. 27:3-5). There are many extrabiblical accounts of suicide. Perhaps the most familiar account is the mass suicide of those at Masada after holding out for several years against their Roman attackers.

The Church's Attitude Toward Suicide

For several centuries the Church did not say much about suicide. Augustine was one of the first to speak concerning it. He felt that suicide was generally unlawful and indicated a weak mind. Thomas Aquinas, in the thirteenth century, stated that the commandment "Thou shalt not kill" refers to the killing of oneself as well as the killing of others.

In the year A.D. 452, the Council of Arles became the first church conclave to condemn suicide. The Second Council of Orleans in 533 ordered that offerings or oblations be refused for suicides. The Council of Brage, in 563, denied religious rites at the burial of suicides. The Council of Toledo, in 693, punished attempted suicides with exclusion from the fellowship of the church for two months.

During the Middle Ages, civil law began to follow the teaching of the Church and prohibited suicide. Desecration of the corpse of a suicide became standard practice. Bodies of suicides were dragged into the street. Stakes were driven through the heart of the victim, and they were sometimes left unburied at a crossroads for animals and birds to consume. Or they were hung on gallows and allowed to rot there. Superstition and fear were greatly in evidence. If the death took place in a house, the body could not be carried out through a door but only through a window, or a portion of a wall had to be taken down. In Scotland, it was thought that if the body of such a suicide victim were buried within sight of the sea or cultivated land, it would be disastrous to fishing or agriculture. In England, the last body to be dragged through the streets and buried at a crossroads was in 1823. In 1882, Britain ordered that suicides could have normal burials. But the strong feeling and reaction toward this kind of death has lingered for many centuries.

Why People Commit Suicide

Ten percent of the people who commit suicide do so for no apparent reason.

Instability. Twenty-five percent are classified as mentally unstable. They have a variety of motivations, justifications and rationalizations for their actions. If a person states that he has been under psychiatric care or confined in a hospital, it is helpful to ask if the doctor prescribed medication for him. It is not uncommon for a person under the care of a physician to forget to take his medication, and this can contribute to his state of confusion.

Impulse. Forty percent commit suicide on an impulse, during a period of emotional upset. They are experiencing some kind of stress, pain, emotion or defeat. It is when the stress is momentarily overwhelming that they decide to commit suicide. These people are most likely to call for help and are easiest to help. They will need to be supported, understood and helped through the stress or crisis situation they are experiencing. They also will need some assistance in handling their problems so they will not turn to suicide as an option again.

Depression. One pattern of suicide is depressive suicide. The person is sitting on a high level of unacceptable rage that has developed because of a series of events in life over which he has no control. Eventually this repressed rage is turned against himself in suicide. Within our churches, we have depressed people who are "suicides waiting to happen." You don't recognize them because they repress their depressive symptoms as well as their rage, and when they die, everyone is taken by surprise and shocked.[4]

Relief of pain. Many people commit suicide for relief of pain. People who have a low threshold for pain and experience chronic pain are candidates for suicide. Those with high levels of pain usually have three choices: a psychotic distortion that reduces the pain, drugs or alcohol, or finally suicide. They often say, "I don't want to die, but I don't know any other way out—I just can't stand it."[5]

Revenge. Others commit suicide for revenge. Some teenagers feel overwhelmed by a hurt or rejection from another person. Their desire to hurt back is stronger than the desire to live. For others, the death of a loved one, family member or friend is too much to handle. Many of the sick and elderly indicate in suicide notes that they couldn't handle being a burden upon others.

Hopelessness. Twenty-five percent commit suicide after giving it quiet consideration and weighing the pros and cons of living and dying. They decide that death is the best option. It may seem strange to us that there are people who think this way. Perhaps this factor can motivate us who know the good news of life to share it with those who have no hope.

Is there a particular kind of person who is most prone to suicide? Doman Lum reports in his book *Responding to Suicidal Crisis:*

> Suicidologists have characterized the suicidal person as a "dependent-dissatisfied" individual who continually demands, complains, insists, and controls; who is inflexible and lacks adaptability; who succeeds in alienating others with his demands; who needs reassurance of self-worth in order to maintain his feelings of self-esteem; who eventually sets himself up for rejection; and who is an infantile personality who expects others to make decisions and perform for him.[6]

What Are the Common Myths About Suicide?

Understanding some of the common myths will help us appreciate what suicide is and is not.

Myth 1: Suicide and attempted suicide are the same class of behavior.

Suicide is committed usually by one who wants to die, whereas attempted suicide is carried out usually by one who has some desire to live. Attempted suicide has been called a cry for help. People who attempt suicide are intent on changing something. Most are hoping to be rescued.

A few people do not plan their attempts carefully and die not really wanting to. One wife attempted suicide about once every six months in an attempt to control her husband. She would turn on the gas shortly before he was to arrive home, and he would find her just on the verge of unconsciousness. Naturally she received much attention from him after that, but it would slowly dissipate until she would again perform her act. One time, however, her husband was two hours late in arriving home. Her miscalculation led to her death.

Myth 2: Suicide is a problem of a specific class of people.

Suicide is neither the curse of the rich nor the disease of the poor. It is no respecter of persons in socioeconomic class, race or age. Teenagers who come from poor families who are constantly moving under stress do commit suicide, but this is a result of isolation and not poverty.[7] There appears to be a slightly higher rate among white males as compared to black males. Males outnumber females in committed suicides, whereas females make many more attempts. At age 15 there are 64 attempts for each girl actually committing suicide. There are less than 6 attempts for each 15-year-old boy who commits suicide. Many of the adolescent attempts are for attention.

Myth 3: People who talk about suicide don't commit suicide.

About 80 percent of those who take their own lives have communicated their intention to someone prior to the act. Any threats or hints about suicide must be taken seriously for most acts are preceded by a warning. Unfortunately, many warnings have gone undetected or have been ignored because no one wanted to believe that the person was serious about his intention. Take it seriously, for this is the distraught person's cry for help. He feels hopeless and is trusting you with his plea.

Myth 4: Once a person is suicidal, he is suicidal forever.

This is not true. Many who have thought of or attempted suicide have discovered the answers to their problems, and they are no longer suicidal.

Myth 5: Suicide is inherited or runs in families.

If another family member has committed suicide, this fact could cause a person to be fearful of his own future behavior. Although suicidal tendencies are not inherited, the family environment and examples of others may be influencing factors. It is a learned behavior.

Myth 6: If a person is a Christian, he will not commit suicide.

This, unfortunately, is not true. Some have said that if a person commits suicide he is not really a born-again person; a true believer could never become so unhappy that he would think of such an act. But Christians as well as non-Christians experience all kinds of physical and emotional disorders. Because of the many factors that could cause a person to consider suicide, we need to remember that none of us is immune.

Myth 7: Suicide and depression are synonymous.

Most people who attempt suicide are experiencing stress, and yet others experience stress without thoughts of suicide. The statement "I can't understand why he did this, he didn't seem unhappy or depressed" indicates the belief that suicide occurs only when there is unhappiness or depression. Depression is not a sign of suicidal thoughts. However, whenever a person is depressed we should be on the lookout for any thoughts or indications of the possibility of suicide.

Myth 8: Improvement after a suicidal crisis means that the risk of suicide is over.

Studies by the Los Angeles Suicide Prevention Center indicate that almost half the persons who were in a suicidal crisis and later actually committed suicide did so within three months of having passed through their first crisis. The period of time immediately following a suicidal crisis appears to be critical. If a person immediately states that his problems are solved and seems overly happy, we ought to be wary and concerned.

Who Is High Risk?

As has been indicated, it is sometimes difficult to obtain accurate statistics on suicidal rates. It could be that the actual rates are twice as high as we know them. However, here are some statistics that may show who is a high risk.

The suicide rate is much higher for men than for women at all ages. Men over 65 account for America's highest suicide rate, 38 per 100,000, a rate that escalates as they grow older, peaking at 60 per 100,000 around the age of 85. And in California it is 103 per 100,000 for those 85 and older. This is in contrast to 12 suicides per 100,000 for the general population.[8]

The suicide rate is significantly higher for the divorced. At age 65, almost 75 percent who committed suicide were divorced. The rate for single or widowed adults is also significantly higher than for the married group.

The Signs of Suicidal Intention

In working with counselees or through contact with people in our everyday lives, it is important to be aware of the verbal and nonverbal hints people give about their suicidal thoughts.

1. *The suicidal attempt.* This is the most clear and dramatic cry for help. One who has attempted suicide needs immediate help and support.

2. *The suicidal threat.* Any kind of threat should be taken seriously. The majority of those who talk about suicide do attempt it.

3. *The suicidal hint.* Some people who consider killing themselves are unclear in communicating their intent. They may make statements such as "You would be better off without me," "Life has lost all meaning for me," or "It's just that I hate to face each day more and more." Some who express keener-than-usual interest in suicide may be hinting at suicide. A Christian may ask, "Does a person who commits suicide lose his salvation?" or "What does God really think of a person who takes his own life?"

4. *Suicidal activity.* There are many kinds of suicidal activity. Making sure all the bills are paid, making out a will, and making arrangements as though the person were going on a long trip could be clues that the person is considering suicide. It is important, however, not to be analyzing every person's activities and seeing suicides behind every bush!

5. *Suicidal symptoms.* A long, serious illness could bring a person to the point of despair, especially if there is no immediate hope or if the illness is terminal. Another symptom is sudden changes in personality, such as becoming very easily upset, moody, anxious or agitated. Remember, too, that among

alcoholics there is a high incidence of suicide. Agitated depression is one of the most serious signs that a person may attempt to take his life. The depressed person who becomes withdrawn by staying indoors for long periods of time, keeping to himself, and shutting off contact from others may be a definite risk. A person thinking of suicide may be bothered by physical symptoms such as loss of appetite, sexual drive, weight and so on. Watch for significant and sudden behavior changes.

6. *Recent crisis.* Many suicides have occurred in response to some immediate and specific stress. Each person evaluates stress in a different manner. A crisis might be the death of a loved one, failure at work or school, marital or home problems, loss of a job, a broken romance, financial reversal, divorce or separation, or a rejection or loss of any kind that involves people about whom the person cares. Any of these may cause the person to question the value of living.

Many suicide prevention scales have been developed because of concern over how to prevent suicide. The purpose is to help the counselor or minister discover what the most valid indicators of suicide are. One of the most helpful resources is William Zung's "Index of Potential Suicide" (IPS). This questionnaire is designed to produce a numerical rating that allows for both objective and subjective evaluation of suicidal risk.[9]

Index of Potential Suicide (IPS)
Interviewer Form

Item	Interview Guide	Severity of Observed or Reported Responses				
		None	Min.	Mild	Mod.	Sev.
1. Depressed mood	Do you ever feel sad or depressed?	0	1	2	3	4
2. Diurnal variation: worse in a.m.	Is there any part of the day when you feel worse? best?	0	1	2	3	4
3. Crying spells	Do you have crying spells or feel like it?	0	1	2	3	4
4. Sleep disturbance	How have you been sleeping?	0	1	2	3	4
5. Decreased appetite	How is your appetite?	0	1	2	3	4

Item	Interview Guide	Severity of Observed or Reported Responses				
		None	Min.	Mild	Mod.	Sev.
6. Decreased libido	How about your interest in the opposite sex?	0	1	2	3	4
7. Weight loss	Have you lost any weight?	0	1	2	3	4
8. Constipation	Do you have trouble with constipation?	0	1	2	3	4
9. Tachycardia	Have you had times when your heart was beating faster than usual?	0	1	2	3	4
10. Fatigue	How easily do you get tired?	0	1	2	3	4
11. Confusion	Do you ever feel confused and have trouble thinking?	0	1	2	3	4
12. Psychomotor retardation	Do you feel slowed down in doing the things you usually do?	0	1	2	3	4
13. Psychomotor agitation	Do you find yourself restless and can't sit still?	0	1	2	3	4
14. Hopelessness	How hopeful do you feel about the future?	0	1	2	3	4
15. Irritability	How easily do you get irritated?	0	1	2	3	4
16. Indecisiveness	How are you at making decisions?	0	1	2	3	4
17. Personal devaluation	Do you ever feel useless and not wanted?	0	1	2	3	4
18. Emptiness	Do you feel life is empty for you?	0	1	2	3	4
19. Suicidal ruminations	Have you had thoughts about doing away with yourself?	0	1	2	3	4
20. Dissatisfaction	Do you still enjoy the things you used to?	0	1	2	3	4
21. Anxiousness	Do you ever feel anxious?	0	1	2	3	4
22. Fear	Have you ever felt afraid for no reason?	0	1	2	3	4
23. Panic	How easily do you get upset?	0	1	2	3	4
24. Mental disintegration	Do you ever feel like you're falling apart? going to pieces?	0	1	2	3	4

Item	Interview Guide	Severity of Observed or Reported Responses				
		None	Min.	Mild	Mod.	Sev.
25. Apprehension	Have you ever felt that something terrible was going to happen?	0	1	2	3	4
26. Alcoholism: pattern	Do you ever take a drink in the morning?	0	1	2	3	4
27. Alcoholism: quantity	Do people ever tell you that you drink more than you should?	0	1	2	3	4
28. Professional help: (M.D., Ph.D., R.N., minister, lawyer, social worker, etc.)	Have you seen anybody professional within the last three months because you have been worried about yourself or your health? Who?	0	1	2	3	4
29. Somatic complaints	Do you ever have aches and pains where nothing seems to help?	0	1	2	3	4
30. Physical health	Do you feel that you are in as good a shape physically as you've ever been?	0	1	2	3	4
31. Drug abuse	Do you take sleeping pills on your own?	0	1	2	3	4
32. Lack of support	Do you feel that there is somebody who cares for and understands you?	0	1	2	3	4
33. Lack of alternatives	Do you feel that there is a way out of your present situation?	0	1	2	3	4
34. Hopelessness	Do you feel that, in time, things are going to get better?	0	1	2	3	4
35. Self-blame	Do you blame yourself for everything that goes wrong?	0	1	2	3	4
36. Guilt	Do you have guilt feelings about your past?	0	1	2	3	4

Item	Interview Guide	Severity of Observed or Reported Responses				
		None	Min.	Mild	Mod.	Sev.
37. Punishment	Do you ever feel that you deserve to be punished?	0	1	2	3	4
38. Available support	Do you feel that when things seem to be at their end, there is someone you can turn to?	0	1	2	3	4
39. Self-control: aggression	Do you ever have fits of anger or lose your temper?	0	1	2	3	4
40. Aggression	Do you ever get into physical fights?	0	1	2	3	4
41. Self-control	Do you take chances when driving a car?	0	1	2	3	4
42. Personal appearance	Does it matter to you how you look in public?	0	1	2	3	4
43. Suicide: projection, idea	How often do you think other people think about suicide?	0	1	2	3	4
44. Suicide: projection, action	How often do you think people who think about suicide actually kill themselves?	0	1	2	3	4
45. Personal responsibility	Is there someone who depends upon you?	0	1	2	3	4
46. Suicide: rumination	Have you had recent thoughts about dying?	0	1	2	3	4
47. Suicide: method	Have you been thinking of ways to kill yourself?	0	1	2	3	4
48. Suicide: prior threat	Have you ever said to someone that you wanted to kill yourself?	0	1	2	3	4
49. Suicide: prior attempt	Have you ever tried to do away with yourself? How?	0	1	2	3	4
50. Suicide: other person	Have you ever known anyone who committed suicide? Who?	0	1	2	3	4

0 = NO   YES = 4

Zung found in his research that people who evidenced no suicidal behavior produced a mean score of 43.2, while a mean score of 72.8 was registered by suicide attempters.

The following guidelines are suggested for effective use of Zung's IPS:

A. Each item should be independently rated without reference to any other item.

B. Each item's rating should be the average of the counselee's range of responses, not the extreme range.

C. The items are rated in terms of intensity, duration and frequency on a five-point scale:

0 = None, not present or insignificant;

1 = Minimal intensity or duration present only a little of the time in frequency;

2 = Mild intensity or duration, present some of the time;

3 = Moderate intensity or duration, present a good part of the time;

4 = Severe intensity or duration, present most or all of the time in frequency.

The severity of the condition can be better established by asking the following questions:

Intensity: "How bad was it?"

Duration: "How long did it last?"

Frequency: "How often, or how much of the time?"

D. Score items positive and present when:

1. The behavior is observed;

2. The counselee described the behavior as having occurred;

3. The counselee admits that the symptom is still a problem.

E. Score items negative and not present (zero) when:

1. The symptom has not occurred and is not a problem;

2. The counselee gives no information relevant to the item;

3. The counselee's response is ambiguous even after clarifying questions have been asked.

Counselors are encouraged to use the IPS or other instruments to help them predict suicides more accurately.

Adolescent Suicidal Behavior

Because we hear more and more today about adolescent suicide and adolescence being a highly stressful period of time, it is important to consider some specific indications of behavior changes that may be a warning indicator. Here are some of the behavioral changes you should be alerted to:

1. A dramatic shift in the quality of school performance;
2. Changes in social behavior;
3. Excessive use of drugs or alcohol;
4. Changes in daily behavior and living patterns;
5. Extreme fatigue;
6. Boredom;
7. Decreased appetite;
8. Preoccupation and inability to concentrate;
9. Overt signs of mental illness, such as hallucinations, delusions or talking to oneself;
10. Giving away treasured possessions;
11. Truancy;
12. Failure to communicate with family members and school personnel; Adolescents who reach despair serious enough to lead to suicide often choose to talk to a peer or to some other interested person outside of his family or school associations.
13. Isolation and morose behavior;
14. Insomnia;
15. Lack of a sufficient father-son relationship. This may have occurred either because the father is absent as a result of death or divorce or because the father has been so wrapped up in his career that he has not taken time to develop a relationship with his son.
16. Difficult mother-daughter relationship, especially in the absence of a strong father figure;
17. Pregnancy;
18. Excessive smoking, indicative of tension;
19. A history of child abuse in the home. Experiences of being battered as a child can spur violence later in adolescence; such violence is usually aimed at the self, resulting in suicide.
20. Apparent "accidental" self-poisoning, especially if the behavior is repeated.[10]

Any one or a combination of these could be present in the life of a normal adolescent who is not thinking of suicide. But you do not know for sure unless you check them out. If you have contact with the person, you could reflect back to the person the behavior you are noticing and ask if anything is the matter. Your purpose is to give him the opportunity to unload what may be troubling him. The same facts we have discussed about suicide in general pertain to adolescents as well.

Consider the Elderly

The other age group to consider is the elderly, because they are the most vulnerable group in the entire spectrum. Remember what was said earlier about the suicidal rate of men over the age of 65. They accomplish self-destruction 5 times more often than the entire population and 12 times more often than elderly females. There are reasons for this.

Older people are often tired, sad, lonely and ill. Men especially have lost much of the meaning of life, for they no longer have their occupations. One of the problems in our society is that men place too much emphasis on their occupations. To them it is the source of identity and self-esteem. And with no other pillars to give them this meaning, let them retire and it is like letting the air out of a balloon. Nothing is left, and this is reflected in their depression and increased suicide rate.

How can you help the elderly? Evaluate the person carefully. Is he ill? Depressed? Mentally stable? Does he have sufficient finances, or has he been denying himself some necessities of life? Has he been forced to give up his independence by living in a care unit or with a relative? How does he handle frustration? Does he talk about the future or live for past memories?

The elderly give hints of their intentions, as do others. If they begin to clean up everything and dispose of property, including treasured keepsakes, be alert. If someone has been depressed over a long period of time and now is suddenly cheerful, he could also be a high risk.

The elderly person may need a physical examination. Help him to feel useful, and give him encouragement and compliments. He needs to hear that someone appreciates his situation. Help family members include the person in their activities. Set up a support team from the church on a continual basis to give him contact with others. One of my concerns about some retirement homes and centers is the refusal to let those living there have pets. A loving cat or dog is appreciated by the elderly and may keep some of them living longer. Whatever you can do, endeavor to alleviate the loneliness.[11] Your task is to get the person to say yes to life again. Help him focus on what he can do and what he has instead of what he cannot do and does not have.

How to Minister to the Suicidal Person

When you come into contact with a person who is suicidal, definite intervention is needed. A person's life is at stake, and whether you want to be involved or not, you are! Your initial task is helping the person stay alive. The second is helping him gain insight into how he came to this place and then guiding him to make the necessary changes to ensure that it will not happen again.

Remember, too, you are not omnipotent and this person's life is *not* on your shoulders. Your role simply is to be as much help as possible.

Many people who are contemplating suicide call a friend, church or agency for assistance. Thus the procedure suggested here focuses upon a plan to minister to those who call. The same principles can be used in face-to-face contact with someone who in the midst of his counseling session indicates suicidal thoughts or intentions.

Step 1: Establish a relationship, maintain contact with the person, establish rapport and obtain information.

For many people, suicide is a gradual process while under stress. They begin to seek solutions to their problems, and they try alternative one, then alternatives two, three, four, and five and perhaps several others, all without success, before they arrive at the solution of suicide. Many struggle against this alternative and again seek other alternatives, but if their way is blocked, they return to this last choice as their solution. Remember that a suicidal person is ambivalent toward life and death. He wishes to kill himself and is tired of what is going on in his life. At the same time, he wants to be rescued by someone. When this person calls, it is important to begin to develop a positive relationship. This relationship could be the reason he decides to stay alive. When the person calls, say something like:

"You did the right thing by calling."

"I'm glad you called."

"I think there is help for you."

These statements are important because they assure him that he made a right decision and that someone else cares for him. This verbal approval could be a way of getting through to him the message that he can make other right decisions. The suicidal person needs you to talk calmly, confidently, with a voice of authority (but not authoritarian), and in such a manner that he will not feel challenged. Caring, acceptance and genuine concern are very important.

As you talk, it is important to find some common ground upon which you and the caller can agree. A place to start is the fact that the caller has a problem and wants help, and you want to help him. Sometimes when a caller is unclear and ambivalent, it takes more work to discover a common ground. It is important to use the word "help" frequently in different contexts.

It is important also to show interest in the caller and attempt to discern his feelings. A relationship of trust needs to be developed. This can be done by giving straightforward answers to questions. You should not be fearful of identifying yourself and your relationship with the church or organization if asked. If asked if you have ever helped a person in a similar situation and you have not, be honest, but also let him know that you feel you have the resources and training to help him.

In establishing the relationship, identify yourself and try to get the person's name, phone number and address. These questions should be spaced throughout the conversation so the person is not unduly threatened by them. If there is a reluctance to give his name, do not pressure the caller at that point. You could ask, "Could I know your first name so I have something to call you by? I would feel more comfortable with that." If he will not give an address, you could ask what part of town he is from. If he gives you a general area, you could respond by saying, "Oh, that is out near..." This statement will perhaps stimulate him to give more information.

You may find that a person asks you to promise not to tell anyone he called. Professional counselors and ministers have the right to keep some information confidential. However, some state laws (e.g., those in California) require a counselor to contact authorities when someone threatens to kill himself or someone else, and you *cannot* make a promise not to do so. But you can assure the person you will do nothing to harm him.

In the conversation, you should also attempt to obtain the phone number of other significant people who could help the person—relatives, neighbors, physicians and so on.

Step 2: Identify and clarify the problem.

Hear the person's story with as few interruptions as possible. Encourage him to tell you (1) what has led him to where he is now; (2) what is bothering him right now; and (3) what he has tried before to cope with his situation. Do not challenge what he is saying. Statements such as, "You should not feel that way" or "Things are not as bad as they seem" are setbacks to the person, and they do not really help him.

Focus on what the person is feeling, and assist him in clarifying his feelings. If he has difficulty expressing his feelings, help him to label them. Try to reflect what you think he is thinking and feeling, as this will help him to pinpoint the problem. His overwhelming helplessness can now be broken up into specific problems, the solutions to which may be seen more easily. He should be helped to see that his distress may be impairing his ability to assess his situation. When he can see the problems, he can begin to construct a specific plan for solving them. And if you understand the nature of the problem he is trying to cope with, you can understand more about his strengths and weaknesses. You want to explore his reasons for wanting to die.

If a person calls and just talks about being down or depressed, statements and questions such as the following may help: "You seem to be depressed much of the time." "How much have you been depressed over the past few weeks?" "When do you get depressed?" "Have you ever thought that life just isn't worth living?" "Have you thought of ending it all?" Inquiries such as these can help a hesitant person put his feelings into words. *The actual threat of suicide needs to be out in the open for you to help the person.*

When a person has trouble talking about suicide, he is usually relieved to find that you are not afraid to talk about it openly. This can at times relieve him of the trapped feeling. Suicide should be discussed in an open and nonmoralistic manner. Suicide is not a moral issue for the suicidal person. It is the result of stress for the most part. Many are already struggling with guilt feelings, and if a discussion of suicide as an immoral act occurs, it can add to this burden and cause further discouragement.

If you are talking in person to an adolescent who is considering suicide, talk with him about his or her beliefs about death. Many of them have never seen a dead person or been to a funeral. They do not understand its finality. They may be thinking only of the attention they will receive. Helping them gain a realistic perspective of death may deter them.[12]

Step 3: Evaluate the suicidal potential or lethality.

A number of factors are involved in making this evaluation. As you listen to the person, you will be receiving pieces of information that will assist you in making this determination.

1. *Age and sex.* Remember that the suicide rate rises with age and that men are more likely than women to follow through. Older single males are more vulnerable. Younger females are less likely to carry out their plan. Persons suffering from alcoholism are considered a high risk. And sporadic drinkers are more vulnerable to suicide than a chronic, heavy drinker. Alcohol often serves as a defense against pain and then becomes a source of new pain. If pain is unbearable in the sober state, suicide may be the choice.[13]

2. *History of the suicidal behavior.* It is important to try to determine if this is the first attempt or if this is one of a series. The more recent the onset of suicidal behavior, the better is the chance to prevent it. But at the same time, the need is greater for active intervention. An extensive pattern of suicidal behavior will require long-term therapy from professionals. If the person has repeatedly attempted suicide, he will probably at some time succeed and actually kill himself. The job of both the paraprofessional and the professional is to help break this suicidal circuit and help the person develop a plan for living.

3. *Evaluate the suicide plan.* The plan has three parts.

a. *How lethal is it?* When a person has admitted planning to end it all, you can ask, "How are you thinking of killing yourself?" Sometimes the harsh words can bring home the reality of the situation. Shooting and hanging are considered the most lethal methods, barbiturates and carbon monoxide poisoning are second. The lethality of a method is measured by how abruptly the point of no return is reached. Other methods are explosives, knives, poisoning and drowning.

b. *How available is it?* If a gun or bottle of pills is at hand, the risk is greater. Ask what kind of pills and where they are. If he plans to use a gun, ask "Do you have a gun? Where is it? Do you have bullets for it?"

c. *How specific is the plan?* If he has worked out the details very well, the risk is higher. If the person says, "I have 100 pills here and I am also going to turn on the gas. I have covered the cracks around the door and windows so the gas will stay in," this is obviously very specific. But if he says that he has to go out and buy the pills or the gun or a hose for the car exhaust, the risk is lower.

Remember that even if you are talking with a person who has a well-worked-out plan and has the means, he still called, which indicates that some small seed of desire to live remains. If a person is in this situation and will not say who he is (or if he has already started the process of taking his life), you may need to work out some system of getting the attention of a coworker. The coworker should notify the police, who will trace the call.

4. *Stress.* This must be evaluated from the caller's point of view. To you it may not seem significant, but to him it is. If he has experienced losses, reversals, or even successes, it could be creating stress or strain.

5. *Symptoms.* What are the symptoms in this person's life? Is there depression? alcoholism? agitation? Is the person psychotic? Remember that agitated depression is the worst symptom. Its stress factors and symptoms are high, so your actions must be fast.

6. *Resources.* What resources does this person have available to help him? Are friends or relatives nearby? Are counseling services available to him in the community or at work? Does he have a place to stay? A lack of resources makes the risk factor higher. If the person is remaining at his home, and it is a sick environment, it would be better for him to be cared for elsewhere. He may need to be away from a parent or spouse who is contributing to his problem. A person living in a depressogenic environment (a negative environment where the person's self-esteem is constantly under attack) would be better off out of its influence.

7. *Life-style.* What is his life-style? If it is unstable, such as a history of changing or losing jobs, changing living locations, drinking, impulsive behavior and so on, the risk is higher.

8. *Communication with others.* Has the person cut himself off from other people, including friends and family? If so, he could be a higher risk. If he is still in touch with others, you can use them to help.

9. *Medical status.* If there are no physical problems, the risk is less. If there is some illness or injury, talk about it and find out how serious it is. Is

it really the case, or is it merely in the person's mind? Has he seen a physician? Some who have a terminal disease may think of suicide as a way of eliminating the pain for themselves and the expense for the families.

Only one single criterion should be alarming by itself, and that is having a lethal and specific plan for suicide. If the situation is serious, do not attempt to handle the problem by yourself. Responsible family members, a family physician or a professional counselor need to be included in the plans.

Step 4: Formulate a plan to help the caller.

It is important to find out what part of the plan he has put into action and to get him to reverse it. If he has turned on the gas and sealed the windows, have him turn off the gas and open the windows. *Do not let him promise to do it when you hang up.* Give specific instructions, and stay on the phone while he carries them out. Ask him to open the door and windows. If he has a gun, have him unload it. If it is an automatic, have him take the clip out of the chamber, then take the bullets out of the clip. Next he should place the bullets in a drawer and put the gun somewhere difficult for him to get to in a hurry. If the person has pills, you might ask him to flush them down the toilet. If he does not want to reverse the plan, continue talking until your relationship is built to the point that he will trust you.

Then get a commitment from him. Ask him to promise to call you if he has any other difficulty or if he is tempted again to take his life. Professionals have found that this is quite effective. The person may let other obligations go, but he will keep his promise to call you. Your word of encouragement on the phone may keep the person alive.

One professional counselor stated that on one occasion when he was out of town, a counselee called and asked for him. The man was very depressed that night, and later it was discovered that he was planning to kill himself that same night. The counselor's wife replied by saying, "My husband is not here tonight, but I know that he wants to talk to you. I will have him call you as soon as he gets back, and I would also like you to call back again yourself. I will let him know, and thanks for calling." Later when the counselor saw this person, he said that those very words kept him alive that night.

Help the person determine his strengths and resources. If he has committed himself to you and agreed not to do anything, help him widen his view of his problem and discover the resources that he has lost sight of during the crisis. Perhaps some other people can help him. In some cases, a person may need to be hospitalized. If the person is quite depressed, be sure to caution him that the process of recovery involves some ups and downs. Perhaps you know of some agencies from which he can obtain the food he needs, the job he needs, or the professional or legal assistance he is seeking. Perhaps a neighbor can stay with him or give him emotional assistance. Be sure to convince him that there are various positive alternatives to suicide. He may not be able to see them right now, but assure him that working together, the two of you can discover them.

Before concluding the call, your last task is to get the person personally involved with someone. You may want to have him come into the church for counseling or go to an agency that you know can help. You could say, "I could see you tomorrow at 11:00 A.M., or I could have you see our pastor. Can you come over then?" Let him know that you are looking forward to seeing him or working with him, and that he can find further help by coming in to see someone personally.

When you see the suicidal individual in person, it may be helpful to have him sign an antisuicide agreement. Even though it is just a piece of paper, the person may feel more committed to following the guidelines because it was signed. You will find an agreement form at the conclusion of this chapter.

In this type of counseling, it is important to convey to the person that you care. It is also important to carefully work in the fact that God cares, as does His Son Jesus Christ. In some cases you may feel led to say this during the first telephone conversation. At other times it may be best to say it face-to-face. Be careful that your approach and tone do not take on a preaching air. The truth of God's love should be explained naturally and honestly, using a direct leading of the Holy Spirit at the right time.

Summary: Three elements are crucial to this phone counseling approach. The person calling must feel:

1. *Activity.* He needs to feel that something is being done for him right now. This assurance can relieve his tension.
2. *Authority.* The counselor must set himself up as an authoritative figure who will take charge. The caller is not capable of taking charge of his life at this time, so someone else must step in.
3. *Involvement of others.* If the caller realizes that others are now involved and caring for him, he will be more apt to feel he is being cared for and will respond.

Barriers to Helping the Caller

In order to be the best possible help to a caller, it is important to be aware of our own defenses that may hurt this ministry. Dr. Paul Pretzel of the Los Angeles Suicide Prevention Center outlines the following barriers to communication with people contemplating suicide.[14]

1. Anxiety on the part of the listener that makes him uncomfortable (and less of a listener).
2. Denying the significance or meaning of previous suicidal behavior that the caller has not made totally clear or the listener has failed to determine.
3. Rationalizing verbal and nonverbal suicidal cues. This is like saying to oneself, "That isn't what he really means."
4. An aggressive reaction to suicidal hints or threats.
5. Fear, which immobilizes the helper and prevents him from really talking about the situation. It could also be a fear of becoming too involved with the responsibility demanded by another person.
6. Manipulating a suicidal person who has "cried wolf" too many times and is no longer listened to by others.

Be alert to the needs of people. They do tell us they are considering a suicide. Be equipped and prepared. But remember, the greatest help you can give this person is you—your concern, your interest, your listening ear and the love of Jesus Christ as reflected through you.

Recommended Resources:

Anthony, T. Mitchel. *Suicide: Knowing When Your Teen Is at Risk.* Ventura, CA: Regal Books, 1991.

Notes

1. Jan Fawcett, *Before It's Too Late* (West Point, PA: Merck, Sharp and Dohme, 1979), p. 2.
2. Keith Olson, *Counseling Teenagers* (Loveland, CO: Group Books, 1984), p. 370.
3. Brent Q. Haden and Brenda Peterson, *The Crisis Intervention Handbook* (Englewood Cliffs, NJ: Prentice Hall, 1982), p. 122.
4. Fredrick F. Flach and Suzanne C. Draghi, eds., *The Nature and Treatment of Depression* (New York: Wiley, 1975), p. 230.
5. Ibid., p. 231.
6. Doman Lum, *Responding to Suicidal Crisis* (Grand Rapids, MI: Eerdmans, 1974), p. 119.
7. Haden and Peterson, *The Crisis Intervention Handbook*, p. 125.
8. "Suicide: Retired Professor Chooses Death" *Los Angeles Times*, 1989, Part V, pp. 1 and 10.
9. William Zung, "Index of Potential Suicide (IPS); A Rating Scale for Suicide Prevention," in *The Prediction of Suicide* (Beck, Resnick and Lettiere, eds.), pp. 221-249.
10. Susan A. Winickoff and H. L. P. Resnik, "Student Suicide," *Today's Education, NEA Journal* (April 1972), p. 32. Used by permission of *Today's Education* and the authors.
11. Haden and Peterson, *The Crisis Intervention Handbook*, pp. 129-131.
12. Olson, *Counseling Teenagers*, p. 382.
13. Flach and Draghi, *The Nature and Treatment of Depression*, p. 241.
14. Paul Pretzel, *Understanding and Counseling the Suicidal Person* (Nashville TN: Abingdon, 1972), pp. 93-95.

Antisuicide Agreement

As part of my counseling, I,_____(your name)
  agree to the following terms:

1. I agree that one of my major counseling goals is to live a long life with more fulfillment and meaning than I now have.

2. I understand that becoming suicidal when depressed or upset keeps me from attaining this goal, and I want to overcome this tendency. I agree to use my counseling to learn better ways to reduce my emotional distress.

3. Since I understand that this will take time, I agree from this point on to refuse to act on urges to injure or kill myself between this day and_____(date)

4. If at any time I should feel unable to resist suicidal thoughts or impulses, I agree to call_____(name)
  at (#)_____ or (#)_____.
  If this person is unavailable, I agree to
  call_____(name) at (#)_____or go directly to _____(hospital or emergency)
  at_____ (address)

5. My counselor or minister, _____ (name) agrees to work with me in scheduled sessions to help me to learn constructive alternatives to these tendencies and to be available as much as is reasonable during times of crisis.

6. I agree to abide by this agreement either until it expires or until it is openly renegotiated with my counselor or minister. I understand that it is renewable at or near the expiration date of_____(date)

_____   _____

Signature   Date

_____   _____

Therapist's or Counselor's Signature   Date

This page may be reproduced for your personal use.

THE CRISIS
of DEATH

7

On Sunday morning, you notice a man sitting in the congregation who has been in attendance for several months. He has kept to himself pretty much, although he is friendly when spoken to. But this morning you seem to notice an air of depression hanging over him. Following the service, you speak to him and ask how he is doing. His response surprises you: "I guess I'm a bit angry and confused right now. I'm wondering where this God is that you're always talking about. I need Him now, but He sure isn't helping me or answering my prayers. I've been praying and reading Scripture, but nothing is changed. My doctor told me three weeks ago that I have cancer. It's terminal...(pause) I've been given six months ...I...don't...want...to...die! Where is *He?*"

Your ministry with this person begins at that moment. How will you reply, and what will you do? Will you be able to handle his feelings without being overly threatened? Can you handle this depression and anger? Can you handle your own feelings of mortality you will be forced to face as you watch this man die? What are the stages he is going to experience?

On Monday morning, you receive a call from one of your board members. He is in tears and you can hardly understand him. But as you listen you begin to understand that his wife and 14-year-old daughter were killed this morning in an automobile accident. He wants you to come over and be with him. He and the 2 younger children are at home. As you leave, you wonder how he will handle this loss. How will he handle the children and care for them? How will the children handle the loss of their mother? What should you expect from them during the next 2 years? How can the members of your congregation minister to them at this time?

These are questions that need to be asked and that require concrete answers.

What Is Death?

What is death? It is the permanent, irreversible cessation of the vital functions of the body. Not all functions stop at the same time. It used to be that the lack of heartbeat was considered final evidence of death, but now the attention has shifted from the heart to the brain for a reliable indication of when death has occurred. Joe Bayly says that death is a wound to the living. Robert Burther said, "The fear of death is worse than death."

The Scriptures have much to say about death. "Precious in the sight of the Lord is the death of His godly ones" (Ps. 116:15). "And inasmuch as it is appointed for men to die once, and after this comes judgment" (Heb. 9:27). "He shall wipe away every tear from their eyes; and there shall no longer be any death; there shall no longer be any mourning, or crying, or pain; the first things have passed away" (Rev. 21:4).

Why is it that we fear death so much? Modern man denies death, and we shrink from even discussing it. We criticize the Victorians because of their attitude toward sex, but they were very aware of and dealt openly with death. Today we have just the opposite attitudes. Our society is very open about sex but closed about death.

People live much longer today than they used to. We strive for not only the good life, but also the long life. In 1900, the infant mortality rate was much different from what it is today. At that time, for every 1,000 live births, 100 of the infants died. In 1940, for every 1,000 live births, 47 died. In 1967, for every 1,000 live births there were 22.4 infant deaths. A significant decline in the death rate of mothers giving birth has also been noted.

We fear physical pain and suffering. We fear the unknown and the things we do not understand. We also fear leaving loved ones and friends. It has been estimated that the average person can go through a 20-year period of time without being exposed to the death of a relative or friend. Today 80 percent of people in our society die away from home or familiar surroundings. This in itself creates a fear response, because we do not want to be alone when we die. Cyris L. Sulzberger says in his book *My Brother Death*, "Men fear death because they refuse to understand it." In order to understand death, we must deal with our fears of it. Joyce Landorf says in her book *Mourning Song:*

> Here, then, is part of the answer as to why death frightens us so much. While, as a Christian, I know Christ has removed the sting of death and death can never kill me for eternity—death still exists. It is still fearfully ugly and repulsive. I probably will never be able to regard, imagine, or fantasize death as being a loving friend.
>
> Whenever and wherever death and dying connects with us—no matter how strong we are in our Christianity or how well we are prepared for it—it still slides and slithers into our lives and freezes us with this fear. Such is the nature of death.[1]

As we talk about death, it is essential to define some terms that describe the grief and loss we experience.

Loss is the state of being deprived of or being without something one has had and valued. Four major categories of loss are: loss of a significant loved or valued person; loss of part of the self; loss of external objects; and developmental loss. Death of a loved one is considered the ultimate loss.

Bereavement is the act of separation or loss that results in the experience of grief. As such, it becomes a precipitating event that starts off the grief process. A different view considers bereavement to be the response that follows the loss and sees it as being made up of two components, grief and mourning.

Mourning is the process following loss of which grief is a part, but extending beyond the first reactions into the period of reorganization of the new identity and reattachment to new interests and people. It is behavior prescribed by the customs and mores of a given society, which determines how a person should conduct himself after the death of another.

Grief is the intense emotional suffering caused by loss, disaster, or misfortune.

It can be anticipatory grief, deep sadness expressed in advance of a loss when the loss is perceived as inevitable, or acute grief, the intense sadness which immediately follows a loss. Chronic grief is sorrow maintained over a considerable period of time.[2]

Grief is tears, an overwhelming sense of loss, a desire to be alone or to have social contacts severed or restricted. During this time, some might even question God's wisdom or love. Feelings of guilt are common. Reactions such as "Why didn't I..." begin to be raised. "If I had treated him better or if I had sought help earlier, or if I had found a better doctor or hospital, this might not have happened."

The first response is a shattering, devastating shock that comes with the news of the death. This shock is followed a month or so later by intense suffering and extreme loneliness. Sometimes during the first or second year there is gradual strengthening and healing of the mind and emotions. For most people, the grief process can take up to two years.

How do most of us respond to the bereaved? We continue to pray for them for 2 or 3 weeks, and we may continue to show them concern in tangible ways for 2 to 3 months—things such as cards, phone calls or taking an occasional meal to them. But at the time when they most need our support, people usually discontinue their ministry. It might be better if the church would develop a program of ministry wherein 12 families would commit themselves for a period of 2 months each to minister to the bereaved over the 2-year period of time and thus help them through the hurt process. Cards, phone calls, including them in family activities, helping them to feel useful and productive, and so on are all part of expressing our concern.

The stages of grief that people pass through are normal and can be immediate or postponed, but the underlying principle is: *People should be encouraged to do their grief work.*

Delayed Grief

Some people delay their grief work, which results in depression. Instead of feeling sad, they appear apathetic and numb. Unfortunately, some churches teach that we must *always* think positively, be in control and take charge of our lives. Such teaching does not help the bereaved.

Denying grief is an unfortunate response. The person is often not encouraged or allowed to go through the valley of his own "little deaths." By rising above his own hurt, he does not admit having been hurt. In a real sense he is refusing to mourn his loss. But eventually it *will* surface. People who carry this unfinished business with them into their future experiences and relationships will suffer unrest, conflict, and ongoing depression.[3]

Within delayed grief you may also find a residue of delayed anger. This needs to be admitted, identified and expressed. You might say to the person, "If I were in your situation, I would be quite angry." Help the person deal with his anger, but also help him accept it as normal. Otherwise, he may experience excessive guilt over being angry.

Roy Fairchild's statement on delayed grief is very insightful:

> The refusal to mourn is the refusal to say goodbye to beloved persons, places, missed opportunities, vitality, or whatever has been "taken away," which is how many religious people view these losses. The refusal to mourn our earlier disappointments condemns us and rigidifies us, as it did Lot's wife. Genuine grief is the deep sadness and weeping that expresses the acceptance of our inability to do anything about our losses. It is a prelude to letting go, to relinquishment. It is dying that precedes resurrection. Our sadness reveals what we have been invested in; it is the cost of a commitment which has been shattered.[4]

Another problem you will come in contact with is an abnormal or pathological grief reaction. Pathological grief may manifest itself in several ways. It is vital to be able to identify these expressions. Dr. V. D. Volkan and Dr. D. Josephthal, psychiatrists, have suggested three processes that underlie pathological mourning.

Pathological Mourning

1. *Splitting.* Splitting is used to help the person survive the trauma without coming apart. It actually supports the mechanism of denial so the person knows the death occurred but still functions ade-

quately. This becomes pathological (sick) when the person admits to the death intellectually but still functions emotionally and in his behavior as though nothing had occurred. If this becomes serious, you will note disturbances in the person's judgment perception. A mourner may be certain that he saw a movement of a corpse's limb as he looked at the body in the casket. This irrational belief helps the person avoid the mourning process, which unfortunately delays recovery and resolution.

2. *Internalization.* The bereaved person wants to avoid the pain of the loss. Thus, he tries to preserve the relationship with the deceased by taking in the person and focusing on his or her internal presence. By failing to release the internalized person, he is rejecting external reality and refusing to let go of the deceased person. He prefers to hang on to his own internal reality.

3. *Externalization.* Externalization is used to avoid the pain of grieving. The person becomes fixed upon some object or item that is associated with the missing person. This could involve anything from furniture to clothing, an automobile, a boat or a photograph. It is used to keep the deceased alive for the survivor. He controls his grieving by keeping this object, but all this really does is postpone the inevitable grief and mourning process.[5]

The Stages of Grief

Following are some normal patterns of response that take place when a person loses a loved one.

Six Stages of Grief

1. *Shock and crying.* We should not deny people this outlet, for it is normal. This is a time of sudden pain and ache. The shock often protects the person from the full emotional impact of the tragedy. Some uninformed and mistaken Christians have made comments such as, "Stop your crying. After all, your husband is with the Lord now." Such comments are not helpful and are quite insensitive. Psalm 42:3 states, "My tears have been my food day and night." Let the person cry. Read also Psalm 38:17 and 2 Samuel 18:33. This is a time of despair and helplessness.

2. *Guilt.* This is almost a universal phenomenon. Statements or reactions such as, "If only..." "Why didn't I spend more time with him?" and "Why didn't we call in another doctor?" are often made. Many guilt reactions are an attempt to gain control once again after this sudden, painful event.

3. *Hostility.* A person may have anger at the doctors for not doing more, anger at the hospital staff for not being more attentive, anger at the person who died. A husband might ask, "Why did she die and leave me with three children to care for?" The person feels abandoned. An adolescent may feel angry at one parent for not doing more to stop the death of the other. Anger could also be directed at God for allowing this to happen. Then guilt and remorse sink in because of the spontaneous feelings of anger. People are helped by knowing that these reactions are normal.

4. *Restless activity.* The bereaved begin a lot of activities but lose interest and switch from one to another. It is hard for them to return to their regular routines.

5. *Usual activities lose their importance.* This brings on further depression and loneliness. Their usual activities were important only because they were done in relationship with the deceased.

6. *Identification with the deceased.* The bereaved person may continue the projects or work of the deceased. A wife may carry on her husband's unfinished hobby. A husband may continue to add to the house when that had really been his wife's project. People begin to do what the other person did, and they do it according to the deceased person's style. Even speech and mannerisms may be altered unconsciously to identify with the deceased. In some cases, people begin having pains where the deceased experienced symptoms. If her husband's back hurt extensively, the wife finds that her own back starts to ache. But all this is just part of the identification process.

Ten Stages of Grief

Granger Westberg expands on these 6 stages in his book *Good Grief.* Here are the 10 stages of grief he believes the normal person must pass through:

1. *Shock.* This is the person's temporary anesthesia, his brief escape from reality. How do we help at this point? Be near the person and available to help. But do not take away from the person what he can do for himself. The sooner he has to make some decisions and deal with the immediate problem, the better off he will be.

2. *Emotional release.* Encourage the person to cry or talk it out.

3. *Depression and loneliness.* Be available to the person, and let him know that whether he can believe it or not, this stage will pass, too.

4. *Distress.* The person may have symptoms of distress. Some of these could be due to repressed emotions.

5. *Panic.* The person may have panic about himself or the future. This can come because the death is ever present in his mind.

6. *Guilt.* The person needs to be able to talk through feelings of guilt with another person.

7. *Hostility and resentment.*

8. *Inability to return to usual activities.* Unfortunately, friends of the bereaved tend not to talk about the deceased. They may remember an important time in the person's life or a humorous incident but refrain from talking about it in the presence of the remaining partner. And yet if they were to do so, they would probably find a positive response. The person may express gratitude that someone talked about his loved one in this way. He is aware that those around him are very cautious about what they say, but fond remembrances talked about are healthy.

9. *Hope.* Gradually hope begins to return. Rabbi Joshua Liebman, in his book *Peace of Mind,* wrote an excellent chapter on "Grief's Slow Wisdom" that speaks most effectively to the temptation not to return to usual activities. Liebman said, "The melody that the loved one played upon the piano of your life will never be played quite that way again, but we must not close the keyboard and allow the instrument to gather dust. We must seek out other artists of the spirit, new friends who gradually will help us to find the road to life again, who will walk that road with us."[6]

10. *Struggle to affirm reality.* This does not mean the person becomes his old self again. When one goes through any grief experience, he comes out of it a different person. Depending upon how a person responds, he can come out either stronger or weaker.[7]

Completing Grief Work

A person needs to complete his grief work. What does this mean? Grief work means (1) emancipating oneself from the deceased (read 2 Sam. 12:23); (2) adjusting to life without the deceased; and (3) making new relationships and attachments.

Grief work is the reviewing by the bereaved of his life together with the deceased. This involves thinking about the person; remembering dates, events, happy occasions and special occasions; looking at photos and fondling trophies or items important to that person. In a sense, all these activities are involved in the process of psychologically burying the dead.

Our tendency many times is to deny the person his opportunity for grief work. We may come into the widow's home and find her looking at pictures in her husband's workshop and crying. How do we usually react? Perhaps we say, "Let's go do something else and get your mind off of this." But it would be better if we could enter her world of grief and feel with her, perhaps even cry with her. Romans 12:15 states that we are to "weep with those who weep."

Tears are a normal expression. Joyce Landorf says, "We must not be ashamed of our tears. Jesus wept on hearing of His friend Lazarus' death (even though He knew He was about to give Lazarus a remission from death!). To weep is not to be guilty of a lack of faith, nor is it a sign of hopelessness. Crying is a natural part of the grieving process."[8]

When grief is not expressed, a higher degree of what we call psychosomatic reactions such as ulcerative colitis and hypertension occur. During the time of grief work, you may notice irritability and some strained interpersonal relationships. Again, this is normal.

Surviving and Rebuilding

Another aspect of grief is called *surviving and rebuilding*. Because women live longer than men, you will probably have more of a ministry with widows than widowers. So we will relate this stage to the widow.

The three periods involved in surviving and rebuilding are (1) bridging the past; (2) living with the present; and (3) finding a path into the future.

Bridging the Past
Even with the pain of loss, during the first few days significant decisions have to be made by the widow. The funeral, financial matters and so on

have to be taken care of and it is the widow's primary responsibility to do so. She may decide to have others make these decisions for her. She may act as though she were still her husband's wife in the sense that she carries out decisions and arrangements as she thinks her husband would have wanted her to do. She does not think of herself as a widow at this time.

But she still has to function in other areas. Buying groceries, preparing meals, caring for children, pets and the household, and perhaps even functioning at work or in the family's business are necessities. This is where family and friends can be of assistance.

The primary task in this period is to loosen the ties with her deceased husband and begin to accept the fact that he is dead. This involves breaking the threads of shared experiences with her husband and translating them into memories. This includes learning to use the word "I" in place of "we."

Living with the Present

The second period is *living with the present*. After the funeral, a shift in the family structure needs to be made. Various roles need to be reassigned in order to take care of daily, routine tasks. Changes in expressive tasks need to be considered. Children will need to be comforted by their mother, even while she is involved in her own grief. This involves her sharing her pain and sorrow with the children even as she at other times has shared her joy and delight with them. Children need support and security from their mother during this time of the loss of one parent.

A mother cannot function as a mother and father. She will wear herself out attempting to fill both roles. Ministers should be careful in what they say to the spouse and children at this time. Statements such as, "You will have to function now as both mother and father" are not healthy. Telling a son he will have to take the place of his father now and be the man of the house is not a realistic statement. It is better for the remaining parent to work on being a better parent rather than attempting to fulfill both roles. Family members will have to accept the fact that some changes must be made and all the father's duties will not be assumed by the mother. Other family members or relatives may be able to fill in some of the vacant places, but not completely.

Role changes will affect everyone. And some of the changes will be unfamiliar, such as a widow's having to handle mortgage payments, inheritance taxes, bank statements, investments, settlement of debts, her husband's business problems and so on.

The issue of housing arrangements is crucial at this time. The home may have so many memories that the spouse will make or be forced into making a hasty decision to sell and move. Your counsel at this time may be important. The widow may be in a panic to ease the pain and the potential financial burden, but good decisions are not usually made at this time of intense emotion. Counsel her to wait if at all possible and consider the consequences carefully. Many widows have regretted selling too soon; they and the children do need the familiar setting. Several months should elapse before significant decisions are made.

This period is a time of giving up old habits and establishing new ones. Many widows report that their ties with their children become stronger at this time. Don't be surprised, however, by conflicts that occur over the will, possessions or family functions.

Significant signs of living with the present are seen as the person goes shopping alone for the first time, takes a job, goes out on a date, redecorates the house and so on.

Finding a Path into the Future

The third period *is finding a path into the future*. During this time the widow finds a stability in functioning and is now able to reorganize her life without her spouse. She has developed new roles and can operate independently in a new fashion.

She now seeks to develop new relationships, not to replace her original spouse but to refocus her own life or find a parent for her children, to ease economic strains and to have the comfort and companionship she desires.[9]

What can we say or do at this time of grief?

1. *Begin where the bereaved person is.* Do not begin where you think she should be at this point in her life. Do not place your expectations for behavior upon her. She may be more upset or more depressed than you feel she should be, but that is her choice.

2. *Clarify her expressed feelings with her.* This can be done by restating her words in your own words. Help her bring her emotions to the surface. You might say, "You know, I haven't seen you cry for a week. If I were in your situation, I would probably feel like crying." If the person is depressed,

be near her and assure her that it will pass in time. She probably will not believe you and could even ask you to leave. Do not be offended by this.

3. *Empathize.* Feel with her.

4. *Be sensitive to her feelings, and don't say too much.* Joe Bayly gives this suggestion:

> Sensitivity in the presence of grief should usually make us more silent, more listening. "I'm sorry" is honest; "I know how you feel" is usually not—even though you may have experienced the death of a person who had the same familial relationship to you as the deceased person had to the grieving one. If the persons feels that you can understand, he'll tell you. Then you may want to share your own honest, not prettied-up feelings in your personal aftermath with death. Don't try to "prove" anything to a survivor. An arm about the shoulder, a firm grip of the hand, a kiss: these are the proofs grief needs, not logical reasoning. I was sitting, torn by grief. Someone came and talked to me of God's dealings, of why it happened, of hope beyond the grave. He talked constantly, he said things I know were true. I was unmoved, except to wish he'd go away. He finally did. Another came and sat beside me. He didn't ask leading questions. He just sat beside me for an hour and more, listened when I said something, answered briefly, prayed simply, left. I was moved. I was comforted. I hated to see him go.[10]

Let them know their feelings are normal. Some of them will apologize to you for their tears, depression or anger. You will hear comments such as these: "I can't believe I'm still crying like this. I'm so sorry." "I don't know why I'm still so upset. It was unfair of them to let me go after 15 years at that job. I know I shouldn't be angry, but I guess I really am. It seems so unfair."

You can be an encourager by accepting their feelings and the fact that they have feelings. Give them the gift of facing their feelings and expressing them. There are many statements you can make to them:

"I don't want you to worry about crying in front of me. It's hard to feel this sad and not express it in tears. You may find me crying with you at times."

"I hope you feel the freedom to express your sorrow in tears in front of me. I won't be embarrassed or upset. I just want to be here with you."

"If I didn't see you cry, I would be more concerned. Your crying tells me you are handling this in a healthy way."

"If I had experienced what you have been through, I would feel like opening my eyes and letting the flood of tears come pouring out. Do you ever feel like that?"

Anger is another feeling that is difficult for many people to express. Use comments such as these:

"It is natural to feel anger and hostility toward everyone and everything that had to do with your husband's death. I feel angry too."

"You must be very angry that your baby has suffered, and you can do nothing about it."

"It is normal and reasonable to be angry and resentful when you have lost your baby, and others have live and healthy babies."

"You have lost your daughter and you have a right to be angry and frustrated."

"It must be hard to find the words to express your anger, helplessness and frustration."

"It is important that you allow yourself to express your anger and rage no matter how much others try to discourage you."

Your encouragement will help grieving persons understand that their expression of feelings will not cause you to withdraw from them. Reassure them that you are not going to leave because of their feelings or try to talk them out of feeling the way they do. Your support is going to remain.

Another positive way of responding is touch. But be sensitive to people you are ministering to who may not be as comfortable with touch as you are. If they seem to reject your physical gestures, such as hugs or touch, be sure to respect them.[11]

5. *Don't use faulty reassurances.* Assurances such as, "You'll feel better in a few days" or "It won't hurt so much after a while." How do you know that?

Remember not to give up helping the person too soon.

It seems when the initial paralyzing shock begins to wear off, the bereaved slowly returns to consciousness like a person coming out of a deep coma. Senses and feelings return gradually, but mingled in with the good vibrations of being alive and alert again is the frightening pain of reality. It is precisely at this time when friends, assuming the bereaved is doing just fine, stop praying, stop calling, and stop doing all those little kind things that help so much. We need to reverse this trend. In fact we must hold the bereaved person up to the Lord more during the first two years of grief than in the first two weeks.[12]

What most of us don't realize is the pattern of peaks and valleys of grief. Look at the intensity of grief as indicated by the following chart.[13]

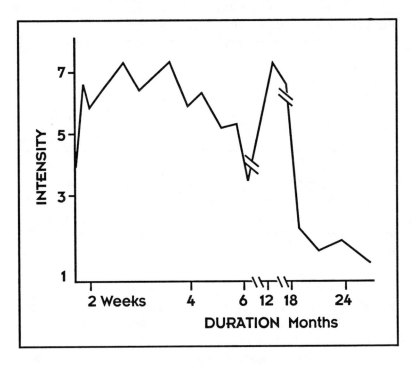

Notice the jagged peaks. The pain and grief actually intensify at three months and then gradually subside, but not in a steady fashion. They go up and down. Most people don't need a reminder of the first-year anniversary of the loss of a loved one. The intensity of grief comes rushing in with pain that rivals the initial feelings of loss. This is why no one should ever tell a person that they should be "over it by now" or "feeling better" at any of these times. It is understandable that most people lack an understanding of the process of grief unless they have been through it themselves. You can share this chart with a grieving person and let them know how normal their responses are and what to expect.[14]

Everyone varies but the average length of time for grief over the loss of a loved one is approximately two years for a natural death. If it was accidental it is three years, suicide death is four years and homicide is five years.

A special concern is the death of a child. This is often the most difficult kind of death to handle. It is easier to come to terms with the death of a person who has lived a long and full life than to accept the death of a child who has yet to experience the potential of life. It is so traumatic that it is estimated that 70 to 80 percent of couples who lose a child in death end up divorcing. The guilt that is so often present turns to blame, and turmoil occurs in marriage. Since the parents feel so responsible for a child, they also feel responsible for death.

Children's life expectancy is greater now than it was 100 years ago, so this type of death is not experienced as frequently. But when it happens it is very hard to handle. Often parents do not receive sufficient social support following the death of a child as compared to the death of a spouse.

In 1990, our mentally retarded son, Matthew, died at the age of 22 following corrective surgery. We have experienced the reality of this kind of loss and grief.

You can help the parents by encouraging them to talk openly and honestly with any of the medical staff who tended their child. The doctors should be able to assure them that everything possible was done for their child. They need to hear that there was nothing more they could do as parents.

Both parents need to express their grief openly and in front of one another. They need to express their sadness in front of the remaining children and even friends. Encourage the man to cry and share his tears with his wife. This is not a time to be stoic and in control. Be sensitive to how much the parents want to talk about the child. This may vary from time to time in your visits with them. In some communities there are support groups of parents who have lost a child in death.

Be sure to encourage the couple to talk freely between themselves. It is not uncommon for a wife to feel her husband is not feeling the loss as much as she because he is not reacting the way she is. The husband may feel that he has to "be strong" for the wife. But she may gain more strength from him by seeing the expression of his feelings. Verbal sharing of pain and loss needs to continue over an extended period of time. They need to know that the child's birthday, favorite vacation spots and holidays will bring back the grief with a new intensity for a while. If they can anticipate this and prepare for it, they will not be thrown by their feelings or by the fact that one parent may react much differently to the occasion than the other.

You may want to give the parents the book *I'll Love You Forever* by my wife, Joyce, and me (Focus on the Family Publishing, 1993) at an appropriate time.

Helping the Grieving Person

Someone, whether it is you or another concerned person, will need to help the grieving person(s) accomplish several tasks. These tasks are especially applicable in the loss of a loved one and will be accomplished over a period of time.

Help them identify secondary losses and resolve any unfinished business with the lost person. For many, these losses are never identified or grieved over. It could be the loss of a role, the family unit, the breadwinner, social life and so on. Sometimes saying aloud what a grieving person never said or had an opportunity to say to the deceased helps to complete some of the unfinished business.

Help them recognize that in addition to grieving for the lost person, grief will need to be experienced for any dreams, expectations or fantasies they had for the person. This is sometimes difficult or even overlooked, as they are not usually seen as losses because they never existed. Yet each still constitutes a loss because these dreams have a high value.

Discover what the grieving persons are capable of doing and where they might be lacking in their coping skills. Help them handle the areas where they are struggling. Encourage positive things they are doing such as talking about the loss. When they do something unhealthy, such as avoidance, alcohol or overmedication, give them other alternatives.

As most people do not understand the duration and process of grieving, provide them with helpful information concerning what they are now experiencing. You want to normalize their grief without minimizing it. But also let them know that their grief responses will be unique, and they should avoid comparing themselves with anyone else. Don't let them equate the length and amount of grieving with how much they loved the person.

Let them know you understand they may want to avoid the intensity of the pain they are presently experiencing. Your empathy, understanding and respect will do much to assist them in knowing that their grief is normal. Encourage them to go through the pain of the grief. There is just no way to avoid it. If they do, it will explode at some other time. They may need reminding that even with the present intensity of their pain, in time it will diminish.

Help them understand that their grief will affect all areas of life. Work habits, memory, attention span, intensity of feelings and response to marital partner will all be affected. This is normal.

Help them understand the process of grief. Sharing the chart in this chapter may be helpful at the appropriate time. Understanding that their emotions will vary and that progress is erratic will help alleviate the feeling that there is no progress. Help them plan for significant dates and holidays in advance. Encourage them to talk about their expectations for themselves and help them evaluate whether they are being realistic.

Help them find ways to be replenished spiritually, socially and physically. Be aware of their eating and exercise habits. Don't let them forego their own regular checkups. Alert them to the possible diminished capacity of the immune system that occurs several months after a major loss.

Help them with the practical problems following a loss, and assist in preventing unwise decisions. Such practical items as helping to arrange for meals, transportation, financial consultation, or eventually training or education needed for survival may be part of your task.

Sometimes grieving people will make major decisions too early, which creates additional losses. Some plan to sell their houses or move to new cities, but this may eliminate their roots or a needed support system. Making major changes during the first year should be discouraged if at all possible. These changes may appear to be wise, but they also bring another sense of loss.

Over a longer period of time, you may be able to assist grieving persons with a number of tasks. Help them discover their new identity separate from the one they lost and what new roles they must either develop or relinquish. These changes must be identified so that such things as lost portions of identity (from married to single) and lost roles can be grieved for.

You may be the one to bring up the fact that a healthy new relationship with the lost person must be developed. (Encourage them to read *Recovering From the Losses of Life* by this author.) This thought will be foreign to many, but it is a major adjustment for everyone who has lost a loved one. It is helpful to ask them how they plan to keep parts of their former life alive, such as special times, routines or mementos, and how reminiscing can be helpful.

One of your future tasks will be helping grieving persons reinvest in new lives. They will be able to start this process at their own time and pace. Some will need direction in getting back into the mainstream of life, especially if they cared for a chronically ill person for a period of time, or if they placed an elderly or handicapped person in a convalescent home. There can be a tremendous sense of loss and resulting adjustment to life following this step.

Sometimes finding support groups or other means of social support will end up providing lasting relationships. You need to be sensitive to the ability and desire of people to get back into the mainstream of life. Be sure you don't encourage them into new relationships too soon. Be especially careful of trying to promote new dating activities for those who have lost spouses through death or divorce.

At some point in time, you will have the opportunity to talk with people about what they have learned through a loss experience. In any kind of loss, there can be growth and gain, but this is not seen immediately. This does not mean we deny the significance of the loss in any way, but we do come to the place where our loss becomes an opportunity for spiritual growth and learning.[15]

When Children Grieve

Children may not experience the losses of adults such as loss of employment, power or status, but they do grieve because of the loss of a loved one. They comprehend death in different ways depending on their emotional development and age. Their grief process normally takes longer than that of adults because of two problems. First, the child does not always grasp the fact that death is permanent, that the dead person is not going to return. Nor does he always grasp that he has to release the strong emotional ties he had with the person. This is difficult if he was especially close to or dependent upon that person.

It is especially hard for a child to experience the death of a parent, for he invests almost all his feelings in his parents. Adults have a multitude of relationships.

How do children mourn? Any child over the age of two will need assistance in understanding what death means. His denial process is usually longer and more intense than that of adults. The younger the child, the more he will probably try to deny the fact of death. A child over the age of five may have fantasies for up to a week about the person's returning, and a child under five may have them much longer. He may carry on as though nothing happened.

It is hard for the child to accept the death all at once. He accepts what it means piecemeal. He may accept that the parent will not be there to play with him, then to bake cookies for him, then to tuck him in at night and so on.

The surviving parent or a helper may experience frustration in attempting to explain death to a child, for children will often change the subject. They need to be approached slowly and carefully. Be sensitive to how much the child can handle at one time. When the loss is accepted, the child may begin to "act out" scenes in which he remembers the deceased parent or sibling. This is healthy, for it helps the person adjust to the loss. The child will remember happy experiences first, and then in months or even years he can handle the pain of the unhappy times.

As the child progresses through the mourning process, it is vital that his physical and emotional needs are met. This relieves him of the fear that those needs will no longer be satisfied. Emotional fulfillment is the most important need.

Remember: The younger a child, the more important it is that a substitute parent be available to spend time with him.

It is interesting that guilt is stronger in a child's mourning than in an adult's. A child may convince himself that his father died because he was mad at him and wished his father was dead after they had a disagreement. He may decide that a parent or sibling died because of something he did or said. You need to help a child express those thoughts and feelings.

Not only is children's guilt more intense, but so is their despair. Some children deal with the loss by withdrawing, and others by becoming rebellious. Regression to earlier stages of development is quite common, including bed-wetting and thumb-sucking.[16]

Helping the Grieving Child

Here are some specific suggestions for you to follow and for you to pass on to parents and others in ministry.

Help a child experience losses in small ways before he is confronted with the larger losses in life. For many children, experiencing the loss of a pet is actually beneficial. In fact, some parents purchase a pet whose normal life expectancy is short for this very purpose. When the pet dies, what has happened is explained to the child, and his questions are dealt with honestly. This does not lessen the grieving process when a person dies, but it does help a child learn about death.

If there is a person who is dying within the family, the child should be helped to understanding the dying process and included as a member of the family unit following the death. He should be given a full explanation of what is occurring, and nothing should be hidden from him. Specific medical details, however, might not be given because of his inability to comprehend them.

A child who has experienced the death of a loved one can be very sensitive about being separated from adults he trusts and loves. If the surviving parent must leave for a while, the child must *have a detailed explanation* about where the parent is going and what he is going to do.

A child should not be sent away anywhere immediately following a death. It could panic the child, and he may wonder if he will be able to return. He may feel he is being punished for the death of the family member. A child needs the familiar surroundings of his own home, toys and bed.

A child should be involved in preparing for the funeral and burial. On the day of the funeral, he can help with refreshments, open the door, clean house, cook or do anything that makes him feel productive.

A child needs to be told about the death immediately. He needs an opportunity to say good-bye to the parent or sibling. This could be done at the funeral home or cemetery. A child should not be forced to attend the funeral, however, if he does not want to go. He needs an explanation of what it is and what it means, but he should make his own decision whether to attend. He may not be ready now but will be ready later.

Parents should not hide their feelings from the children following death. Open and honest responses can help the child grieve. A parent can explain that the dead person is now at peace and if he was a Christian, he is now in the presence of God. The parent's grief is for the loss of this important relationship. It is a normal feeling, and it will pass in time. The child is probably feeling the same loss and is sad. Those feelings are also normal. A child's questions must be answered honestly, and he should be given the opportunity to ask the parent any question. The language used with the child should be at that child's level of comprehension.

Phrases such as, "going to sleep," "resting," or "going away" to describe death should *not* be used with a child. It creates too much anxiety and is not truthful. The Christian perspective on death and heaven can be described, but carefully, and according to the child's level of response. Several Christian books on death can be used with a child. But ministers and parents alike should read these books carefully before using them, for not all may be helpful in dealing with children.

Do not overlook the feelings and inner turmoil a child may be experiencing. Recognizing and responding to his feelings helps him accept and work through them. Physical symptoms in a child may indicate an excessive amount of fear. If a parent dies of a lingering illness, a child may experience some similar physical responses at times. Or any pain the child experiences may be a threat in his mind. The child thinks that if his mother died in pain, maybe the pain he feels means he now has the same disease.

Every child will vary in his response, and that response may be a source of stress for a parent. Some children adapt well. Others may appear to be unfeeling, some angry and some rebellious.[17]

Ministry to the Terminally Ill

Another crisis ministry will be to those who know they are going to die. The terminally ill person has special needs and responses during his last days.

What does a person experience when he knows he is going to die? It is important for us to know what he is going through for two reasons: (1) some of us may be aware prior to our death that we are going to die; and (2) in order to minister to another person who is in this state, we need to know the stages. Dying means change. Even when we think we are prepared, we also live with the fear that we will not be able to cope. We are afraid of what kinds of changes will occur in us and what these changes will do to others as well.

When a person knows he is going to die, he usually experiences five different stages of emotional response. His loved ones go through these same emotional reactions as well.

1. *Denial and isolation.* The first reaction is that of, "It can't be. They're wrong. It's not me they are talking about." Some people make statements such as, "They'll find that someone in the lab made a mistake, and then they'll come and tell me that I'll be all right." Or the person may go to doctor after doctor seeking another diagnosis and a ray of hope. Not only does the person himself not want to hear that he will die, but his relatives and loved ones do not want to hear it either. The disciples didn't want to hear Jesus speak about His dying. Again and again He told them about His betrayal and crucifixion, but they did not want to hear it.

Often a person experiences a shock reaction upon hearing the news. One way shock manifests itself is through denial. Denial has been called the human shock absorber in time of tragedy. Through denial our emotions are temporarily desensitized. Our sense of time is somewhat suspended because of our attempt to delay the consequences. Not only can the denial aspect of shock manifest itself in a reaction such as, "Not me! No, I won't believe it," but in some cases denial can take the form of displaced concern. Some relatives who are shocked with the news about the loved one may try to act as though they are emotionally detached. But denial freezes the emotions, and they must be thawed out eventually.

Joyce Landorf says:

We need denial—but must not linger on it. We must recognize it as one of God's most unique tools and use it. Denial is our special oxygen mask to use when the breathtaking news of death has sucked every ounce of air out of us. It facilitates our bursting lungs by giving them their first gulps of sorrow-free air. We breathe in the breath of denial and it seems to maintain life. We do not need to feel guilty or judge our level of Christianity for clutching the mask to our mouth. However, after breathing has been restored and the initial danger has passed, we need not be dependent on it.

I think God longs for us to lay down the oxygen mask of denial, and with His help begin breathing into our lungs the fresh, free air of acceptance on our own.[18]

What do we do to help a person at this time as we visit him at home or in a hospital? Don't judge him for what he is saying, no matter how difficult he seems or what he says. Do not expect too much response on the first, second, or even third visit. He may not feel like talking. Do not become discouraged and quit visiting him. Eventually he will respond because he needs someone with whom to share his loneliness. Perhaps the example we find in Job can be a pattern for our response to the person (see Job 2:13).

2. *Anger.* In the second stage the person experiences anger, rage, envy and resentment. "Why me, God? Why me? Why not someone else?" The person is angry at those around him who are well—friends, relatives, doctors. He is angry at the doctors who cannot make him well. He is angry at God for allowing this to happen and for not immediately healing him.

In Job 7:11 we read, "Therefore, I will not restrain my mouth; I will speak in the anguish of my spirit." Perhaps this is what the person is experiencing at this point in his life. You may become the object of his anger simply because you are there, and you should not take the anger personally. Nor should you become judgmental and say he should not feel this anger. Anger is part of the normal process any person will experience. Through his anger the person could be demanding attention. Honest and open communication can help him feel understood.

3. *Bargaining.* "Spare me, Lord! Let me recover and be filled with happiness again before my death" (Ps. 39:13, *TLB)* is the prayer of so many people facing death. The person makes promises: "If I can get well, I will serve the Lord more than ever," or "If only I can live until June to see my son get married." Then, if the person lives until June he may say, "If only I can live to see my grandchildren," and the bargaining goes on and on. This stage usually lasts only a brief while, but it can be intense while it lasts.

Hezekiah, a man noted in the Old Testament, was told by the Lord, "Set your affairs in order, for you are going to die; you will not recover from this illness" (Isa. 38:1, *TLB).* When he received the news, he turned his face to the wall and bargained with God. He reminded God of how he had served and obeyed Him, and then he broke down and cried (see Isa. 38:3). Hezekiah's prayer was heard by God, and he was given 15 more years to live.

Hezekiah's response to this experience is recorded in Isaiah 38:17-20: "Yes, now I see it all—it was good for me to undergo this bitterness, for you have lovingly delivered me from death; you have forgiven all my sins. For dead men cannot praise you. They cannot be filled with hope and joy. The living, only the living, can praise you as I do today....Think of it! The Lord healed me!" *(TLB)*.

Part of the bargaining process could reflect our reaction to death and to God. We feel that God doesn't know what He is doing, in some cases, and we need to straighten Him out. Others may be allowed to die, but in this case He is wrong. Joe Bayly writes in *The Last Thing We Talk About:* "Death for the Christian should be a shout of triumph, through sorrow and tears, bringing glory to God—not a confused misunderstanding of the will of God to heal."[19]

Joyce Landorf tells the story of a lady who tried to bargain with God about her husband's terminal illness:

> She had lost her first husband after thirty years of marriage. Two years later she had married again and had seven happy years with a second husband. Then he got cancer.
>
> She told me they had been so very happy and the seven years so short that she pleaded and bargained with God to heal her husband. He was very close to dying and she knelt by his bed and begged the Lord to heal him so he wouldn't die. She said the Lord's voice spoke so clearly that she was quite startled by it. She heard Him say very distinctly in her mind, "Your husband has prepared himself to accept death and to die right now. Tell Me, do you want him to prepare himself for death again—later on?" She opened her eyes and looked at her husband—he was at peace—he had reached acceptance. She said, "Oh, Joyce, I knew right then I'd have to release him. I didn't want to make him go through that again—later on—so I released him. At that moment a great peace settled over me. He died a few hours later. Both of us were at peace." If she had hung on, begged God to let her husband live, she would have missed what God wanted to do in their lives.[20]

Our ministry to the terminally ill is to be a listener. James 1:19 in *The Amplified Bible* states that we are to be "a ready listener." This is a time to listen and not to give the dying person false hope. False reassurances do not help him. Simple reflection, a touch and listening will minister to him.

4. *Depression.* Denial has not worked, anger has not worked, bargaining has not worked; thus the individual facing death concludes that nothing works, and now the depression sets in. This depression has two parts. One is

what is called reactive depression—thinking about past memories—and the other is called preparatory—thinking about impending losses. This is a time when the person needs to express sorrow, to pour it out. You can minister best at this point by sitting silently with the person or holding his hand and letting him know that it is all right to express his feelings. Do not argue or debate with him, for the consequences can only be negative.

5. *Acceptance.* The person now rests in the knowledge of what will happen. This is a somewhat peaceful acceptance of the inevitable death. There is nothing else to do but accept the inevitable. The person may lose all interest in what goes on around him at this point and even become less talkative. You need to be honest with him. He might ask how long he has to live, and you should never give a time limit.

Ministering to Family Members

The family members of the terminally ill person need as much or more help and support as the person himself. They may not want the person to be told he is terminally ill, but it is better for all concerned that he be told. The family members should be encouraged to face this crisis of life with the patient and not isolate him.

One of the problems that can occur is the Abandonment Syndrome. Dying people express the fear that their condition will make them so unacceptable to others around them that they will be abandoned, and in many cases studies have confirmed their fears. Some of the ways this abandonment occurs are as follows:

1. *A brief and formal monologue.* A relative or even a doctor may come in, ask a few rhetorical questions, and then leave without letting the person express his inner fears and hurts. People breeze in but seem to respond only on a superficial level. Some come in and inform the person how he ought to be feeling and promise to come back, but never return.

2. *Treating the person as though the disease or accident has turned him into a nonperson.* He feels badly when others talk in front of him as though he were not there any longer. But even some unconscious people can hear what is being said. Many who have survived a coma have said that the faithful, verbal prayers of others were heard and meant so much to them. You should pray with the person whether you know he can hear or not.

3. *Ignoring or rejecting the cues that the person attempts to give.* He

may want to talk about what is happening. What would you say to the person who says, "I think I am going to die soon"? Many respond with: "Nonsense. You're going to live on for many years." That is not what he needs to hear. His feelings and interpretation are important to him.

4. *Literal abandonment.* Sometimes people in nursing homes as well as terminally ill patients are actually abandoned. People say they want to remember the person as he used to be or that he receives better care at the home than they could give. Often this is a reaction to the fears they have of their own deaths. Because of the implications of the loved one's death, they try to separate themselves from him in some way. It also has been observed that some loved ones initially have close contact with the terminally ill person such as kissing him on the lips. Then they begin to kiss him on the forehead, then the hand, and finally they simply blow a kiss from across the room. The patient can sense this form of rejection.

Let me pause briefly to raise the question of whether the person should return to his home to die. For some this may be best if they so desire, but others would feel more comfortable staying at the hospital. It is where they can feel the most secure in an honest atmosphere and receive the best care.

Many people do much of their grief work in advance of the impending death of a terminally ill family member. They experience the same grief stages as the terminally ill person. Ministers can help such people by having them actually visualize the sequences of the death, the funeral, the mourning and the people involved prior to this time. It is an act of preparation that is needed.

I have talked to many people who are unaware of the process of grieving before the death. Recently, a distant relative experienced the death of her mother. She was a bit taken back when her father remarried eight months after her mother's death. And yet, he had grieved during the last three years of her impending death and was able to readjust and go on with his life in a brief period of time.

Stages of Anticipatory Grief

Grieving over a loss that you know is going to occur may be less severe than grief following a sudden, unexpected death. Here are four basic stages in anticipatory grief.

1. *Depression.* This depression occurs following the diagnosis.

2. *Heightened concern for the ill person.* In an unexpected death, often there is guilt over such things as not being kinder, not showing sufficient love, having argued with the person and so on. In anticipatory grief, much of the guilt can be eliminated through the opportunity to increase love, concern and compassion for the person. Personal business can be concluded with the person prior to his death.

3. *Rehearsal of the person's death.* It is very common for the person to rehearse in his mind what he will do when the family member dies. He anticipates how he will feel, how he will be comforted, what he will actually do. Many arrange for the funeral in advance, which also helps them prepare for the person's death.

4. *Adjustments to the consequence of the death.* Those who are left adjust to life without the family member and begin to consider the future.[21]

Remember the following three key points as you minister at this crisis time.

A bereaved person, no matter what his age, needs *safe places.* He needs his own home. Some people prefer to withdraw because their home reminds them of their loss, but giving up the home and moving creates more of a loss. A brief change may be all right, but familiar surroundings are helpful.

The bereaved also needs *safe people.* Friends, relatives and a minister are necessary to give him the emotional support he needs. It is better to visit the person 4 times a week for 10 minutes than to come once a week for an hour. This is more of a continual support without becoming exhaustive.

Finally, the bereaved needs *safe situations.* Any kind of safe situation that provides the bereaved person with worthwhile roles to perform benefits him. The roles should be uncomplicated and simple and should not be likely to create anxiety. One pastor called upon a home in which the woman had just lost her husband. He could tell that people had been coming in and out all day long and that she was tired of receiving them and their concern. As he came in he said, "You know, I've had a tiring day. Would it be too much to ask you to make a cup of tea or coffee?" She responded and fixed the coffee. When he was leaving she said, "Thank you for asking me to make you the coffee. I started to feel worthwhile and useful again."

Perhaps what we most need to minister effectively to others is a clear understanding of what death is. For the Christian, death is a transition, a tunnel leading from this world into the next. Perhaps the journey is a bit frightening because of leaving what security we can feel here for the unknown, but the final destination will be well worth the present uncertainty.

John Powell, in *The Secret of Staying in Love,* has a thought for us to consider.

This book is gratefully dedicated to Bernice. She has been a source of support in many of my previous attempts to write. She has generously contributed an excellent critical eye, a cultivated literary sense and especially a confident kind of encouragement. She did not help with the preparation of this book. On July 11 she received a better offer. She was called by the Creator and Lord of the Universe to join the celebration at the banquet of eternal life.[22]

Notes

1. Joyce Landorf, *Mourning Song* (Tarrytown, NY: Fleming H. Revell, 1974), p. 26.
2. Bertha G. Simos, *A Time to Grieve: Loss as a Universal Human Experience* (New York: Family Service Association of America, 1979), pp. 10,11,28,29.
3. Roy W. Fairchild, *Finding Hope Again: A Pastor's Guide to Counseling Depressed Persons* (San Francisco: HarperCollins, 1980), pp. 113-114.
4. Ibid., p. 117.
5. V. D. Volkan and D. Josephthal, "The Treatment of Established Mourners," in *Specialized Techniques in Individual Psychotherapy,* T. B. Karasu and L. Belleck, eds. (New York: Brunner-Mazel, 1980), no page indicated, adapted.
6. Joshua Liebman, *Peace of Mind* (New York: Simon and Schuster, 1946).

7. Granger Westberg, *Good Grief* (Philadelphia, PA: Fortress, 1962), pp. 30-37, adapted.
8. Landorf, *Mourning Song*, p. 147.
9. Naomi Golan, *Passing Through Transitions* (New York: The Free Press, 1981), pp. 171, 175-82, adapted.
10. Joe Bayly, *The Last Thing We Talk About*, originally titled *View From a Hearse* (Elgin, IL: David C. Cook, 1973), pp. 40,41.
11. H. Norman Wright, *Recovering From the Losses of Life* (Tarrytown, NY: Fleming H. Revell, 1991), pp. 182,183.
12. Landorf, *Mourning Song*, p. 145.
13. Glen W. Davidson, *Understanding Mourning* (Minneapolis, MN: Augsburg Publishing House, 1984), p. 59.
14. Wright, *Recovering From the Losses of Life*, p. 59, adapted.
15. Therese A. Rando, *Grieving: How to Go on Living When Someone You Love Dies* (Lexington, MA: Lexington Books, 1988), pp. 227-250, adapted.
16. Brenda Q. Hafen and Brenda Peterson, *The Crisis Intervention Handbook* (Englewood Cliffs, NJ: Prentice Hall, 1982), pp. 43,44.
17. Ibid., pp. 44-48, adapted.
18. Landorf, *Mourning Song*, p. 53.
19. Bayly, *The Last Thing We Talk About*, n.p.
20. Landorf, *Mourning Song*, pp. 83,84.
21. Richard Schult, *The Psychology of Death, Dying and Bereavement* (Reading, MA: Addison-Wesley, 1978), pp. 140,141, adapted.
22. John Powell, *The Secret of Staying in Love* (Allen, TX: Argus Communications, 1974), Dedication, n.p.

THE CRISIS
of DIVORCE

~~~~~~~~~~~~~~~~~~~~~~~~~~~

8

The young couple sat in my office for their first session of premarital counseling. After we had discussed some of the preliminaries, the woman explained something that was really bothering her.

"When I was three years old," she said, "my parents divorced. I've only seen my natural father eight or nine times in my life. I think of my stepfather as my real dad and love him very much. In fact, I felt abandoned by my real father. Now our wedding is coming up and my natural father called me and told me he is looking forward to giving me away!"

Then her fiancé spoke up. "And that isn't all," he said. "Jane's parents divorced and have both remarried, and my parents divorced three years ago and have since remarried. Where do we have everyone sit during the ceremony?"

The divorces were over and the parents were reestablished in their new marriages. But were the divorces really over? There is no final ending to the pain of divorce. Couples do not marry with the intention of getting a divorce. But when it happens, it affects many people besides the husband and wife.

Divorce is a crisis that affects the couple, their children, their relatives, their friends and their business associates. The changes brought about by the divorce create feelings of failure on the part of both husband and wife and disequilibrium for everyone involved. Children experience a gamut of emotions. Many people find they lose their partner as well as other significant people.

Divorce is a life-long, ongoing experience during which each person becomes crisis prone at different times. The main paradox of divorce is that the marriage may be dead and legally ended, but the relationship continues.

When a loved one dies, a dignified finality to the relationship and mourning rituals take place. And the person usually receives tremendous support from other believers as well. But in a divorce, support is often lacking and there are no mourning rituals. The person has to continue to interact with his or her former spouse during and following the legal proceedings. In the death of a spouse, the loss of a person and a relationship occurs; in a divorce, only the death of the relationship is experienced.

Six Stages of Divorce

A person experiences six overlapping stages through the course of a divorce. Although divorced people do not experience the stages in the same order or with the same degree of intensity, most of them experience all six stages. You will need to know the various stages as well as specific stress that divorce brings in order to minister to the person or couple.

1. *Emotional divorce.* This is the first visible stage. This begins during the marriage when one or both spouses start to withhold emotion from their relationship. Their attraction to and trust for each other has diminished, and they have ceased to reinforce feelings of love for each other. Unfortunately, you probably have couples in your church who live in this state throughout the duration of their marriage. They may never separate or divorce, but they remain emotionally detached from each other and fail to improve their relationship. In emotional divorce, the reality of no longer being "number one" impresses itself more and more upon the person. During this time, feelings are concentrated upon the negative areas of the spouse's personality rather than upon the positive areas of the two lives.

2. *Legal divorce.* One or both spouses may retain a lawyer and decide

to plan his or her own divorce and complete the multitude of forms. The laws have been written to make dissolution of a marriage a relatively simple procedure. But one of the reasons divorce is a trying emotional experience is that the legal process, although providing for the dissolution of marriage, does not provide for the release of emotions.

During the period of emotional divorce and either before or during the legal phase, a decision must be made for one parent to leave the family. Here is where the sense of loss and finality can really hit. Even when people change their residence for positive reasons, they can experience stress. When the move is the result of a divorce, even more stress is experienced. Often parents hesitate telling their children the truth at this time and indicate that they are trying a separation to see if it will help the marriage. But children usually figure out what is taking place.

This period of separation is a major disruption for everyone. The entire family has to undergo a massive reorganization concerning rules, roles, standards and boundaries. During this time, the people involved may receive emotional support from relatives or close friends, which can be helpful. But one of the dangers is that the people involved in the divorce may perceive their friends and even the church and its members as either allies or enemies. This is the time for an objective helper such as a counselor or pastor in addition to a lawyer.

3. *Economic divorce.* This stage may alter a couple's life-style. An unemployed mother may find herself seeking a job out of necessity. Does your church have any provision to help during this time of adjustment or job search? Some mothers may choose to seek employment as an exercise of their newly found freedom. Perhaps this is the first time they have had an opportunity to work. Decisions concerning who gets the car, the stereo, the pets and so on are made during this stage.

Alimony, child support and community property (or other property rights depending upon the state of residence) are issues to be discussed with a lawyer and decided upon by the parties or the court. Some couples are able to agree on property division and financial responsibility, but others find that resentments, hostilities and feelings of revenge prevent equitable solutions. The restructuring of the financial area of a person's life makes him even more aware of the realities of divorce.

4. *Coparental divorce.* The most enduring hurt can be experienced at this stage. The word "coparental" indicates that parents are divorced from

each other but not from their children. It should be expressed to the children that even though adults can be divorced from one another, parents and children cannot. Unfortunately, many children do feel that they have been divorced from one of their parents.

The divorce process can be as easy or as hard upon a child as his parents wish to make it. Loss of perspective by a parent is one of the most dangerous problems that can occur at this stage. Controlled by anger and bitterness, a parent may try to justify himself by placing all the blame on the other parent. By attacking his ex-spouse, he forces the child to take sides. As you minister to divorcing couples, make them aware of this tendency before they do it, and help them avoid making this serious mistake.

5. *Community divorce.* This stage is characterized by loneliness. This may be caused by a change in social status. If the divorced person was in a social club for couples or an adult couples' Sunday School class, he may now feel out of place and ill at ease. He or she may have been a board member of the church or a Sunday School teacher. What is the policy of your church? Do you encourage the person to continue on in that position, or do you ask him to resign? Perhaps you struggle with this, wondering what is best for the Body and what is best for the person. It is a difficult issue since asking the person to resign means another loss that feeds his feelings of guilt and isolation.

6. *Psychic divorce.* During this stage a divorced person becomes autonomous—separate from the influence, presence and perhaps from thoughts of the former spouse. Achieving autonomy is the process of creating distance between one person and another. This is one of the most difficult stages, but it can be a time of learning to become a whole person, independent and creative. It can be a time of reflection upon one's own responsibilities and actions and a time to begin making positive changes.

The divorced person must be aware of the emotional adjustment and even mourning that continues during this stage. Divorce can bring with it separation shock. The longer the marriage, the greater the possibility of this malady. The termination of a relationship can bring waves of depression, self-pity, guilt, remorse and fear. The intensity of these reactions is determined by the degree of importance the marriage had in shaping the divorced person's identity. This is the time for the person to become an autonomous person again, without someone to lean on and also without someone to support.[1]

Reactions of Friends

Often people at church do not know what to say and what not to say to a person experiencing the process of divorce. Some married people are threatened by the presence of a divorced person. Their reactions are more often a reflection of their own insecurity than a rejection of the divorced person. Close friends can be a source of support at the time of divorce and can be therapeutic. The person in the process of a divorce should be encouraged to rely upon his friendships but should also be made aware of some of the common reactions of others he may experience.

Here are 12 common ways friends react to a divorced person:

1. A friend may experience some *anxiety* or *fear* upon hearing of the person's divorce. Perhaps if he has looked up to the person and the marriage relationship as a model, part of his own security now begins to crumble. He may begin to reflect upon his own marital relationship and question its direction.

2. A second reaction is *shame*. Friends may be experiencing the very same difficulties as the divorcing couple and know they are not dealing with those problems. They have not chosen divorce, nor have they chosen to take any constructive steps to improve their marriage. Now they are confronted with someone who has taken a step, and they feel uncomfortable for ignoring their own relationship.

3. Sometimes a friend is *overly preoccupied with the subject of divorce*; it is on his mind constantly. He talks about it every occasion and seeks out additional information. He may feel as though he has been let in on a secret, especially if the divorce came as a surprise to him. He shows little tact and sensitivity by asking too many personal questions.

4. It often happens when a separation or divorce occurs that friends have *fantasies* and desire for a sexual relationship with one of the partners. Fantasies that occurred before the divorce may become intensified and may even be expressed openly after the divorce. A divorced woman could suddenly be given an inordinate amount of attention from male friends. Such attention is given in the guise of interested help and support.

5. Strange as it may seem, some *experience pleasure* from the suffering and failure of others. If the couple occupied a place of prominence or have wealth, social status or an abundance of talents, the failure of the marital relationship might be looked upon with pleasure by those who have been envious.

6. People have been known to *feel superior* to their divorced friends. They are proud of their own marriage relationship. They look upon divorced people as weak and inferior, or as quitters and second-class citizens who have sinned.

7. *Surprise* is another common reaction. Some friends cannot imagine that this couple had any difficulties. Sometimes the surprise takes the form of a protest: "It can't be, not you! You don't mean it! Go for some help! Think of the children!" If the surprised person is a close friend or business associate, he may also be afraid that the divorce will be a reflection upon his own marriage.

8. Friends of the divorced couple may experience some degree of *emotional loss and grief.* The stability of the divorcing couple's marriage may have been an emotional support in their own lives, and now that support has been removed. If the relationship between the couple is close, feelings of empathy are natural.

9. If their is bitterness between the divorcing parties, friends may experience *conflict over allegiances.* Taking sides may mean losing an emotionally significant friend, which can intensify the person's emotional turmoil and grief. And if feelings of rivalry, envy and preferences are aroused, the loss could also produce feelings of guilt and shame.

10. Another reaction to which some people are especially vulnerable is the feeling of *disillusionment* about the trustworthiness of friends and the permanence of relationships. Depression is not uncommon, especially if the person's self-esteem is partially built upon this relationship. Often people are not aware of the intensity of their friendships, and when divorce occurs they become disillusioned.

11. A *personal identity crisis* may also occur. Friends who were involved in the mutuality of the marriage and in the lives of the individual spouses may need to assess who they really are and what is important in their own lives.

12. Finally, some friends are *curious* about the settlement. Some actually become preoccupied with it. They want to know how much money was involved, who received what, whether a good lawyer was retained, who had the advantage and what was decided about support for the children. If the inquisitive friend strongly identifies with one spouse more than the other, his curiosity may be more intense.[2]

Friends and members of the congregation need instruction on how to minister to those in the process of divorce. Has anyone ever preached a message or taught a lesson in your church on what people experience as they divorce and what others can say and do to help them? Perhaps they need to hear the 12 common reactions to divorce listed above and consider where they fit on that list.

Facing Up to the Divorce

The transitional period of divorce is a process that may take two years or longer. Concurrent with the six stages of divorce are a series of overlapping phases, each with its own goals and tasks. It is important to be aware of these so you can identify which phase the person is in who comes to you for help.

1. *Denial.* This phase starts long before the intense stress arises that pushes the marriage into a state of crisis. People use denial to keep the marriage relationship going. Over the years in my marital counseling, I have seen this time and again. Men are often more hesitant to face marital problems and may simply state what their wives say about the marriage. They tend to interpret the issues in a bit more positive manner, and the wife ends up feeling either that she is wrong for her perception or that her husband does not care.

During this time, one or both of the spouses may be aware of the problems but feel they can accommodate themselves to the difficulties. They may even prefer leaving the marriage the way it is to facing the effort necessary to change. This leads to a very fragile relationship, and even a minor amount of stress can create a crisis.

2. *Loss and depression.* When a couple can no longer cope with their problems together, they may decide that being together is a bigger problem. One spouse's feelings may cause him to look for help from a pastor, physician or counselor at this time. Help the person verbalize his fears about the future of the marriage and the possible consequences.

3. *Anger and ambivalence.* This occurs as the end of the marriage becomes a reality. The depression that was present begins to lift to reveal an underlying feeling of anger. Feuding and haggling often occur over the various legal decisions facing the couple. It is not uncommon to see one of the spouses behaving like a rebellious adolescent and the other an irate parent. Feelings of anger toward the person's partner are mixed with ambivalence over terminating the marriage.

4. *Reorientation of life-style and identity.* In time, each spouse spends less time regretting the past and experiencing anger toward the spouse and starts to look to the present and future. If divorce is a reality, one needs to move on with one's life. This upheaval raises the question once again of, "Who am I?" A new identity needs to be formed in every area of the person's life—personally, vocationally, sexually and socially. The person's confidence is shaken regardless of who desired the divorce. This can be a time of sexual difficulty, too, as self-esteem may be lowered and the person may feel sexually undesirable or inadequate.

Damaged self-esteem prompts the person to attempt to rebuild it, but often in ways that can damage it even more. Too often the person plunges into relationships too soon in order to make sure others see him as sexually desirable. But he is hesitant to enter into serious emotional involvements during this time.

5. *Acceptance and achievement of a new level of functioning.* Now as the person works through his feelings, he is able to move toward deeper and more lasting emotional commitments. Some are able to once again accept their former partner and the fact of the divorce, which can lead to better relationships with the former spouse, children and in-laws. This is also the time when interactions without the former spouse have been established and the children's relationship with the absent spouse are into a routine. A balance comes into

the person's life at this time as the mourning over the past relationships is settled.[3]

Ministering to Divorced People

As you minister to a person in divorce, remember that the counseling principles suggested for helping a person in any type of crisis apply here. Be sensitive to the feelings of a divorced person about his divorce in light of the teaching of Scripture and your own church. He may even hesitate coming for help because of his concern over the church's feelings and teaching.

One of the most difficult situations is attempting to help the spouse who does not want the divorce to occur. He wants you to devise a solution that will succeed. But you need to remember that, even though you may be the most skilled pastoral counselor available, the spouse who wants the divorce will divorce, regardless of your ability. In most states, nothing can be done to stop a divorce. The hurting spouse will hang onto every promise from the Word of God to give him hope. He may say, "I know God will bring my spouse back to me. I have read His promises, and I know He hates divorce. It is His will that we stay together, and I will just wait and pray. Don't tell me otherwise. I don't want to make any plans for divorce or talk to an attorney. That would be doubting God."

Often these people feel that if they do not resist anything in the settlement, their spouses will see this as an act of love and desire them once again. But it doesn't work that way; I have rarely seen that approach succeed. Many of my counselees have appreciated knowing this before they consult an attorney. I have seen many couples in marriage counseling put their marriages back together and move from the brink of a divorce to a healthy relationship. It is possible. But you must be realistic when you work with the person who is being rejected. Unfortunately, he often comes in having read some book that states that if he will follow the 13 principles outlined in the book, his spouse will return to him. This gives false hope, makes the impact of divorce even worse, and delays the resolution process.

It is important for you to be aware of some of the legal steps and procedures in divorce and have competent, honest, Christian attorneys to whom you can refer people. Do not attempt to answer legal questions, but encourage the person to seek the counsel of a lawyer.

When the person comes to see you, try to determine which stage he is in. At some point discuss with him the different stages he will experience so he will be able to anticipate the process and not be thrown by it. Inform him, perhaps in print, of the various reactions of friends so he will be aware and forewarned. Establish in the first session where the person is in this transitional process, and identify the specific issues with which he is struggling.

One of the biggest steps involved in this process is "letting go" of the past relationship that includes the spouse, the children, the life-style, the home and so on. You will need to help him express his feelings of depression, grief, anger and frustration. As the counseling progresses, you may help him deal with past issues that may have created some of his problems. Such a person does need specific advice for problems and issues confronting him.

This is a time for the mutual help groups that so many churches have available. Just as a recovering alcoholic needs both the Alcoholics Anonymous meetings and individual counseling for the greatest progress to be made, so a divorced person needs a group as well as the individual counseling. (See the list of groups and books to use in your counseling at the end of this chapter.) The person needs both anticipatory guidance and assistance in learning new living skills. Recommend helpful books and other people to talk with who have worked through a similar situation.

One of the main concerns to look for in helping a person is the amount of resentment and bitterness that seem to be present. Anger over the hurt and rejection is very normal, but there needs to come a time when that is resolved. Unfortunately, some continue to be wounded people and to allow this experience to plague them for decades.

Following are 24 questions to have the person answer, preferably during the week and on a piece of paper. These should not be used during the early phases of the crisis but at a time when you feel it is appropriate. Duplicate these questions and have them available to use. Ask the person to answer them fully and to bring them to your next meeting.

Self-evaluation Questionnaire

1. What grudges and resentments do I hold against my spouse?
2. How long have I held these?
3. Am I truthfully recalling the events that I am now holding onto? How would someone else recall them?
4. Who reinforces my grudge? Who agrees with me?
5. What value am I receiving from that reinforcement from others?
6. Describe what you will gain by punishing the other person.
7. Who am I really punishing?
8. Do I really want to hurt this other person?
9. Describe all the accusations you have made against your spouse.
10. Now write down all the ones you know to be true.
11. Notice any difference in the length of the lists.
12. What could my spouse do or say concerning me that would make me feel better about him or her?
13. What is one thing I would like that person to agree with me on?
14. Describe what you need to tell that person in order to be more truthful with him or her.
15. Describe everything you feel that person has done to you.
16. What are all the things I feel I did "for him or her"?
17. What are all the things I feel he or she did "for me"?
18. Am I receiving value from making that person appear "wrong"? If so, what is it?
19. Do I receive a reward from telling my "soap opera" to my friends and relatives? What are the rewards?
20. Am I telling the facts concerning what the other person has done?
21. What am I willing to do to get on with my life?
22. Describe how you pray for your spouse at this time.
23. Describe how you feel God feels about you at this time.
24. Is this perception consistent with Scripture?

This page may be reproduced for your personal use.

Learning to Forgive

I find that many people have difficulty letting loose of their resentments. Not too many people are born with the capacity of forgiving. It is a response that must be learned. The believer has the greatest opportunity to learn and practice this because of being a forgiven person.

One of the questions I gently ask in counseling when we are dealing with resentment and forgiveness is, "Are you aware that by holding onto the resentment toward that person, you are giving that person control of your emotional life?" Counselees often look startled and say, "What do you mean?" What I mean is, they are allowing the other person's responses and attitude to so influence them that the person is actually controlling their emotions. Often the counselee says, "I never thought of it in that light." After considering this new perspective, many people decide it is not worth being resentful.

The major question is, "How do I learn to forgive that other person?" Following is an approach I have used, one that incorporates some of the better techniques currently practiced by therapists.[4] These suggestions can be effective whether the person resented is still living or is deceased. I have people begin by completing the following steps, in writing.

Steps to Forgiveness

First, list all the resentments you have toward the particular person you are allowing to continue to limit your life. List each hurt or pain you recall in as much detail as possible. Write out exactly what happened and how you felt about them and feel now.

Please be aware that you may experience considerable emotional upheaval as you make your list. Other old, buried feelings may surface at this time, and you may feel upset for a while. Prior to and during this writing ask God to reveal to you the hidden and deep pools of memory, so your inner container can be emptied. Thank Him that it is all right for you to wade through and expel these feelings at this time. See Jesus Christ in the room with you, smiling and giving His approval of what you are doing. He is saying to you, "I want you to be cleansed and free. No longer do you have to be lame, blind, or deaf because of what happened to you."

Don't show these lists to anyone else.

Second, after writing as many resentments as possible, stop and rest for a while. By doing this you may be able to recall others you need to share. You will probably not remember every one, and you do not need to.

Third, upon completing the writing, go into a room with two chairs. Imagine the other person sitting there and accepting what you are verbally sharing with him. Take your time, look at the chair as if the person were there, and begin reading your list. At first you may feel awkward and even embarrassed. But these feelings will pass. You may find yourself amplifying what you have written as you share your list.

Next, after you have read your list of grievances, sit back, relax, and imagine this person responding to you in a positive manner. In your mind see him saying to you, "I want to hear what you have to share with me, and I will accept it. Please go ahead and tell me. I need to hear what you have to say."

Imagine the person you resent actually hearing you, nodding in acceptance, and understanding your feelings. You may find yourself becoming very intense, angry, depressed, anxious, and so on. Share how you are feeling with that imagined person. Remember, not only is that other person giving you permission to share all of your present and past feelings, Jesus is there, also giving you that permission. You may find that sharing and talking about just one resentment will be enough for you to handle at one time. If you find yourself emotionally drained, then it is important to stop and rest and relax. After you have done this, you can resume your normal tasks for the day. At another time you will continue to share your list of resentments.

Finally, before you conclude your time of sharing, close your eyes and visualize you, the other person, and Jesus standing together with your hands on one another's shoulders. Spend several minutes visualizing this scene. You may wish to imagine the resented person verbally accepting what you have said to him.

Once you have completed all the steps, you may find that you will need to repeat them several times, over a period of weeks, until the past is purely a historical memory. If there is more than one person involved, you will need to complete these steps with each one.

Another helpful method is to write a letter to the resented person. Be sure that you do not actually give this letter to the individual in mind. For some, the written sharing may be more helpful than the verbal.

Start your letter as you would any letter: Dear_____. This is not an exercise in style or neatness or proper punctuation. You are simply identifying, expressing, and draining your feelings. At first it may be difficult, but as you begin you will feel the words and feelings flowing. Do not hold back! Let out all the feelings that have been churning underneath. This is not a time to evaluate whether the feelings are good or bad; right or wrong. They are there and need to be drained. Once the letter is complete you may need to rest from this experience.[5]

As I work with clients in therapy and have them write such a letter I ask them to bring it to their next session with me. Often they hand me the letter as they enter the room. "No," I say, "I'd like you to keep the letter, and we will use it in a little while." At the appropriate time I ask them to read the letter aloud. Since there is an empty chair in the room, I ask them to imagine that the resented person is sitting in the other chair, listening to the reading of this letter.[6]

Suggest that the person read the chapter, "Relinquishing Your Resentments," from this author's book *Making Peace With Your Past.* It contains another exercise that can be very beneficial. Also encourage them to read *Forgive and Forget* by Lewis Smedes (HarperCollins).

You may feel that the crisis is finished once a person has worked through the various stages and gone on with his life. For a time it is, but when the person moves toward marrying again, the crisis often reappears. If you are going to work with couples as they remarry, please be sure you read *Help for Remarried Couples* and *Families* by Richard Olson and Carole Della Pia-Terry. The practical suggestions and questions in this book will give you the direction and structure you may be seeking.

We will look for a moment at the new crisis that arises from marrying again. Many who marry again to start a new life enter a relationship with unresolved issues left over from the previous marriage. Not only will there be adjustments to the new spouse, but often to an "instant" family as well, because a second marriage frequently involves children from the first marriage. It usually takes what we call a "blended family" about six or seven years to stabilize. Premarital counseling for couples in this situation needs to be more extensive than the few routine sessions you give a couple anticipating their first marriage. Some sessions should involve the children also.

Before a second marriage is attempted, a person needs to have resolved the issues from his former marriage. How can you tell whether this has occurred? Richard Olson and Pia-Terry suggest the following guidelines:

A person has appropriately resolved his or her previous marriage when he or she

- has accepted the death of the marriage relationship and the reality of the divorce;
- has made decisions about the divorce settlement and the children that both former spouses can live with, with a minimum of continuing bitterness;
- has put into practice these decisions, such as financial payments, visitation, custody, holidays, and so on, and the arrangements are working;
- has learned not to be "hooked" by the former spouse's behavior. In some cases the previous two items cannot be true; one can only be responsible for one's behavior. Therefore, the person should not "give in" to his or her spouse's behavior or manipulation.[7]

Stages of Forming a New Family

The stages involved in forming a new family are different from those the person experienced when starting the first family. Three sequential but overlapping stages are involved.

1. *Recovery from loss.* The mourning of the first relationship must be completed. Sometimes it is delayed until or reopened when the divorced person begins to consider remarriage. If both people considering remarriage are at different stages in overcoming their loss, or if only one has been married before, complications in their new relationship can occur.

2. *Planning the new marriage.* Two major tasks need to be accomplished during this stage. First, each person needs to come to terms with (1) his own positive lack of confidence regarding his ability to sustain a close and lasting relationship; and (2) his fear of repeating the mistakes and problems of the first marriage.

The second major task is to help all the family members invest in each other emotionally. This will take patience and time. A child in particular may struggle with the fear of being rejected by the new stepparent. He may also be concerned about giving up his or her emotional attachment to his real parent. In fact, at the time of remarriage children have to deal once again with the feelings of loss and divided loyalties. They may have difficulty feeling that they actually belong in the new family. They struggle with how to handle membership in two households. They may have unreasonable expectations for themselves and others, fantasies about their natural parents reuniting, and guilt over causing the divorce.

3. *Reconstituting the family.* The primary task here is restructuring the roles. And the two major areas in which a second family must redefine its roles are discipline and nurturing. The role of the stepfather to his wife's children and the relationship between children of each spouse must be defined. And the final task is to delineate the appropriate relationship with the divorced biological parents. If this sounds complex and potentially stressful, it is! The potential for continued stress and major crisis is abundant.

This has been a simple overview of what will be involved. If you plan to develop a ministry with the divorced and those about to be remarried, please study extensively in this area, or else ask some lay couples who have experienced divorce and remarriage to become the specialists.

I am sure some ministers would prefer not to be involved in the whole issue of divorce and remarriage. But the divorced population in churches is large. These are hurting people who need someone to minister to them. Instead of investing our energy in lamenting the problem of divorce and its increase and preaching against divorce, which really does not stop people from divorcing, let me suggest a constructive ministry that will have a dramatic effect upon the divorce statistics. These recommendations will not be expanded here, but through further reading and education you can create an effective ministry to the divorced in your church.

Divorce Ministry Suggestions

1. Have a thorough program of individual premarital counseling for every couple who seeks to be married in your church. This would involve a minimum of 6 or 7 sessions with a minister or qualified lay person. Have each person take the Taylor-Johnson Temperament Analysis, the Prepare Inventory and the Family History Analysis described in this author's book *The Premarital Counseling Handbook* (Moody). Each person should put in approximately 50 hours of outside homework, reading books and listening to tapes.

We need to remember that the task of the church when it comes to marriage is not to perform weddings but to nurture marriages.

2. Develop a two-fold program of ministry to married couples. Provide an annual marital checkup for couples. This usually takes 2 meetings with a minister or trained lay person who helps the couple evaluate how their marriage has developed over the previous year and establish goals for the coming 12 months. In addition, have several marriage enrichment or renewal retreats each year and make a strong push to have every married couple of the congregation in attendance.

3. Set an example of a positive marriage relationship for the congregation by continuing to court and date your own spouse. Unfortunately, many ministers neglect their own wives and children in their zeal to help others. Actions speak louder than words.

4. Help people through your teaching and preaching to learn to *apply* the Scriptures to their lives. Many are "knowledgeable" of the Word of God but have not learned to apply it in a practical manner.

5. Finally, develop a strong preparation ministry for the divorced who are contemplating remarriage. Second marriages have a higher risk, but that can be greatly reduced with careful evaluation, preparation and helping people experience Jesus Christ in their lives in a very practical way.

Recommended Resources

Support for Divorced People

Dalke, David. *The Healing Divorce: A Practical and Theological Approach.* Available from Learnings Unlimited, 516 4th Ave., Longmont, CO 80501. Dalke, an ordained United Methodist minister, has created a model of divorce recovery using the story of liberation of the children of Israel found in the biblical book of Exodus. He provides input on tapes and then suggests a group process in an accompanying workbook entitled *The Healing Divorce Guidebook.* He also includes a tape of background information dialogue between biblical faith and the circumstances of the divorced persons that we located.

Fisher, Bruce. *Rebuilding: When Your Relationship Ends.* San Luis Obispo, CA: Impact Publishers, Inc., 1981. This is Fisher's readable description of the 15 building blocks of divorce recovery that he located in doctoral research. The book is a valuable discussion tool. Fisher conducts training seminars for persons who want more insight in using his concepts and process. For information about these, write Family Relations Learning Center, 450 Ord Dr., Boulder, CO 80303.

The Church's Ministry with Singles, Including Single Parents

Baptist Leader, vol. 45, no. 1 (April 1983). Most of this issue is devoted to the church's ministry with single adults. The following suggestions come from its bibliography:

Brown, Raymond K. *Reach Out to Singles: A Challenge to Ministry*. Philadelphia, PA: Westminister, 1979.

Carter, Velma T., and Leavenworth, J. Lynn. *Caught in the Middle: Children of Divorce*. Valley Forge, PA: Judson, 1985.

Christoff, Nicholas. *Saturday Night, Sunday Morning: Singles and the Church*. New York: HarperCollins, 1980.

Claussen, Russel, ed. *The Church's Growing Edge: Single Adults*. New York: Pilgrim Press, United Church Press, 1980.

Etzler, Carole. *Single*. Joint Educational Development, 1980. A three-minute motion picture on the struggle of singles for acceptance in the church. Available from American Baptist Films, Valley Forge, PA 19481, or Box 23204, Oakland, CA 94623.

Aid for Stepfamilies

Much more material is available when one turns from remarriage to the stepfamily. Some are the following:

Burns, Bob and Whiteman, Tom. *The Fresh Start Divorce Recovery Workbook*. Nashville, TN: Thomas Nelson Publishers, 1992.

Burt, Mala S. and Robert B. *What's Special About Our Stepfamily: A Participation Book for Children*. New York: Doubleday, 1983.

Capaldi, Fredrick, and McRae, Barbara. *Stepfamilies: A Cooperative Responsibility*. New York: Franklin Watts, New Viewpoints, 1979.

Clubb, Angela Newmann. *Love in the Blended Family*. Deerfield Beach, FL: Health Communication, Inc., 1991.

Flanagan, Bill. *Divorce Recovery Video Series*. Muskegon, MI: Gospel Films.

Maddox, Brenda. *The Half-Parent*. New York: New American Library, Signet Books, 1975.

Reed, Bobbie. *Stepfamilies—Living in Christian Harmony.* St. Louis, MO: Concordia, 1980.

Visher, Emily B., and John S. *How to Win as a Stepfamily.* New York: Brunner-Mazel, December 1982.

Divorce—Remarriage

Hershey, Terry. *Beginning Again: Life After a Relationship Ends.* Laguna Hills, CA: Merit Books, 1984.

Richards, Larry. *Remarriage: A Healing Gift from God.* Dallas, TX: WORD, Inc., 1981.

Smoke, Jim. *Living Beyond Divorce: The Possibility of Remarriage.* Eugene, OR: Harvest House, 1985.

_____. *Every Single Day.* Tarrytown, NY: Revell, 1982.

Notes

1. Paul Bohannan, ed., "The Six Stations of Divorce," *Divorce and After* (Garden City, NY: Doubleday and Anchor, 1971), pp. 33-62, adapted.
2. Ibid., n.p., adapted.
3. Reva S. Wiseman, "Crisis Theory and the Process of Divorce," *Social Casework* 56 (April 1975), pp. 206-211.
4. H. Norman Wright, *Making Peace With Your Past* (Tarrytown, NY: Revell, 1985), pp. 69-71.
5. Ibid.
6. Ibid.
7. Richard P. Olson and Carole Della Pia-Terry, *Ministry with Remarried Persons* (Valley Forge, PA: Judson, 1984), p. 37.

MINISTERING
to CHILDREN
in CRISIS

9

"You're a child again. Seven years old. Your parents have just moved, and this is your first day at a new school. It is strange and big and scary. You didn't sleep well. Your stomach doesn't feel good, and you have to go to the bathroom a lot. As you walk down the hall to the room, you would rather turn around and run. The door opens and 35 strange faces turn around and stare at you. You are about to enter a crisis!"

Perhaps for you as an adult that experience would not be a crisis (although some adults today would experience a new situation like that as a small crisis). But each day can produce a miniature or major crisis in a child's eyes. Moving, separation or divorce of parents, rejection by a friend, loss of a pet, a poor grade on a test—these and many other events can produce an upset equal in intensity to the emotional upheaval of a crisis.

Children experience many upsets and crises. Their fears and potential fears abound. Ministering to children will involve ministering to the parents of these children, too. It also will involve training all those who work with children in your church to identify the signs of crisis problems, and then equipping them to help as much as they can. Some people assume they will never work directly with children. Perhaps so, except when a crisis occurs and they are forced into it. All of us need to be prepared.

As a minister or lay counselor, in some cases you will see the parents initially. You may work through them, giving them guidance and suggestions in order to help the children. There will be other occasions when you will help the child directly. You need to be capable of doing both.

Several specific problems of children will be considered in this chapter. They tend to overlap in some cases, and yet they are distinct. The suggestions given in this chapter will help you deal with the situations discussed, and with other problems as well.

Crisis in a child can have long-lasting effects because it may make the child less capable of dealing with trauma in the future. This is a fact supported by formal research.[1]

Children Have Limited Coping Skills

Children cope with crisis events in a different way from adults. They are more limited in their coping skills.

For children, there are two stages of crisis resolution. The first-stage reaction involves the initial shock and then a high level of anxiety. Adults handle this better because of their previous experience with crisis. Children do not have the experience to draw upon. They do not know that the problem will be resolved, and they feel as though they are in the midst of a tornado. The child's mind and emotional state are not yet developed enough to solve problems as an adult. Adults can fall back on resources and established routines—children fall back on chaos. In a way they lose their identity or sense of self.

The second stage is similar but less intense. The child's reaction is less crippling, and he is able to look at the crisis and evaluate it instead of just responding to it.

But children often lack the verbal skills and the creative fantasy available to an adult. They may find a poor solution and cling to it even though it is not good for them. A child needs to discuss and sort out his fears with an adult because he probably does not realize he has other options.

If a child remains anxious and does not live up to his potential, he is stuck in the second stage and has not yet resolved the crisis. In uncontrollable events, a child feels helpless. When he experiences helplessness repeatedly, he learns to despair at the lack of control. Children with repeated experiences of loss of control soon lose control totally. Some adults are capable of handling crisis by restricting their activities in some way, but this approach is not available to children. They must face daily challenges—they are not allowed to skip school.

One of the characteristic responses of a child under crisis is regression. When a child responds at his appropriate age level, he knows how to use his skills and capabilities properly to relate to others and confront daily tasks. But if he becomes upset, such as in a crisis, he loses his capability to coordinate all his abilities to meet the needs of the situation. He becomes confused and disorganized. Those attempting to help the child may need to take charge of part of the child's life and guide his or her behavior.

Factors in Helping Children

As you or your Sunday School staff or other lay counselors work with children in crisis, consider these facts:

- Helping a child resolve a crisis can become a crisis for the counselor.
- Your tendency may be to put a lid on the child's crisis too soon and thereby hinder a proper resolution.
- You do not have any magical solutions, so do not convey to the child the idea that you do.
- Things may get worse before they get better. This is true in many types of counseling.
- In working with a child, you may vacillate between feeling confident and uncertain.
- If you have a greater investment in helping a child than the child has in being helped, the results will be negligible.
- A child will influence you as much as you influence a child. You may find yourself being friendly toward a friendly child and angry toward an angry child.
- A very anxious child will tend to agree with most anything you say. And a child can be led, simply by the structure of a question, to make false statements.
- You may struggle with your own limitations and your desire to provide follow-up help.

- Most people attempting to help a child experience some or perhaps all the above responses.[2]

Empathy

One of the main approaches with children is the use of empathy. Empathy means entering the private world of the child and becoming comfortable with it. It is realizing that the child's thinking and perception are different from yours as an adult.

Empathy means moving into the child's world for a time *without* making judgments.

Empathy means sensing meanings of events of which the child is not aware.

Empathy means putting your thoughts and help into words the child can understand.

Empathy means not attempting to unravel and expose unconscious feelings for the child. That would be too threatening and counterproductive.

One of the main tasks of empathy is clarifying the child's jumbled feelings, for he may experience a number of confusing feelings all at the same time. Unraveling these will help him solve problems according to his ability.[3]

Communication

Communication is a key in counseling children in crisis. If you have not talked with children for some time, you are going to feel like an alien invader from outer space trying to understand these creatures. Some of you think you can communicate with children, but do the children feel that you are communicating with them? Children have their own style of reasoning, meanings for words, and connections for events. You must enter their frame of reference if you are going to be able to minister to them. A child's thought pattern will follow its own logic and not yours. And what makes sense to you may not make sense to the child.

It is important to look at children's thinking and communication at different states in order to minister to them in crisis. William Van Ornum and John B. Mordock have developed an interesting classification of children's thinking and communication.[4]

The Magic Years of Childhood

The magic years (ages three to six) are the years of early childhood, nursery school and kindergarten. And children of this age do experience crisis. We call this the time of magical thinking because the child's belief at this age includes believing that his own thought processes can influence objects and events in the world outside himself. He is unable to understand how and why things happen, how and why life is unpredictable. Adults accept sudden events as just a part of life. Scripture teaches us that life is uncertain and we should expect problems and upsets to occur. But children have difficulty grasping this.

Children at this age do not understand that their thoughts do not cause an event to occur. A child's thinking reflects omnipotence. He believes he is at the center of life and can affect what happens. Children do not understand why they become ill. They become quite disturbed with the unfamiliar bodily changes that accompany illness. And they often believe that they caused the illness. They feel that they were bad and a cold is a punishment.

Help Child Express Feelings

If this is how they think, what do you do if called upon to help? Sometimes it will be impossible to fully change the child's pattern of thinking. You need to accept this as a fact of life and lessen your own frustration. Helping a child fully express his inner thoughts and feelings is one of the best approaches. This helps him gain greater self-control in a crisis event. By expressing his thoughts aloud, he moves to a new position. Patiently repeat your questions to the child, and encourage him to think aloud. Help him discover the most probable or real reason for what occurred. And try to help him discover this himself instead of giving him the reason. Look for any indications of guilt the child may be experiencing.

A young boy lost a mother through divorce, and he was now living with his father. The helper said, "You know, Jimmy, it could be there were times when you wanted your mother to go away. And now she has gone away. Tell me about those wishes you had." After the child related his feelings, the helper replied, "Your mother had several reasons for leaving, and none of those reasons had to do with you. Let's find out what those reasons were. Who could you ask?"

Remember that young children are egocentric; they are centered on themselves. They fail to consider the viewpoints of others. This has nothing to do with being conceited, it is just a normal part of the developmental process. Children of this age talk past one another. They have their own private speech and may not be talking to anyone in particular. They are not concerned whether the listener understands their words or not. They just assume their words have more meaning than is there. They take things for granted and do not realize that other people need clarification. When a child reaches the age of seven, he begins to learn to distinguish between his perspective and someone else's.

Use Child's Language

As a helper, you need to use the child's language and be flexible in your communication. You must actively guide your conversation with a young child or you will end up with a failure to communicate.

A young child takes things at face value, very literally. When a parent says, "I'm sick and tired of the way you are acting," what does a child think? He catches the parent's anger but also believes that the parent may be getting both "sick" and "tired." Think of the other phrases we say that are misunderstood. "Keep your shirt on," "hold your horses," "that's cool," and so on. Try to enter the child's mind. If you could hear what he is thinking, you would be amazed!

A child puts two and two together and does not necessarily come up with four for an answer. His connections are unique. Those connections make sense to him but to no one else. A child may see illness and going to the football game as related because his father became seriously ill the last time he went to the football game. A child may even become very anxious and avoid going to a game because of the connection he made between the game and his father's illness.

Young children often center on one aspect of an event to the exclusion of all the others. They cannot see the forest for the trees. If you throw too much information and too many events at a child in your conversations, he cannot handle them. You need to introduce other aspects of the situation to a child gradually as he is ready to handle them. Your task will be to help him see all the aspects, to organize his thoughts, to explore other reasons for what happened. One of the best descriptions I have heard is that helping young children is like working on a jigsaw puzzle. You help them by asking them to discover the other pieces, by pointing out some of the pieces, and by helping fit the pieces together.

Whenever you are called upon to help a young child, remember these facts: the child feels responsible for what happened; he makes different connections from yours; he is egocentric, and he centers on one event to the exclusion of others.

The Middle Years of Childhood

Children from 7 to 12 have changed considerably in their thinking. They have advanced in their ability to think conceptually. They are now able to work out problems in their heads instead of just by trial and error. They can see the viewpoints of other people, and they recognize the feelings of others as well. Even their world of fantasy has changed. They now fantasize about real people and events instead of so much make believe.

Use Game Playing

Children in the middle years are usually enjoyable and uncomplicated, calm and educable. But they still have a difficult time dealing with anything that resembles a crisis situation. They prefer to avoid the issue and often will change the subject when you attempt to draw them into a discussion of their problem. They try to avoid the pain and anxiety. This is why many who work with children of this age use games and play in the therapy process. Play allows children an outlet for what they are feeling and gives the counselor the information sought after. Communication toys such as tape recorders, phones, drawing materials and puppets are very helpful.

Even though these children have developed considerably in their thinking processes, they still tend to jump to conclusions without considering all the facts. In fact, children of this age group have a tendency to listen to contradictory information and not see the inconsistency. They often do not understand what they are hearing. Sometimes these children will not understand adults who are talking to them, and the problem is that the adults do not realize they are not being understood. As you work with a child, you need to make your statements very clear and even rephrase the statement several times. Repeat and repeat. What may be clear to you may not register with the child.

Based upon the way children think, listen and reason, what additional approaches can you take when you minister to a child in a crisis situation? Be flexible, and be able to shift gears as you work with children of different ages. Don't be fearful of disqualifying yourself if you are not comfortable working with children. It is best to have children work with those who are most gifted and skilled in working with them.

Communicate at Child's Age Level

Be sure you do not attempt to force the logic of an adult upon a child. Listen to the way children communicate, for that is a key to knowing how to communicate back to them. Children are walking question marks. They ask questions for information and as their roundabout way of letting you know something is bothering them. An innocent question such as, "Do your children ever fall down and get bruises?" or "Did your mother ever drink?" may be informational, or they could be questions indicating the child has been abused or lives in a home with alcohol problems. Some questions can be a cry for help or a test to see if you think their question is dumb. Giving them simple answers with an occasional, "That's a question a lot of children ask" or "Lots of children want to know about that" may help to keep the questions and information flowing.

Do not ask questions that can be answered with a yes or no. They will be of little value to you. General questions may not bring a direct answer. Asking for comparisons can be helpful, however, such as asking a child to describe two different events or two different people.

If you don't understand what a child is saying or what a child means, don't be afraid to let him know. You might say, "John, I think I understand what you are wanting to tell me, but I am not sure. Could you tell me that again with some different words?" Reflect on how the child looks as he is talking. This lets the child know you are receiving part of the message. "John, you looked a bit puzzled and hurt when you were telling me that. Tell me that story again, and I would like to know how you feel about it."

Be Nonjudgmental

If a parent or Sunday School teacher has asked you talk with a child, be sure to let the child know your intentions. This can be a fearful time, for the child may be thinking he is going to be punished rather than helped. He may hold back telling you his difficulty because of this fear. Don't force your behavioral expectations upon the child. Most adults sit still, and most children do not. Especially under duress a child may wiggle and fidget in the chair. Let him. Some children stand up and walk around. This may enable them to talk with you more easily.

Van Ornum and Mordock suggest some practical summary guidelines when talking with a child in crisis. Your role as a helper or counselor differs from that of an authority figure. Therefore, be sure to avoid:

- Sounding didactic and professional;
- Overwhelming the child with authority and wisdom;
- Joining forces with the child in criticizing other authority figures in his life;
- Ending statements with "Isn't that so?" "Get what I mean?" or "That's right." Also avoid nodding or shaking your head in response or producing an inflection in the tone of your voice at the end of a sentence. These cues set up children's responses—they'll say what they think you expect from them;
- Leaving the door open or talking within earshot of others (this limits privacy);
- Approaching the child with misconceptions gleaned from others or from file records;
- Defending feelings, ideas or friends that are attacked or denied by the child;
- Becoming so confused during the interview that you can only ask, "What else is on your mind?";
- Feeling inferior in the presence of a gifted child, or superior in the presence of an average one.[5]

Understand Child's Defense System

Children often need to hang on to their defenses while they are in a crisis situation. Helping to change a child's personality by interpreting what a child is doing, and clarifying his hidden motivations, is appropriate for those who are *not* in a crisis. Taking this approach while a child is *in* crisis creates too much anxiety for the child. If you point out to a child the defenses he is using to cope with his problem, his anxiety level will be raised. Children in crisis handle their problem by increasing their defenses. This is what works for them. Here is a listing of some of the defense mechanisms to help you understand better what games children, adolescents and adults use.

- Fantasy—daydreaming about solutions to a problem.
- Hypochondriasis—using illness as an excuse not to deal with a problem.
- Projection—blaming other people and things for their problems.
- Displacement—taking out their feelings on someone or something other than the original source.
- Repression—unconsciously blocking out strong feelings.
- Suppression—consciously holding back feelings.
- Sublimation—substituting one set of feelings for another set of more socially acceptable feelings.

How do you support a child's use of defenses? Simply go along with what the child is doing at the time as long as it is not hurting someone. A child may need to use fantasy, rationalization or displacement. A minister was talking to a child about the child's dog, which had been run over and killed. The child had been talking about the dog and all of a sudden stopped talking.

Child: "I don't want to talk about this anymore."
Minister: "You feel real upset about talking about your dog now."
Child: "Yes, I don't want to."
Minister: "Not talking about him helps you not feel so upset. Is there anything else you could do to not feel so upset?"
Child: "Oh, I don't know..."
Minister: "Well, do you ever use a memory or a fantasy to feel less upset? What might you think about?"
Child: (Pause–smiles) "I thought about playing a game now."
Minister: "Good. That might help."

This is an example of encouraging the child at the time the child needs his defenses.

Here is another way of helping children in crisis to encourage positive feelings that have a calming effect.

Child: "I was upset at the club meeting today."

Minister: "You sound like you were upset. Do you feel upset now?"

Child: "Not too much...but a little..."

Minister: "When did you start to feel less?"

Child: "Hum...oh, when I left."

Minister: "What did you do?"

Child: "I thought about playing with my brother."

Minister: "That sounds pretty good. Maybe you could do that the next time you're at the meeting if you start to feel upset."

You can also calm a child by encouraging him to use his positive feelings for another person.

Minister: "Are there times when you feel less nervous?"

Child: "Yeah. When I get to see my father."

Minister: "Tell me what that feels like."

Child: "I feel good, like I'm safe and don't have to be afraid."

Minister: "You feel protected when you're with your father."

Child: "Yeah, but when he isn't around I don't feel very good."

Minister: "Well, maybe when you don't feel good, you could think about being with your father—think about what you do with him and what it's like."

These are simple but effective techniques that work well with upset children.

Remember that crisis counseling with children is supportive counseling. It is used when the child is about to be overwhelmed, to help him recognize his problems and put them in perspective. As a child develops trust in you, this too will help him gain strength. Remember that when a child becomes distressed in a crisis, his thinking capability begins to deteriorate. Therefore, his unreasonable beliefs need to be replaced by reasonable ones. His self-defeating behavior needs to be explained, and he needs to be encouraged to develop problem-solving behaviors with your assistance.[6]

Let us look now at some of the most common types of crises children experience.

Depression in Children

Perhaps it seems odd to discuss depression in children as a problem, but depression is not a respecter of persons. And it often goes undetected by parents and professionals alike. Children may be the most hidden age group of all in terms of incidence of depression. Parents often deny that their child is chronically unhappy. They fail to recognize, accept and respond appropriately to the child's depression. After all, who wants to admit his child is depressed? How do you recognize depression in a child? Here is a composite picture of how a child would appear *if every characteristic* of depression were included.

Appearance. First of all, a child may appear sad, depressed or unhappy. He does not verbally complain of this, and he might not even be aware of it. But his behavioral responses give that impression.

Withdrawal. Another characteristic is withdrawal and inhibition. Interest in activities is very limited. The child appears listless, and the parent thinks the child is bored or sick. Often the parent begins looking for some symptoms of a hidden physical illness, and indeed there may be some physical symptoms that further blur the fact of depression. These symptoms include headaches, stomachaches and sleeping or eating disturbances.

Discontent. A common mood is discontent. The child gives the impression of being dissatisfied and derives little pleasure from what he does. Often people wonder if someone else is responsible for the way the child feels.

Rejection. The child may feel rejected or unloved. He may tend to withdraw from anything that might be a disappointment to him. As with other age groups, a negative self-concept and even feelings of worthlessness are present.

Irritability. Irritability and low frustration tolerance may be seen. Often the child is unaware of why he is bothered.

Some depressed children, however, act just the opposite. Clowning around and provoking others are their attempts to deal with their depressive feelings. They may act this way at a time of achievement because they find it difficult to handle something positive. This provocative behavior usually makes other people angry.

Children do not always experience and express their depression in the same way as adults. Because of their limited experience and physiology, they may tend to express their depression as rebellion, negativity, anger or resentment. The depression expressed when parents divorce, for example, may be manifested by bed-wetting, attacking friends or siblings, clinging to parents, failure in school and exaggerated story telling.[7]

The signs and symptoms of depression vary with the child's age. An infant who is depressed may simply not thrive. A parent's depression may also affect a small child. For example, a mother who is depressed may withdraw from her child, who in turn becomes depressed. But the child may not be able to overcome the depression until the mother overcomes her depression.

Reasons for Child's Depression

Why do children become depressed? It could be caused by any of the following: a physical defect or illness; malfunction of the endocrine glands; lack of affection, which can create insecurity in the child; lack of positive feedback and encouragement for accomplishments; death of a parent; divorce, separation or desertion by a parent, parental favor toward one sibling; poor relationship between a stepparent and stepchild; economic problems in the home; moving to a new home or school; punishment by others.[8]

Parents can handle many depressive experiences without taking the child for counseling. But if the depression is severe and the child does not respond, he should have professional help.

As with adults, look for any type of loss that may have occurred in the child's life. This could be a divorce situation, loss of a pet or friend, or a severe rejection experience. Try to see this loss from the child's point of view. It is easy to misinterpret a child's perspective, especially if you have not been around children much.

Accept depression in the child as a normal reaction to whatever the cause may be. If the child is grieving over some loss, allow the child a period of time to adjust to the loss. Let the child know that everyone experiences sadness and depression at one time or another. But be sure to put it into terminology the child can handle. Explain that feelings like this are normal and that in time they will pass and the child will feel better. Let him know that God understands our down times as well as our happy times.

As a child goes through the grief process, remember the characteristics of the magic and the middle years of the child. If a child's loss is the death of a parent, keep in mind the characteristics of the grief process, which were discussed in an earlier chapter. A child's thoughts and feelings over the loss of a parent through divorce may be similar to those experienced when there is a loss through death. In both age groupings the child needs to:

- Accept the pain of the loss;
- Remember and review the relationship with the loved person;
- Become familiar with all the different feelings that are part of grief, anger, sadness, despair;
- Express his sorrow, anger and sense of loss to others;
- Find an acceptable formulation for a future relationship with the deceased;
- Verbalize feelings of guilt;
- Find a network of caretakers. He needs many people to support him at this time.[9]

Encourage children to tell God about their feelings. Assure them that their down feelings are not permanent and will go away.

A child needs to be helped to experience the depression as fully as possible. Resisting the depression does not help. It merely prolongs the experience. Encourage the child to be as honest as possible in admitting that he is depressed or sad. If grief is involved, you need to allow the child to do the grieving naturally. If the grief is over divorce, do not expect the child to get over the grief quickly. This type can last longer and can recur from time to time.

Help the child find some type of activity that will bolster him. A new game, a hobby, a sight-seeing trip or anything that would interest him may be helpful.

Find a way for the child to experience some type of success. Discover what he does well or fairly well, and help him use a special ability. His self-esteem can be elevated and rediscovered by small successes.

Help the child break out of his routine. Even such simple items as new food at a meal or taking him to a special restaurant may help. Taking a day off from school for an outing may be helpful unless he enjoys school more than the outing.

Listen to the child without being judgmental or critical. He needs your support.

The Crisis of Child Abuse

Although we have seen a great deal of media exposure recently about child abuse, it is nothing new. For centuries, in all cultures and social strata, children have been abused. Parents in your community and church abuse their children physically and sexually. And in most cases it is well hidden. Whether you want to or not, you will be confronted with these cases. A parent may come in and tell you that her child has just told her of being sexually molested by an uncle, her father or a man in the neighborhood. A parent may come in and confess to you what he has been doing to his own child. It is important, as expressed earlier, that you become knowledgeable of the laws of your state in regard to reporting such cases.

The abuse of a child may involve being neglected or abused physically, emotionally or sexually. Each type of abuse carries with it its own distinct characteristics that help you to identify an abused child. Below are some of the characteristics that are common to all abused children regardless of the type of abuse.

- A child may appear to be different from other children in emotional or physical makeup. In some cases, parents of this child may describe him as being "different" or even "bad."
- A child may seem overly fearful of his own parents. He may be hesitant to go to the parent, and he expresses his fear through his hesitancy.
- The child has extremes in behavior such as crying too easily or being overly sensitive. Or he may block his emotions and appear not to care.
- A neglected child will show evidence of poor overall care. Clothes may be dirty or torn or may not fit well. In the winter, he may not be wearing proper clothing.
- A child may be cautious or wary of physical contact, especially when it is with an adult. There also may be the other extreme, where an abused child appears starved for adult affection, but his methods of getting it are inappropriate.
- Some children show a radical change in their general overall behavior.[10]

Have you ever considered how an abused child feels? Most children want to love their parents. Home to a child offers the greatest amount of love the child has ever experienced, and the child wants to be in his home. But many abused children feel they are the cause for the abuse. They come to believe the many statements made to them that they are bad. They experience parents who yell and cuss at them and threaten to abandon them or make them leave home. Many grow up feeling unwanted. They learn to suffer silently from inconsiderate and inappropriate punishment, for they never know when they will be punished. They do not have to flagrantly disobey or violate a major rule to be beaten—there seems to be no reason except for parents' rage.

Abused children feel anger and rage, but at home they cannot express those feelings. They learn both to deny and to repress fear, anger, bitterness and hatred. Any expression of their feelings leads to further repercussion that they want at all costs to avoid.

Further, the abused child grows up feeling he can never do anything right, he can never meet his parents' unrealistic expectations. Whatever problems occur within the family, the child is blamed.

The abused child grows up with a classic love-hate tension. He needs his parents and wants to love them, but when he tries to draw close to his parents, the abuse pushes him away. This tension begins to eat away at him. And if he cannot get his feelings out against his parents, he becomes defiant and hostile with others as a means of release.[11]

An abused child has difficulty trusting other people. Treating such a child usually involves play therapy in a safe environment in which the child can express his feelings and learn to cope with the reality of abuse. Most of the cases you become aware of should be treated by a professional who specializes in working with children. Develop a network of professional counselors whom you can call on when you become aware of this unfortunate crisis that is all to prevalent in our society.

Children of Divorce

One of the most frequent distressful situations that will occur with children of your congregation will be the divorce of their parents. Divorce can be one of the most traumatic experiences a child as well as an adult can face.

Newsweek magazine has estimated that 45 percent of all children will live with only one parent at some time before they are 18. Twelve million children under the age of 18 now have parents who are divorced.

The results of studies on children of divorce indicate that the effects of divorce on children are more serious and long lasting than many divorced parents are willing to admit. Studies released in England in 1978 showed that children of divorce have a shorter life expectancy and more illness than families where no divorce occurred. These children leave school sooner as well. In New York City, which has a very high adolescent suicide rate, two out of every three teenage suicides occur among teenagers whose parents are divorced. Many others carry a pattern of insecurity, depression, anxiety and anger into their adult years.[12]

In divorce, children experience many types of losses. These can include not only the loss of one of the parents, but also the loss of a home, neighborhood, school friends, the family standard of living, family outings, family holiday get-together, self-esteem and so on. Have you ever wondered what it would be like to learn, as a child, that your parents were divorcing, and then in this panic to begin telling your friends? Fear becomes a daily companion.

When there is the loss of a parent, there also may be a loss of hope for the future. An uncertainty occurs, and a child can feel out of control to a greater extent than ever before. The stable parents upon whom he depended are no longer that solid rock. This may occur in such a practical area as finances. If a divorced father has promised to take care of the family through his monthly payments, what must a child feel when payments become irregular and eventually cease?

Divorce affects children in different ways depending upon the age of the child.

Children—Three to Six

Young children of three to six become fearful. The routine separations of life become traumatic. A parent's going shopping or the child's leaving for school is a stressful experience. Children tend to regress to earlier behavior and become more passive and dependent. More and more they ask "What's that?" questions, which is their effort to overcome the disorganization of the crisis.

Three- to six-year-olds have a great need for affection. They may refuse to feed themselves, and some even revert to a need for diapers. The child can create wild and imaginative fantasies in his mind because he is puzzled by what is happening to him. He is bewildered. Play does not have the same sense of fun. Throughout all the stages of childhood, a common thought is, *Did I cause my parents' divorce? Am I responsible for not having a family anymore?* These preschoolers may become aggressive with other children.

Children—Six to Eight

The six-to-eight-year-old child has his own set of reactions. Sadness is there, but his sense of responsibility for the parents' breakup becomes stronger. He has deep feelings of loss. He is afraid of being abandoned, and sometimes even of starving. He yearns for the parent who has left.

Frequently these children are angry with the parent who cares for them all the time. They have conflicting loyalties. They want to love both parents but struggle with the feeling that loving one is being disloyal to the other. Thus they feel torn and confused. Symptoms can include nail biting, bed-wetting, loss of sleep and retreating into fantasy to solve family problems. Children of both age groups become possessive.

Preadolescent Children

Preadolescent children of 9 to 12 usually experience anger as their main emotional response. This anger is directed toward the parent they feel is responsible for the family breakup, and this could be the custodian parent. But anger, instead of coming out directly at the parent, may become directed at peers. They may alienate others at the time when they most need them. Their self-image is shaken. Sometimes they throw themselves into what they are doing with great intensity as their way of handling the disruption of their lives.

This is a time of conscience development, and the divorce may have a shattering effect upon that process. Psychosomatic illnesses are not unusual at this stage.

The child's reaction at any age will vary and often is dependent upon the behavior and reaction of the two parents. When there are hateful responses between the parents, child custody battles, visitation battles, and going through the child or using the child to get back at the other parent, we can expect emotional turmoil in the child. Children do not have the resources necessary to cope with this amount of stress. Some parents actually use bribery in an effort to win allegiance of a child. Unfortunately, some children learn to manipulate both parents and use one against the other. The more emotional turmoil involved in a divorce, the more potential for harm to a child.

Children's Major Concerns

In all the turmoil, children seem to have two major concerns.

They dream of their parents' reconciling. If this occurred, all their problems would be over. They believe, in spite of previous problems, that the family was better when both parents were there. The child may have seen the conflict, but he is usually willing to have the conflict in order to have an intact family. After all, this is the only family he knows.

His second concern revolves around himself—*he is concerned about what will happen to him.* He is afraid that the parent he is living with will abandon him. One parent already did abandon him. Why shouldn't the other?

If one parent was forced to leave, as many are, the child's fear centers on being thrown out as his mother or father was.

Another fear concerns being replaced in the parents' affection by someone else. As the custodial parent begins to date, the child wonders if this new person is going to become important to his parent. And if so, he fears he may lose the time and attention he now receives.

In order to help the child or his parents, it is important to understand what a child of divorce experiences. Remember that the feelings experienced by a child from the divorce of his parents will change in time. There are fairly clear emotional stages through which the child passes as he struggles to understand and deal with the divorce. These stages are normal. They cannot be avoided or bypassed. They have nothing to do with the spirituality of the child. Your goal as you counsel the child or parents is to help the child pass through these stages in order to produce positive growth and minimize the negative effects.

Whether a child's home is quiet and peaceful or filled with visible conflict, the child rarely expects a divorce to occur. He may not like the conflict but hopes it will settle down eventually. Discovering that a separation or divorce is going to occur is usually a great shock to a child.

Fear and anxiety. These occur because a child is now faced with an unknown future. A home and family with two parents is the child's source of stability. It is now about to be shattered.

Various indications of fear and anxiety may manifest themselves in restlessness, nightmares, sleeplessness, stomach problems, sweating, and aches and pains. These are normal problems. Parents at this time need to give reassurance and discuss their plans in detail. It is important to give facts, because a child's imagination may run wild. And knowing is better than wondering. A child may tend to think up worse problems than actually exist.

Abandonment and rejection. After fear and anxiety come feelings of abandonment and rejection. The feelings of the initial stage recede and are replaced by this struggle. The child may know at one level that he will not be rejected or abandoned, but he is still concerned that it might happen. A younger child has difficulty distinguishing between the parents' leaving one another and their leaving him. And he may focus upon this. This stage may be perpetuated by unkept promises on the part of a parent who leaves.

Aloneness and sadness. These soon replace abandonment and rejection. As the family structure changes and settles down, the reality of what has occurred begins to settle in. A child feels this stage with a pain in the stomach and a tightness in the chest. This is a time for depression, and regular activities tend to be neglected. Many children do a lot of thinking, which is usually wishful daydreaming. And the fantasies follow the same theme—parents getting together again and everything being all right. Crying spells may become more frequent at this time.

Frustration and anger. And then come frustration and anger. Children whose parents divorce or separate are angry children. This is a natural response to the frustration they feel. In addition, they have seen angry and upset parents, and this modeling of anger is emulated by the child. This anger may continue to be the pattern for many years and may carry over into many relationships.

The anger may not show itself directly. It is an inward basic feeling that may be suppressed or masked. It may come out through negativity and moodiness. Whether expressed or not, it can be damaging. If it is there, it is far better for it to be admitted and handled rather than buried and waiting for an eventual explosion.

The child's anger is there for several reasons. It serves as a protection and a warning signal, just like depression. It is alerting the person to a problem and is often a reaction to hurt, fear or frustration. It is an involuntary response, and parents and counselors alike should not be threatened by the anger or attempt to deny its presence in the child. If it is not allowed a direct expression, it will be expressed in a passive and indirect manner, which is far more dangerous.

The child's anger may be expressed through a negative perspective on life, irritability, withdrawal, self-isolation, and resistant to school chores or whatever the child wants to resist.

The feeling of anger should never be denied. Rather, help the child learn to express and drain it. According to his ability, help him to understand the cause for his anger and its purpose.

A child needs time alone with the parent each week. This can be difficult if there are several children in the family, but it is needed. Urge the parents to be good listeners and help their child express his feelings, which will help resolve the anger.

Be on the lookout for the signs of indirect expression. Sarcasm and resistance are fairly easy to spot, but the manifestations may occur in physical complaints such as asthma, vomiting, insomnia and stomachaches. Accept the normalcy of the child's anger. Encourage the child to talk it out but not act it out.

Rejection and resentment. Eventually the child's anger moves into rejection and resentment. The child is not over his angry feelings but is now attempting to create some emotional distance between himself and his parent. This is a protective device. Pouting can be one of the forms of rejection, as can the silent treatment. The child won't respond to suggestions or commands and often "forgets" to follow through with what he is supposed to do. He becomes hypercritical.[13] This behavior is actually a reaction formation. As a child pushes a parent away, he really wants to be close to the parent. He says hateful statements and yet wants to be loving. He is just trying to protect himself from rejection, so he rejects others first.

Reestablishment of trust. The final stage in the process of dealing with divorce is the reestablishment of trust. It is difficult to say how long this will take, as it varies with each situation and child, and can range from months to years.

Advice to Parents

What advice can you give to the parent or parents who are concerned about the effect of their divorce upon the child? Provide them with some of the basic principles of helping people in crisis discussed in this book. Listening, encouragement, reassurance and being available are very helpful to a child. As a youth pastor for almost seven years, I was amazed at how this gave support to the adolescents with whom I worked. And in talking with others who worked with children, I found they used the same principles.

Suggest to the parents that they do the following:

1. Do not be overconcerned with your own feelings to the neglect of the child's feelings. Each day give him some time to discuss what he is experiencing and feeling.
2. Give the child time to process his feelings. There are no quick solutions or cures.
3. A stable environment is beneficial to the child. If possible, live in the same home and neighborhood with as much the same as possible. The greater the change, the greater the stress and discomfort to the child.
4. Give positive feedback to the child, and build the child's sense of self-confidence.
5. Reassure him that he is not the cause of the divorce or separation. Both parents need to give consistent and equal amounts of love.
6. According to the child's level of understanding, help him to know in advance the different types of feelings he will be experiencing. Keep the child informed at all times of any expected changes so he can prepare in advance.

Give Child Assurance

When you are counseling a three- to six-year-old child whose parents are divorcing, help the child verbalize his hurt and his idea of why his parents are divorcing. Remember that at this age, the child may feel as though his behavior or thoughts actually caused the divorce. And it is not easy to convince him otherwise. Help him to see other possibilities.

Minister: "You've made a mess at the table before—did your father leave then? Did your older sister ever make a mess?"

Let him know his feelings are the same as other children's.

Minister: "Perhaps you are afraid that you'll never see your daddy again. Lots of children feel that way."[14]

Comments such as this help children open up and talk about their inner thoughts and feelings.

Children need the assurance that even though their mother and father will be working through their own struggles, they will still be taken care of by their parents. Parents, friends and other relatives need to repeat this to the child so the child begins to realize that more than one person is supporting him with this belief. Assist the child in selecting some task that he can accomplish to help overcome the feeling of helplessness.

Teach the parents of your congregation how to minister to their own children during a crisis time. This can be an opportunity to equip children to handle the crises of life.

Life Events

1. Death of a parent..100
2. Divorce of parents...73
3. Separation of parents 65
4. Parent's jail term 63
5. Death of a close family member
   (e.g., a grandparent)..63
6. Personal injury or illness...53
7. Parent's remarriage 50
8. Suspension or expulsion from school.......................47
9. Parents' reconciliation 45
10. Long vacation (Christmas, summer, etc.)................45
11. Parent's or sibling's sickness..................................44
12. Mother's pregnancy..40
13. Anxiety over sex...39
14. Birth of a new baby (or adoption)..........................39
15. New school, classroom or teacher 39

16. Money problems at home 38
17. Death (or moving away) of close friend 37
18. Change in studies 36
19. More quarrels with parents 36
20. (Not applicable to a child or teen)
21. (Not applicable to a child or teen)
22. Change in school responsibilities 29
23. Sibling going away to school 29
24. Family arguments with grandparents 29
25. Winning a school or community award 28
26. Mother going to work or stopping work 26
27. School beginning or ending 26
28. Family's living standard changing 25
29. Change in personal habits (e.g., bedtime,
     homework, etc.) 24
30. Trouble with parents—lack of communication,
     hostility, etc. 23
31. Change in school hours, schedule, or courses 20
32. Family's moving 20
33. A new school 20
34. A new sport, hobby or family recreation activity 19
35. Change in church activities—more involvement
     or less 19
36. Change in social activities—new friends,
     loss of old ones, peer pressure 18
37. (Not applicable to a child or teen)
38. Change in sleeping habits—staying up late,
     giving up nap, etc. 16
39. Change in number of family get-togethers. 15
40. Change in eating habits—going on or off diet,
     new way of family cooking. 15
41. Vacation. 13
42. Christmas. 12
43. Breaking home, school or community rules 11

Totaling the score, you may be surprised to find how quickly an average child can reach the 300-point level of severe stress potential. Changes occur rapidly in a child's life, far more rapidly than in the life of his parents. Six hours of school alone can subject him to the possibility of any combination of life events 8, 10, 15, 18, 22, 25, 27, 31 or 43 on almost a routine basis. In addition, the ups and downs of his social life add the chance of stress from life events 13, 17, 32, 36, 39 or 41. He is especially susceptible to personal injury because of the high percentage of his time spent in physical activities such as bike riding or skating. In addition, he may fall victim to any contagious disease that strikes the school.[15]

Recommended Resources:

Fraiberg, Selma H. *The Magic Years—Understanding and Handling the Problems of Early Childhood.* New York: Scribner, 1981.

Hart, Archibald D. *Children and Divorce: What to Expect and How to Help.* Dallas, TX: WORD Inc., 1982.

Van Ornum, William, and Mordock, John B. *Crisis Counseling with Children and Adolescents: A Guide for Non-professional Counselors.* New York: Continuum, 1990.

Wallerstein, J. S. and Kelly, J. B. *Surviving the Breakup: How Children and Parents Cope with Divorce.* New York: Basic Books, 1990.

Notes

1. J. Isherwood, K. S. Adams, A. R. Harnblow, and A. R. Lifte, "Life Event Stress, Psychological Factors, Suicide Attempt, and Auto-accident Proclivity," *Journal of Psychosomatic Research,* 26 (1982), pp. 371-383.

2. William Van Ornum and John B. Mordock, *Crisis Counseling with Children*

and Adolescents: A Guide for Non-professional Counselors (New York: Continuum, 1983), p. 15, adapted.

3. Carl Rogers, "A Way of Being" (Boston, MA: Houghton-Mifflin, 1980), adapted.

4. Van Ornum and Mordock, *Crisis Counseling with Children and Adolescents*, pp. 21-39, adapted.

5. Ibid., pp. 37,38, adapted.

6. Ibid., pp. 62-67, adapted.

7. Archibald Hart, *Children and Divorce: What to Expect and How to Help* (Dallas, TX: WORD Inc., 1982), pp. 124,125, adapted.

8. Brent Q. Hafen and Brenda Peterson, *The Crisis Intervention Handbook* (Englewood Cliffs, NJ: Prentice-Hall, 1982), pp. 110,111, adapted.

9. E. Lindemann, "Symptomatology and Management of Acute Grief," *American Journal of Psychiatry*, 139 (1982), pp. 141-148, adapted.

10. Hafen and Peterson, *The Crisis Intervention Handbook*, p. 83, adapted.

11. Van Ornum and Mordock, *Crisis Counseling with Children and Adolescents*, pp. 146,147, adapted.

12. Hart, *Children and Divorce*, pp. 9,10, adapted.

13. Ibid., pp. 66-74, adapted.

14. Van Ornum and Mordock, *Crisis Counseling with Children and Adolescents*, pp. 94,95, adapted.

15. Thomas H. Holmes and Richard H. Rahe, "Stress Rating Scale," *Journal of Psychosomatic Research*, Vol. 2 (1967), p. 216.

THE CRISIS of ADOLESCENCE

~~~~~~~~~~~~~~~~~~~~~~~~~~~~~~

10

You have a full day planned at your office. The church secretary has been informed that you do not want to be interrupted. You are settling in to work on your sermon. But there is an interruption. A young teenage girl whom you recognize from the youth group barges in, visibly upset, and says, "Your secretary said you were busy, but I have to talk to someone. This can't wait. Please, could you talk to me for a few minutes?" You stop what you are doing and ask her to sit down. The story unfolds.

I didn't know who to talk to about this. (pause) I've been dating this boy in the youth group, you know who he is, he's the president of the high school youth group. (pause) We've—well—I just found out I'm pregnant. I don't want to be pregnant! (starts to cry) But I am. What can I do? He wants me to have an abortion. What should I do?

The next morning you sit down once again to begin preparing your sermon. Another interruption. This time it is John, a 14-year-old who is in his first year of high school. You chat with him for a minute and then he says:

I'm not sure what's wrong. I didn't bother going to school today. It's not much use, since I just can't seem to learn anything anymore. I try to, I really do. But I read the stuff and it doesn't register. And I'm tired all the time. I get enough sleep, but I am just tired. And I think there must be something wrong with me, too. I get all these aches and pains I never had before. I didn't want to talk to my parents about this, but I've got to tell someone. You spoke to our class three weeks ago and said if we ever wanted to talk to you, to come see you. So, I'm here. What's wrong with me?

That afternoon you receive a frantic call from a parent who tells you she will be there in 15 minutes with her 16-year-old son. When she arrives, her son follows her in looking sullen. "You've got to talk to him and find out what he's been up to!" she says. "He won't tell me, and I found these pills and other things in his room. I don't know what they are, but I'm sure they're drugs and maybe marijuana. I think he's been using these. Can you talk to him?"

The next morning you are called by one of your members who is a physician. He tells you he has just admitted a young girl to the hospital who has attended the youth group from time to time. He asks if you would call on her in the hospital. You agree and later that day make the call. As you walk in the room, you are taken back a bit by what you see. A 15-year-old girl is sitting up in bed, but she looks more like a skeleton. She is 5 feet 8 inches tall but weighs only 93 pounds. Her parents are there looking very concerned. She is suffering from anorexia nervosa. They are all looking to you for help.

Every case I have just described is a crisis situation.

The Transition of Adolescence

For some young people, adolescence is a time of continual crisis with a few respites in between. For others, their development is a bit smoother. But overall, adolescence is one of the most difficult transitions of life. It is a roller-coaster experience, a time of stress and storm. This can be the time when self-doubt and feelings of inferiority are intensified and when social pressures are at their peak. The adolescent's self-worth is dependent upon one of the most unstable pillars in existence—peer acceptance. Dr. Urie Bronfenbrenner, an eminent authority on child development at Cornell University, says the junior high years are probably the most critical to the development of a child's mental health.

The young person from 13 to 19 is becoming independent from his parents and at the same time experiencing a radical identity crisis. Many are able to establish their identity at this time, while others postpone it until adulthood.[1]

Today's generation of young people faces a unique set of pressures. Young people experience instant information and a media bombardment that usually transmits values antithetical to the Christian faith and beliefs. It is important to remember that children and youth are being raised in a promiscuous, violent, non-Christian society. And being a Christian can create additional stress that produces inner conflict.

Moral choices are being made at a younger age today. These choices include sex, drugs, friends and drinking. The latest research indicates that one out of five junior high students has already had sexual intercourse.

This present generation also lives under the potential of being the last generation. Young people face the possibility of having no future. Wars have always been a part of life, but never before have we had a generation that lives under the threat of being destroyed instantaneously. What do they hear from the media? The threat of war, the bomb, pollution, social security payments being exhausted and other frightening prospects. And thus many young people seek to avoid these possibilities by finding pleasure wherever they can.

More and more teens are coming from unstable homes. Divorce is commonplace, and the role models of stable marriages and stable family life are lacking.

This is also a generation unsure about and unable to understand and follow through with commitment. Perhaps that is partly because this generation has been given much more than the previous generation. Today's teens have not had to struggle as much as previous generations. It is difficult for them to delay rewards. They don't know how to handle discouragement and disillusionment very well, and thus they are prone to experience crisis more readily. They look for instant solutions. Many of them use drugs as their escape, and in some cases when nothing else will work, they opt for suicide.[2]

This is a disparaging picture, but, unfortunately, many teenagers fit into this scenario. Many others are committed, well-adjusted future adults, but they, too, will experience crisis situations.

The time of adolescence is a transitional period between childhood and adulthood. Teenagers need to accomplish three important psychological tasks. Dr. Keith Olson describes them in this manner:

1. To develop a sense of personal identity that consistently establishes who he or she is as an integrated individual throughout each life role, separate and different from every other person.
2. To begin the process of establishing relationships that are characterized by commitment and intimacy.
3. To begin making decisions leading toward training and entry into a particular occupation.[3]

What happens in adulthood is really based upon the successful completion of these tasks. Part of the crisis of adolescence will be tied into these developmental issues. (For a practical and thorough amplification of these developmental tasks, see chapter 1 of *Counseling Teenagers*, by Dr. Keith Olson.)

To be successful as an adult, the adolescent needs to move away from the childhood dependence upon his parents. But this move toward independence often creates a crisis for the adolescent's parents because they are not in control of how this movement occurs. If the parents resist the breaking away, stress occurs for both parties. We'll look at some of the normal breaking-away behaviors.

The adolescent needs quantity time alone and with his peer group. He is not eager for family get-togethers nor as interested in them as he used to be.

He may withdraw from involvements, including church attendance. He tends to be secretive around his parents and does not confide in them as he used to as a child. Parents who use their children for their own identity needs and self-esteem have difficulty handling this lack of confiding and wish for a return to the "good old days."

Teenagers are reluctant to accept advice or criticism from their parents. They are overly sensitive to suggestions because their insecurities seem to arise when they are given advice or criticism. Their lack of properly formed identity and low self-esteem tend to make them more sensitive at this time. They resent criticism. Discipline, criticism, and advice are interpreted as domination, and they feel out of control. They need to be in control.

Rebellion is a very common reaction. But the more secure the teenager, the less rebellion will be seen. The more insecure, the more radical the rebellion.[4]

During the late teenage years, allegiance and commitment is shifted more to individual peers of both the opposite and same sex. The strength of this transition on a teenager's life is illustrated in the following chart.[5]

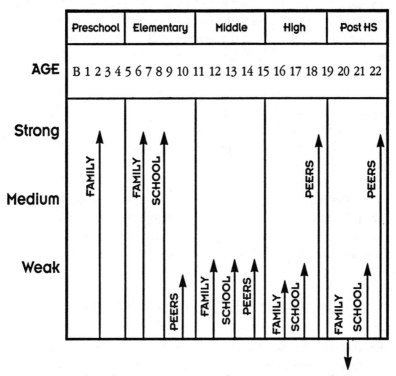

	Preschool	Elementary	Middle	High	Post HS
AGE	B 1 2 3 4	5 6 7 8 9 10 11	12 13 14 15	16 17 18 19	20 21 22

Increased involvement with peers often creates anxiety for parents. Evenings spent talking on the telephone and constant demands to be with friends are the norm. Changes in manners of dress, speech, musical taste, enjoyable activities and general behavior are usually related to the peer group.[6]

Adolescents often are absorbed with their own world and are limited by self-centeredness. They react in a subjective manner. If they are self-critical, they tend to assume others are also critical of them. They think of themselves as unique and special. They are satisfied with old friendships that sustain them rather than wanting to build new friendships. Moving to a new location at this time of life can become traumatic.

Social fears are high on their list. They do not like feeling rejected, disapproved of or ignored, nor do they want to look foolish or be out of control. Authority figures are among those to be feared.

The thinking process of adolescents is different from that of children. They recognize both possibilities as well as actualities. They tend to overidealize and think conceptually in abstract and universal terms. In addition to a strong search for personal identity, their strong sense of idealism creates anger and frustration. They know the way things should be and are intolerant when things are not that way. Their views on life's issues and values can fluctuate daily.

They are overly dependent on feedback from their peers and may behave differently in different groups.

When faced with an unexpected crisis, they may lose the ability to see value in things. They become disillusioned, and when this occurs they tend to become cynical and even degrade others. This all leads to a resistance to change that makes counseling more difficult.[7]

The counseling approaches discussed in earlier chapters apply as you counsel with a teenager, and also the techniques for dealing with depression and suicide. But it is essential to be able to identify some specifics that are unique to the teenager when he or she appears in a crisis state.

Depression in Younger Adolescents

Because teenagers are in transition between childhood and adulthood, their depression shares the characteristics of the depression of both these periods of life. Some of their depressions are related to their developmental struggles.

Because they are separating from their parents and endeavoring to establish their own identities, they will frequently experience the feeling of loss. And as we have seen before, loss is at the basis of so much depression. Probably the most common loss of the adolescent is that of self-esteem.

Depression is actually more normal for this developmental stage than for some other stages. Unfortunately, some of the depression of adolescence goes undiagnosed because the person is considered to be going through the "normal adolescent" throes of adjustment.

There is a difference in the depression of adolescents 13 through 16 or 17 as compared to older adolescents. Teenagers at the younger end of the scale have strong needs to deny self-critical attitudes. They avoid admitting personal concerns to others. Because of this, they do not exhibit or even experience the hopelessness, gloom and self-depreciation seen in adult depression. They are also at a developmental stage in which, like children, they are oriented less to thinking about something than doing something. They are more likely to express their depression through overt behavior than through the introspective preoccupations that characterize adults.

As you observe the behaviors of younger adolescents, you will note three manifestations of depression: (1) some of them are reflective of the inner state of being depressed; (2) some represent efforts to get rid of or to avoid the depression; and (3) others are an appeal for help. Let's look at the symptoms of early adolescent depression from these three manifestations.

Inner State of Being Depressed

Depression reflecting the inner state of being depressed usually is evidenced by three major symptoms.

1. The teenager experiences an excessive amount of fatigue. If he complains of fatigue even after adequate rest, it could be that he is suffering from depression he can neither resolve nor express.
2. Hypochondriasis is another symptom. Young adolescents are concerned about the ongoing changes that are normal for their age group, but when there is an excessive preoccupation with their bodily changes, it could reflect depression concerns about their own inadequacy. The young person has difficulty admitting this to himself and expressing it to others.
3. Inability to concentrate is possibly the most common complaint that leads the person to seek help. It may be seen in school performance but may appear in other situations as well. The young adolescent often denies being apathetic or having anything on his mind that is bothering him. You may hear him say that his school work is going downhill. No matter how hard he studies, he cannot grasp the material or retain it. When you hear this, look for depression.

Attempts to Defend

Depression characterized by attempts to defend against the depression reflects two very common symptoms. The first is boredom and restlessness. One way to avoid feeling depressed is to keep busy so you can keep your mind off of things. And because the young teenager wants so much to avoid the feeling of depression, his activity level may become excessive. He seems to be driven and is very restless and bored. He alternates between a high level of interest in new activities and becoming quickly disenchanted with them. Notice those teens who have difficulty handling the routines of life and are constantly searching for new and exciting activities. This may be a defense against depression.

The second characteristic is a flight to or from people. These adolescents frequently dread being alone and look for constant companionship. But they move from person to person searching for those who can give them time and attention. They want people for company who are not preoccupied with their own activity. Unfortunately, this frantic search leaves them with little time for their necessary functions. Sleep, chores, obligations and schoolwork receive the leftovers.

On the other hand, some teenagers prefer to be alone because being around others increases their fear of being rejected or abandoned. If the teenager takes this avenue of avoidance, he will pursue his own private activities with a tremendous intensity. He may have a higher interest in hobbies, pets or anything that does not hold the potential for the rejection he so greatly fears.

An Appeal for Help

The third manifestation of depression is represented by some type of an appeal for help. This is usually evidenced by some kind of behavior that can include temper tantrums, running away, stealing and a variety of other rebellious and antisocial acts.

Acting out in an attempt to deal with depression has definite purposes for the teenager. When he is engaged in some act, if it is exciting and new, it helps him avoid coming to grips with what is bothering him. If the new behavior is getting positive feedback from his peer group, his self-image is bolstered. The behavior may also be manifested by a person who does not have much impulse control, and this in itself is a cry for help. It is a message to others that he is in pain and cannot handle his own life. His misbehavior is rarely carried on secretly. The actions are usually public in some way and conducted in such a manner that he is going to be caught.[8]

Depression in Older Adolescents

Older adolescents tend to manifest their depression in ways similar to those of adults. And yet they may still express depression indirectly, through maladaptive behavior. What are these manifestations?

Drug use is one means of expression. Yes, there are a multitude of reasons for drug use, but some of it is related to depression. It can serve several purposes. It can help the young person defend himself against being depressed. The secrecy of obtaining illegal drugs can add a sense of excitement to the person's life. And sharing the drug experience offers peer relationships.

Sexual promiscuity also is used as a defense against depression, more frequently by girls than boys. The attention and the feeling of being needed and wanted can overcome the feelings of sadness and being alone and unloved.

Suicidal behavior is another manifestation. A significant rise in suicidal behavior and actual suicide with both early and later adolescents has been occurring. It may be a manifestation of depression, or it could be tied in with other causes. William Blackburn suggests seven influential factors contributing to the increase. These are (1) a changing moral climate; (2) society's high mobility; (3) the high divorce rate; (4) alcohol and drug abuse; (5) popularization and glorification of violence in the mass media; (6) the easy availability of weapons; and (7) the already high suicide rate.[9]

Loneliness, with its accompanying depression, is a key factor for those who actually complete suicide. These teens tend to be isolated rather than simply withdrawn. Blackburn gives a simple explanation of how a faltering support system can lead to suicidal behavior.

The sources of support become shaky foundations. When the foundations become shaky, some young people turn to alcohol and other drugs for solace. The agents, when mixed with a teenager's romantic notions of death, a society that glorifies violence, and easy access to suicide, combine into a powerfully lethal mixture that spells death for more and more adolescents. Finally, suicide becomes suicide. Suicide attempted or completed plants the idea of self-generated death in the minds of others. Also, suicide in the family especially pulls other family members closer to that option.[10]

Often an adolescent responds with behavior that has a hidden message. For example, self-mutilating teens, through their deliberate and radical behavior, express their independence. This behavior can also be their way of trying to control their fear or sexual thoughts, their violent and aggressive impulses. In talking to a young person, you may hear him say, "It's my body and I will do with it what I want, and nobody can stop me. Just try. It won't work." Any efforts to control their outward behavior without dealing with their feelings will be ineffective.[11]

Alienation and personality restriction is yet another manifestation of depression. Older, depressed adolescents feel apathetic and out of touch with themselves and others. They do have some social contact with others that gives the pretense of intimacy and belongingness. However, the group often reinforces depression because of the membership. This alienation and personality restriction is characterized by inaction. The young person avoids anything that might lead to a failure and any aspiration that could bring disappointment. He will not expose himself to any heartache. He is not a risk taker.

Losses Are a Cause of Adolescent Depression

What are the causes of depression in adolescence? They are very much the same as adults experience, with the transitional struggles thrown in as well.

Real and Fantasized Losses

Many of their actions stem from loss, which again must be seen from the adolescent's perspective. Rejection by another, losing an athletic event, having to wear braces at 16 and so on, are real losses to an adolescent. So are fantasized losses. A fantasized loss is unconscious or unrealistic concern that causes the person to feel deprived in the absence of any objective evidence to justify this overconcern.[12]

A very important difference between a real and a fantasized loss is this: A real loss tends to bring on a reactive depression in which the depressive characteristics are readily observable. A fantasized loss tends to be the type of depression in which the manifestations are not apparent to the young person or to an untrained helper.

Death

There are other more serious losses. Grief is a part of loss, and the type of grief will differ with the type of loss. When adolescents lose a parent in death, they often deny it in order to protect themselves from this threatening experience and the ensuing feelings. If the relationship was close, there will be intense pain and anger at being left alone.

The death of a brother brings a sense of loss, but there are disruptive feelings because of the mixture of both positive and negative feelings that siblings have for one another.

If an adolescent loses a friend in death, there is strong anxiety. Teenagers are aware that adults die, but the death of a peer is shocking and unnerving. They have to face their own mortality at an age when they are not prepared to do so.

Divorce

Another loss that many face is the divorce of their parents. When this occurs, there is a loss of security and confidence in the future. Anger at the parent who left usually is stronger and lasts longer than if the person had died. In death, the parent did not make a choice to leave. In divorce, the person does have a choice. So why did he leave?

The guilt the young person feels over the part he thinks he played in the divorce is strong and difficult to resolve. He does not blame himself for the divorce as much as younger children do, however. He may tend to spend more and more time away from home because home is no longer as safe and secure as it once was. He may experience too much freedom and temptation that he is not yet equipped to handle. He may fear losing his friends now. If the person already has a tendency toward depression and withdrawal, it will be accentuated at this time. (We will discuss loss through death and divorce in more detail later in this chapter.)

Illness of Loved One

Another loss teens face is when a parent, sibling or friend has a chronic, debilitating illness. This creates fear about his own vulnerability. His fear may cause him to withdraw, which then creates guilt because he is not responding as he should.

Moving and Changing Schools

Even a friend moving away brings a sense of loss. The pain suffered is as severe as rejection. The same sense of loss can occur when the person has to change schools or make any other type of move.[13]

Loss Threatens Self-esteem

Another factor to consider is that the normal developmental process presents teenagers with a number of real losses and threats to their self-esteem. During this time they are expected to loosen their dependence upon their parents, which they may do. But some are tied closer to their parents than others and are hesitant, whereas others break away as fast as they can. Now they are expected to receive emotional fulfillment from their peer group, which is a far less secure and stable group than their parents. They are also expected to take responsibility for their future and eventually the running of their lives. They are learning to live without some of the previous sources of gratification, which can be another underlying factor for depression.

Remember that the better a teenager is prepared to meet the transitional challenges of adolescence, to give up his earlier attachments and to cope with real and fantasized losses, the more likely he will be to avoid depressive episodes during this age. When you are confronted with the depressed teenager, these are some of the issues to consider and deal with in your treatment plan.

Loss Through Parents' Death or Divorce

When an adolescent loses a parent in death, he is often cut adrift. Van Ornum and Mordock describe the process in this way:

> Adolescence is a time of separation from parents. When this happens abruptly, the gradual process required for healthy identification with a parent cannot take place. Adolescents first develop their own ideas by

resisting the ideas of others. Through rebellion they discover who they are. When a parent dies, the process of resisting, developing independent ideas, and then rediscovering the parent's viewpoint has not been allowed to come full circle. Death of a parent can throw an adolescent into a tailspin.[14]

The person becomes preoccupied with himself, but this may create worries. For example, if a parent died because of an illness, a young person may develop intense fears of sickness, pain or disfigurement.

Encourage the adolescent to express his anger. He does not need to judge the anger or experience the judgment of others against his anger.

Other adults need to be available to fill in the gap the death of a parent creates; this will help the young person continue to develop.

Normal Development Hampered

The divorce of parents hampers the normal development of the adolescent for a period of time. The adolescent feels abandoned, and his need for strength from the family is disrupted. What occurs is the adolescent's acceleration of autonomy—he has to grow up too soon. Parents divorcing can have a lasting effect upon both attitudes and values. The young person becomes disillusioned about commitments and relationships. "If your own parents divorce, who can you depend on? How do I know that if I marry, it will last?"

Symptoms of difficulty with handling parents' divorce include feeling empty, fear, concentration problems and fatigue. These teenagers become critical about their parents and their behavior. They feel betrayed and are afraid of talking about their pain and embarrassment for fear of having others see them as a failure. How do they defend against this? Through anger and rage.[15]

Some feel relief over the divorce because there is no more fighting. But it is difficult to express this. The grief process is involved in both the death of a parent and when parents divorce. But in death there is a finality to the grief process, whereas in divorce there is no closure. The hurt and wounds can continue for years.

The actual counseling approach with the depressed young person is the same as working with an adult. I would encourage you at this time to reread the counseling principles discussed in the chapter on depression.

Keeping in mind the concept of loss in the life of the adolescent, your involvement in his life has important implications. As you express both respect and interest in him as a person, this may provide a relationship that helps to make up for some of his loss and will aid in lifting his depression. And now you can direct the young person's efforts usefully toward coming to grips with what is creating his depression and finding some solutions.

Teen Needs Purpose in Life

As you work with an adolescent on a real loss, help him through your discussion of the event to take a different perspective such as seeing it as less tragic and less permanent, if that is possible. If the loss is a fantasized loss, your task will be more difficult. You may need to use more speculative interpretation of what has occurred to help him discover what has previously been unknown to him.[16]

Some adolescents who experience stress and crisis respond by running away. This is a logical solution for them. But they not only run away from stress, they also run toward something. They usually run toward less alienated feelings and additional control of their lives. When a youth is disillusioned by a crisis, he needs to reestablish commitment bonds, increase his self-esteem, and find some purpose in life. He wants this immediately but fails to realize he needs to work through the shock state of the crisis that is blocking his efforts to end his stress.

Remember that insight, in and of itself, is not sufficient. The person needs to do something about the symptoms and the direction of his life. You may become frustrated in counseling an adolescent because you may be putting adult expectations for change on a person who is not yet an adult. Because of the teenager's depressive helplessness, he may expect too much from you, including an instant, magical cure.

It is very common for the adolescent to say simply, "I don't know what to do. You tell me what to do." And, as you know, this can be a deadly trap if you respond as he wishes. The counselee then is directing the counseling session, but you are supposed to be in charge of what occurs. And remember, if you do not give him the answer or help as he perceives it, you will receive his anger in one way or another. This is just part of the risk of counseling.

Insight for the Counselor

When adolescents come in to see you, either on their own or because some-one makes them come, you may see a range of reactions. Some will be very hesitant to converse with you. You may have to use some indirect procedures such as reflecting their silence or responding to their nonverbal communication. Those who are reluctant to talk are usually afraid. They may be afraid of you or even of themselves. Their fear is of their own vulnerability, of your dominating them in the session, of your telling others what they will say, of not being able to find the words to tell you what they are feeling and so on. Some may be angry with you. Let them be angry, and just accept it. Let them know that you might be angry, too, if you were in their place.[17]

Referral Sometimes Necessary

Not all of us can work effectively with teens, and we need to face that pos-sibility. Referral is not a sign of lack or weakness on our part, but a positive step in order to give the greater amount of help to the person in crisis, whether child, adolescent or adult.

Dr. Keith Olson suggests some characteristics of those who work effec-tively with depressed adolescents. Evaluate yourself on the basis of this list.

1. They have a very strong capacity for developing immediately warm and empathetic contacts with depressed youth.
2. They are dependable and consistent in their responses.
3. They control themselves and the counseling setting through an intel-ligent use of their authority that in no way demeans or devalues the adolescent counselee.
4. Their presentation of themselves offers a positive picture for the formation of an ego ideal for the counselee.
5. They are able to tolerate being mistrusted without feeling angrily defensive or self-doubting.
6. They can develop relationships comfortably with their teenage counselees that are marked by narcissistic self-absorption on the part of their counselees.
7. They are able to be very encouraging and supportive of their coun-selees' movements toward independence.

8. They are able to tolerate their counselees' hostile, angry attacks without reacting with anger, defensiveness, or self-doubt.
9. They should be counselors who, because of their appearance, personality, counseling style, and overall presentation, are generally accepted and well received by teenagers.[18]

Keep Confidentiality

Adolescents may not be overly impressed with seeing a minister for a crisis situation unless a relationship has already been established. To help the process of counseling, be sure you inform the person about any limits to confidentiality. The adolescent is concerned that you may inform his parents. He needs to know that what he says will be held in confidence. However, you may want to tell him that if he is involving himself in some kind of behavior that is extremely destructive, and if he cannot stop after working with you, you may have to resort to letting others know what he tells you for his own protection, even though he may not want you to do so.[19]

Be Positive

Because of the adolescent's tendency to focus on the negative and on unpleasant experiences, you will need to bring out the positive and attempt to reflect hopeful feelings. He will begin to feel more able as you help him develop his strengths. He has solved problems before. Help him to remember how he accomplished his prior success. There are times to relate what has worked for you, but be sure it does not appear to be advice or moralizing.

Help Adolescent Express Feelings

In working with an adolescent, it may be helpful to encourage him to write out his feelings, since many of them have difficulty expressing themselves face-to-face. Writing is private and helps them uncover avoided or denied feelings. By writing, they can focus on their situation and feelings and become involved in looking at the feelings without embarrassment.

T. J. Tuzil, in working with adolescents, has suggested the use of a daily writing log. As a young person works through a crisis experience, this kind of writing helps him clarify feelings and raises his level of objectivity.

This daily log is organized into two different categories, "situations" and "myself." Using the "situation" column, the adolescent writes accounts of at least two situations that happened to him that he had not initiated. He then writes his reactions to what occurred and how he feels about the reactions. This is important since so many crises happen to the person from an outside source.

In the "myself" column, the young person writes actions or behaviors he chose to initiate, giving his reasons, reactions and feelings. After completing this log for several days or weeks, the person becomes more aware of his feelings and why he behaves as he does.[20]

Sometimes writing letters, which are not sent, can help an adolescent work through his crisis feelings. For example, he might write to a parent or sibling who is no longer there because of divorce, separation or death.

Help Adolescent Develop Support System

If an adolescent is disillusioned by a crisis, help him develop a support system, build his self-esteem, and discover meaning and purpose. How? By following the steps necessary to help any person in crisis, but especially through empathy and listening and then problem solving. A young person receives support when you listen and understand his feelings. He wants his point of view to be heard and respected. As you listen to him, he in turn will listen to you as you offer your suggestions.

Notes

1. Jay Kesler, *Parents & Teenagers* (Wheaton, IL: Victor, 1984), p. 17, adapted.
2. Ibid., pp. 151-155.

3. G. Keith Olson, *Counseling Teenagers* (Loveland, CO: Group Books, 1984), pp. 27,28.

4. Ibid., pp. 55,56.

5. Fred Steit, *Parents & Problems: Through the Eyes of Youth*, quoted in Peter H. Buntman and Eleanor M. Saris, *How to Live with Your Teenager* (Pasadena, CA: Birch Tree Press, 1979), p. 14.

6. Olson, *Counseling Teenagers*, p. 57.

7. William Van Ornum and John B. Mordock, *Crisis Counseling with Children and Adolescents* (New York: Continuum, 1983), pp. 41-43, adapted.

8. Frederic F. Flach and Suzanne C. Draghi, *The Nature and Treatment of Depression* (New York: Wiley, 1975), pp. 104-106, adapted.

9. William Blackburn, *What You Should Know About Suicide* (Dallas, TX: WORD Inc., 1982), p. 24.

10. Ibid., p. 31.

11. R. R. Ross and B. McKay, *Self-mutilation* (Lexington, MA: Lexington Books, 1979), n.p., adapted.

12. Flach and Draghi, *The Nature and Treatment of Depression*, pp. 104-107, adapted.

13. Olson, *Counseling Teenagers*, pp. 495,496, adapted.

14. Van Ornum and Mordock, *Crisis Counseling with Children and Adolescents*, p. 76.

15. J. S. Wallerstein and J. B. Kelly, "The Effects of Parental Divorce: The Adolescent Experience," in E. J. Anthony and C. Koupernik, eds., *The Child in His Family: Children at Psychiatric Risk* (New York: Wiley, 1974), adapted.

16. Flach and Draghi, *The Nature and Treatment of Depression*, pp. 106-111, adapted.

17. William Van Ornum and John B. Mordock, *Crisis Counseling with Children and Adolescents*, p. 50, adapted.

18. Olson, *Counseling Teenagers*, pp. 360,361.

19. R. A. Garner, *Psychotherapeutic Approaches to the Resistant Child* (New York: Jason Aronson, 1975), p. 62, adapted.

20. T. J. Tuzil, "Writing: A Problem-Solving Process," *Social Work*, 23 (1978), pp. 63-70, adapted.

CRISIS in
the TRANSITIONS
of LIFE

~~~~~~~~~~~~~~~~~~~~~~~~

11

From birth until death, life is a series of transitions. A transition is a bridge between two different stages of life. And involved in this transition is the process of change as one stage is terminated and a new one is begun. Any new change carries an element of risk, insecurity and vulnerability.

In the Introduction, this concept of transition was introduced and considered briefly in relation to the mid-life crisis. Some suggestions were offered in terms of the church's ministry and resources. In this chapter, I would like to deal with the topic a bit more, since the crisis aspect of many of life's transitions could be avoided if they were handled in a constructive manner. Planning ahead and incorporating the Word of God into our lives are two of the keys for success.

The Family Life Cycle

Let us look first at the process of transition and then at one unexpected event that produces a crisis in many marriages today. The family life cycle is a popular topic of conversation in both secular and Christian circles. It helps us identify where we are in our journey of life. The family life cycle in some ways corresponds to that of the individual life cycle. In most families we have what are called normative events. These include the following:

- marriage;
- birth of a child;
- the child entering school;
- the child becoming an adolescent;
- the child launching into adulthood;
- birth of a grandchild;
- retirement;
- senescence.

Each transition carries with it the death of the previous state and the birth of a new one, which quite naturally produces the potential for a crisis. This potential is present without anything extraordinary occurring. Look at just a few of the unexpected events that could occur through a time period of 50 years, for example:

- miscarriage;
- marital separation and divorce;
- illness, disability, and death;
- relocations of the household;
- changes in socioeconomic status;
- catastrophes outside the home with massive
  dislocations of the family unit.[1]

During this time of change, a person must restructure his way of looking at his role and at life and develop plans for living within the change. He needs to put forth effort to give up old patterns of thinking and activity and develop new ones. Whether or not a crisis occurs depends upon the person's ability to handle this process of change. A crisis occurs when the accomplishment of tasks associated with a particular stage of development is disrupted or made difficult.

Timing of Events

One of the greatest determinants of whether a transition carries excessive stress and crisis potential is the timing of such an event. We all have timetables for our lives. In premarital counseling, I ask couples when they plan to become parents, graduate from school, move to the level of management in their careers and so on. Many have a very precise timetable. Most people have their own expectations for when certain events will occur. And some have a "mental clock" that tells them whether they are "on time" or "off time" in the family life cycle.

When an event does not take place on time, a crisis may result. An example of this is the empty nest stage. Many mothers face an adjustment when the youngest child leaves home. But this is a predictable stage that can be planned for in advance. It is when the child does not leave home at the intended time that a crisis often occurs for both parents and child.[2]

My wife and I entered the empty nest stage approximately 7 years ahead of schedule. When our daughter left home to be on her own we should have been left with a 13-year-old son at home. But he had left home at the age of 11 to live at Salem Christian Home in Ontario, California. He was a profoundly mentally retarded child who was like an infant. We had planned for his leaving for 2 years by praying, talking and making specific plans and steps to follow. Therefore, his leaving and our daughter's leaving were fairly easy transitions. But when our daughter told us a year and a half later that she wanted to come back home and live for a while, it was a more difficult adjustment. Why? We had adjusted to the empty nest, we liked it, and we did not expect her to come back home.

One of the transitions of life that has the potential for being a long-term, low-key source of crisis or unhappiness is retirement. This is a stage of life when one must come to grips with the past and the future in terms of work. With proper preparation for the actual rite of retirement and years of building a strong marital relationship and a proper sense of personal identity, it can be a time of continued growth.

As a person considers retirement, it is important for him to define his expectations and develop a plan. One such plan I have used with counselees is divided into three parts. Plan A is to make a list of all the desires you have for retirement, along with their possibilities. Plan A assumes you have good health and good finances, and that you and your mate are together or you are alone. Plan B and Plan C allow for certain variables that need to be taken into consideration.

Plan A	Desires and Possibilities
Good Health	
Good Finances	
Alone	
Together	

Plan B		Desires and Possibilities
One Good	Health	
One Bad	Finances	
Alone		
Together		

Plan C	Desires and Possibilities
Poor Health	
Poor Finances	
Alone	
Together	

The Unexpected Transitions

Thinking about, discussing and preparing for as many options as possible makes a person feel more secure. This means that part of your ministry is helping people handle not only the predictable transitions, but also the unexpected and untimely events.

But why is a normal transitional event so threatening? There are three basic reasons.

Deprivations

First, having an event happen too early or too late in our plan can deprive us of the support of our peer group. A woman who desires a child early in life but does not have one until age 37 does not have the support of many other women her age. Many women having their first child are 15 years younger, and these are not likely the ones with whom she has friendships at this time of her life.

A second reason is that by being off schedule, we may be deprived of the sense of pride and satisfaction that often accompanies such an event.

Some seek after advancement and promotion in their work and actually have it timed out. But what happens if that sought-after promotion occurs 2 years prior to retirement rather than 15 years before? Is it really recognition for accomplishment or merely a token gesture? When an event occurs later than expected, its meaning is often lessened.

Third, having an event occur too early can limit us from preparing adequately. A young mother who is widowed early has to support her family during a time when most of her friends are couples. An oldest son who suddenly has to quit college and take over the family business because of some unexpected event does not have time to prepare for this new role.

Multiple Untimely Events

Another situation that creates crisis is when many events happen all at once. "Oh, no! Not something else!" we cry. "This is the last straw." And then we fold.

Many people cope well with sudden, hidden and untimely events in life. They are able to take one crisis event at a time and delay responding to others. Thus they are able to stay in control. We would assume, for example, that if two of our important issues or goals were threatened at the same time, we would experience an overwhelming drain on our resources. But perhaps not. Here is a man whose wife is seriously ill in the hospital. The next day a major crisis threatens his business. Instead of attempting to juggle both and deal with them, he may decide that his wife's recovery is too important and nothing is going to deter him from helping her. Thus the business crisis recedes in importance. The second event then does not add to his level of distress as we would have expected.[3]

Many people develop the ability to handle the trials of life and allow them to be a time of growth and strengthening. This is where our teaching and preaching ministry, interspersed with the testimonies of those who have handled life's stress, can be helpful in the church.

Counseling in a Transitional Crisis

What can you do when a person in the midst of a transitional crisis seeks your counsel? It is important to identify what his difficulty is in making the adjustment. His problem may be a normal change of life or one of the variations just mentioned. But most problems encountered during this time center on one of the following:

1. The person may be having difficulty separating from the past stage. He may be very uncomfortable with his new role or time of life and is fighting separation from the previous stage.
2. He may be having difficulty making a decision concerning what new path to take or what plan of action to follow to make this new transition.
3. He may have difficulty carrying out this new decision because of a lack of understanding of what is involved in making the change. He may be lacking information concerning expectations for himself and others. He could also be struggling with his own lack of preparation for this transition.
4. The person may already be in this transition but having difficulty weathering the period of adjustment until the new changes have stabilized. He may be lacking information or resources that are needed to make the change secure.

To be effective in helping a person in this type of crisis, an orderly progression of steps need to be followed.

First, identify the target problem. This is the difficulty the person feels at this time and the problem he is *willing* to work on.

Second, identify the target goal, that is, the situation in which the person would feel he or she would no longer need your assistance. Help him identify what it would take for him to feel competent to run his own life.

Third, identify the tasks that need to be accomplished for this to occur.

Again and again we go back to the problem-solving approach in which a specific plan needs to be constructed and then carried out.

During the initial portion of counseling, you may need to identify more specifically some of the transitional tasks that may be overwhelming the person. This can include helping him cope with the threat to his past security or sense of competence, as well as with the loss of feelings of self-esteem. He may be feeling a great deal of loss and actually longing for the past. Help identify and clarify any anxieties and frustrations he may have with making decisions about the new changes. Also help him adjust to the stress and frustration of implementing the changes necessary in this new role.

Further, since lack of satisfaction leads to lowered self-esteem, help him accept the feelings that accompany this new stage of life and the fact that he will be feeling some discomfort for a while. Eventually, as he works toward his new role and redirects his attitude toward the change, he will become comfortable with it.

One of the most helpful steps you can take is to put the person in contact with another person who has made the necessary adjustment and has something to offer from his own experience. A transition is a normal growth experience, but some people need help in order for real growth to take place.[4]

The Crisis of an Affair

When couples marry, they make a commitment to fidelity. Unfortunately, many of them break that commitment. An extramarital affair can be one of the most devastating crises an individual experiences, for with it his dreams, hopes and trust are shattered. There is an intense feeling of hurt, rejection and anger. Affairs do not occur out of the blue. In most cases there has been a long buildup, but most of it has been internal and thus not easily observed. If an affair comes as a complete surprise, it can mean that the couple was drifting apart without a conscious awareness. Or it could mean there was a strong level of denial over the problems.

When a person comes to you for help, it is important that you become aware of the dynamics and causes for affairs. (For assistance in this area, please read *Broken Promises,* by Dr. Henry A. Virkler, WORD, Inc., 1992, and *Torn Asunder*, by Dave Carder, Moody Press, 1992. Virkler's book is must reading for those counseling in this field and Carder's book is for the person experiencing the affair.)

Victim Stunned

When the affair is first discovered, the offended person is stunned by the news. He may travel through the four stages of a crisis described in chapter 1 in a shorter period of time than normal. As the person brings his hurt to you, your ministry is twofold. One is helping him work through his feelings, and the other is helping him take constructive steps instead of taking some action that will make matters worse.

Experiences Array of Emotions

The offended person experiences an overwhelming tide of emotions. At first there is amazement, disbelief and even confusion. Some may have an attitude of, "I knew it all along!" If there is too much evidence so the affair cannot be denied or if the offending spouse has confessed, the person enters the next phase of raging emotions. Anger, betrayal, anxiety, hurt, resentment, wounded pride, sorrow, personal guilt and a sense of irreparable loss are all part of the pattern. Many people say they feel abandoned or worthless and raise the question, "What will happen to me now?" New emotions now emerge such as disillusionment, loneliness, self-pity or a deep resentment and the desire to get even and punish the spouse.

Needs All Details

Unfortunately, the person then moves to wanting to know all the details and facts about the affair. A few do not want to know anything, but they are the minority. The desire to know is prompted by a desire to feel even more pain or to gain more evidence with which to punish the spouse. One of the most helpful approaches you can take is advising the person not to ask for specific details such as how many times did they have intercourse, what was it like, where did they meet and what restaurants did they frequent. The person does not need this information, and it will make the healing of the marriage even more difficult. A person's mind will use that detail and run it around again and again as he relives the hurt. He may want to avoid a certain hotel, song or restaurant he is now aware of because of his probing.

Evaluates Situation

After these phases pass, the person begins to assess and evaluate himself, his spouse, and their relationship and family. As he becomes calmer, he can begin to think about the future. Now he is able to consider the alternatives. Those who want their marriage to continue will look to you for some magic formula with a guarantee that if they follow your guidelines, their spouse will return. There are no guarantees, of course, and you cannot promise any. It will take much time and effort to rebuild the relationship. But it can be done, for I have seen many couples who have overcome the hurt and devastation and have rebuilt and developed a stronger marriage than they had before.

As you minister to the offended person, share with him the most common mistakes most people make so he can avoid them.

1. The spouse rages and denounces the partner, which pushes him or her even further away. If there are no positive overtones along with the anger, the spouse involved in an affair may feel justified.
2. Do not ask for specific details of the other relationship.
3. Do not tell other people about the affair. Too often the offended person gets on a campaign to tell as many people as possible, such as family, people at work and the children.
4. Do not ask your spouse's close friends or parents to talk with him to straighten him out. It will backfire.
5. Do not ask to see the person your spouse is seeing if you don't know the person. Often a person will do this to satisfy his curiosity, or to plead with, attack, or berate the individual. Some wives, after seeing the other person, say, "I can't believe that he would be involved with her. She is older and less attractive! What does he see in her?" But often a man is attracted to a caring, listening, attentive person rather than simply physical beauty, especially men in their forties.
6. Do not go on a campaign at home to make the person suffer or force him to leave. It may give the person just the excuse he is looking for.

Seeks to Resolve Situation

As the person you are ministering to begins to recover, find out what he or she would like to do. Help him clarify the alternatives and then move to some type of plan. If he wants the marriage to stay together (and that would be my first approach, if at all possible), try to determine what the other spouse desires. If the person involved in the affair wants the marriage to stay intact, he must disengage from the extramarital partner. You as a counselor or minister cannot compete with that third party, nor can the spouse. The affair cannot be ended piecemeal or slowly. There will be hurt and there is no way to overcome that. Unfortunately, people don't think that out in advance.

A spouse is at a distinct disadvantage as long as the affair continues.

That which is new, exciting, and doesn't have much of the daily, mundane aspects of marriage attached to it usually takes precedence over the spouse. And with a new partner, one has only a positive history, whereas with one's own spouse there is both a positive and negative history. Unfortunately, the negative part is usually the part that is remembered.

The offended spouse will often ask, "Is it possible for a marriage to be rebuilt after an affair?" The answer is "Yes." It is a crisis, and even though it is painful and you wish it had never occurred, let's take this opportunity to make something constructive happen.

A few people will grasp at the affair as their opportunity and excuse to end the marriage. Often there is little that can be done to convince them otherwise. Even so, I try to encourage them to consider the other alternative of using the crisis to rebuild their individual lives, the marriage and the family life. Some are able to forgive quite readily, whereas I have seen others who have made the choice never to forgive their partners.

Counseling Victims of an Affair

Here are some suggestions to follow as you help the person sort through his shattered marriage dreams and rebuild his life and marriage.

1. Help the person work with his feelings. He may be overwhelmed by them since many of the felt emotions are harsh—anger, hate, resentment, feeling violated. These feelings may run alongside others that are softer such as sadness, love and compassion. Help the person discover these feelings, for they can aid him in working through the crisis. Building upon these emotions will help heal the marriage relationship and will help the person continue to be a trusting person regardless of the risks.

If the person is emotionally healthy, this process will be easier. Help the person identify the feelings. "What is it you are feeling? Is it fear? Is it anger? Is it hurt? Is it feeling abandoned?" Encourage the person to talk out the emotion in detail. Ask about the positive feelings by saying, "Often in the midst of experiencing these feelings, a person still has others such as love, care, empathy. But they are overshadowed and we are afraid of being hurt, so we protect ourselves. I am wondering what other feelings you have toward your partner." Help the person recognize at some point that whatever his emotions are, they belong to him and he must take responsibility for them.

2. Encourage the person to communicate in a new way with his spouse in order to discover new information. Many crises occur because of lack of information, which is often due to lack of communication. Guesswork, assumptions and mind reading do not work in a marriage.

Because of the secrecy and embarrassment of the extramarital affairs, the offended persons often make wild assumptions and guesses. They assume that their spouse is in love with the other person or that the affair has been satisfying. These issues can be discussed in time. Both spouses need to reveal their hurts, dissatisfactions, concerns and dreams for the marriage. A better understanding through communication can help the process of rebuilding. This may occur outside your office or while you are assisting the couple. Suggest that as they talk with their partner they follow these suggestions:

A. Try not to be hostile or vindictive. Don't show sarcasm or ridicule. Don't try to demean or embarrass the other person.

B. If your spouse is reluctant to open up, do not push too hard. Your spouse needs to feel he or she can trust you as well.

C. If your spouse continues to be reluctant, don't give up. Gently encourage without nagging.

D. Don't assume you know what your spouse is thinking or feeling.

E. Don't ask, "Why did you feel that way? Why did you do it?" These are too hard to answer, and if put on the spot a person may make up a response.

F. Encourage your partner to let you know how he or she feels about you. Don't defend yourself.

G. Your openness and nondefensiveness can be a positive model for your spouse.

H. Encourage your partner to discuss his feelings. Do not judge his feelings or he will stop talking.

I. If you are too angry or upset, do not discuss at that time.

J. If you sit around and dwell on the offense, write out how that will help you reconstruct the marriage.

Encourage the person to read *Forgive and Forget*, by Lewis Smedes (HarperCollins), and the chapter on "Relinquishing Your Resentments" in *Making Peace With Your Past*, by this author (Revell).

3. As communication improves, insight into what really happened and

why can occur. This will be painful but can be growth producing. Sometimes I have found it helpful to ask the offended spouse, "Now that your partner has shared with you what was distressing him about the relationship, what will you do with that information? Do you have any plan in mind?"

4. Help the couple negotiate and rebuild their lives. Here is where you may move into some extensive marital counseling. For additional help in this area see *Marital Counseling* by this author (HarperCollins).

Affairs can happen to any of us. I don't know how many times I have sat in the counseling office and heard a man or woman say, "I can't believe it would happen to me." And many of these people are ministers or spouses of ministers. Lest we ever become judgmental, we in ministry must place our marriages on a high priority *above* the ministry or we may be setting up our relationships for crisis.

Many a marital crisis could be avoided by helping the couples in your congregation become aware of the warning signs of an affair. One of the most unfortunate attitudes I have seen in church members and ministers is the belief that, "It cannot happen to me or people in my congregation." It can and it will. But it is possible to alert people to the causes and help prevent a crisis.

As I teach couples' classes on this subject, I begin the class time by making the following statement:

"Most of you in class today have had an affair at one time or another during your marriage."

I wait and slowly look around the room before proceeding in order to let the statement sink in and gain everyone's attention.

I continue by saying, "Yes, most individuals have had an affair at some time or another in their marriage. Unfortunately, the thinking of most of us toward marital unfaithfulness is limited to sexual involvement. In a broader sense, a large portion of couples have been unfaithful through involvement with other things rather than some person other than their spouse. When our thoughts are preoccupied with any divergence and our energies drained and sapped so that even leftovers are few and marriage is neglected, we are involved in an affair. Men and women have affairs with their jobs, the TV, their hobbies, the church. When some event, activity, or person takes precedence over our spouse and interferes with the development and growth of our marriage, a nonsexual affair is in progress. And this could become the groundwork for a real sexual affair's taking place. Let me share with you some of the warning signs of an impending affair."

By this time every person is listening and thinking. I would encourage you to consider teaching in this way. A preventative ministry is easier and is also appreciated by those who want to avoid an avoidable crisis.

Notes

1. Elizabeth A. Carter and Monica McGoldrick, *The Family Life Cycle—A Framework for Family Therapy* (New York: Gardner Press, 1980), p. 41.
2. B. L. Neugarten, "Time, Age, and the Life Cycle," *American Journal of Psychiatry* (1979), pp. 136, 889.
3. Richard S. Lazarus and Susan Folkman, *Stress, Appraisal and Coping* (New York: Springer, 1984), pp. 108-111.
4. Naomi Golan, *Passing Through Transitions* (New York: The Free Press, 1981), pp. 265-268.

STRESS and the TYPE-A PERSONALITY: A POTENTIAL CRISIS

12

Life alternates between times of calm, stress and crisis. For some more than others, it seems as though life is a continual movement from the tempestuous winds of crisis to calmness and back again to some other crisis. You are already aware of the characteristics of a crisis that needs to be resolved in a certain period of time. But stress is a different condition from a crisis. Stress can be seen in the surgeon performing brain surgery and in the young mother getting three children ready for school. Moderate degrees of stress are necessary to motivate us to move through life and to accomplish things. Many people attain their greatest accomplishments when they are under stress, but it is stress that they can handle. They use it and keep it within bounds.

Stress is any type of action or situation that places conflicting or heavy demands upon a person. These demands upset the body's equilibrium. Stress is any situation that chronically irritates or upsets a person. The indicators are a worried anticipation of future events that cannot be avoided and then being preoccupied with and ruminating about these events for a period of time after they occur.

People vary in their reaction to life's pressures. What is stressful to one person is not to another. If too many sudden events occur at one time, it becomes more difficult to handle the pressures. A person's background, neurological structure, and his previous experience with pressure affect how he will respond. One person loses a job and is devastated, whereas someone else feels the loss but in addition sees it as an opportunity to move on and find a new position that might be better.

How does stress relate to crisis? A person who has a number of steady or minor upsets has more difficulty handling a serious crisis experience. On the other hand, if a person can learn how to handle some of the typical, daily stress-potential situations, he is better equipped to handle the crises of life. This is where our teaching in the church can become a stress-preventive ministry. It is our job to help our church members handle stress in a positive manner by identifying what can be stressful in their lives, then preparing for some of the typical stressors by developing a biblical perspective on life.

What actually causes stress? There are several factors. I would encourage you to look for these indications in people you counsel and talk with in your church. Much of the following material can be amplified and passed on in your teaching or preaching. Additional resources will be suggested for your continued study in a number of these areas.

Contributing Factors to Stress

1. Boredom or lack of meaning in what a person does leads to stress. This may sound strange, and yet many people do not find a challenge and meaning to life. This is an opportunity to help a person discover the meaning of life that Christ gives. Helping a person see life through God's perspective can bring meaning no matter what a person is doing vocationally or no matter what is happening to him.

2. Time pressures and deadlines can create stress. Often this is our own doing.

3. An excessive workload can create pressure in one's life, and again this is often self-induced. Sometimes this occurs because the person does not feel he can count on other people to get the job done. Or he feels that others will do it differently and at a slower pace—or maybe even better than he could do it!

4. Unrealistic expectations of oneself or of another person can lead to dissatisfaction and tension. Suggest to those with whom you minister that

they itemize each of their expectations and identify where each came from, why it is important, and how their life would be affected if that expectation were not met.

5. Role conflicts can create tension. I have met many ministers who are in a staff position that is not suited to their individual abilities and gifts. They felt like a square block in a round hole. Married couples also can feel pressure because of the role conflicts in which they find themselves and the feeling that there is no possibility of change.

6. Job insecurity and financial problems can be a major stressor. Most of us have felt this uncertainty at one time or another.

7. A relationship in which open communication and an open show of emotions are blocked is not only stressful, but it also can lead to depression in the life of a person who already has low self-esteem.

8. Those who build their sense of identity and self-esteem upon an inadequate basis such as work will experience stress and tension.

9. Lack of understanding of normal adult developmental stages can create individual pressure and marital pressure. For both this cause and the previous cause, see *Seasons of a Marriage* (Regal), by this author.

10. A major cause of stress for themselves as well as family members and fellow workers is the Type-A personality. This will be discussed in detail later on.

Here is a list and an evaluation form I use with people concerning the causes of stress. Some of the causes listed here are similar to the previous list. You may want to reproduce this and have it available for those you counsel as well as to use in your teaching.

Causes of Stress

1. *An unresolved relationship.* If a person has uncertainties about a relationship in a friendship or marriage, stress could be present. If one wonders if his partner is unhappy or is thinking of leaving the marriage, not only is stress present, but this might easily lead to a crisis. This type of burden could color a person's attitude toward all other areas of life. (Read and apply Philippians 4:6-9.)

2. *Environment.* A person's environment could contribute to stress. A

monotonous and repetitious environment can be just as much a problem as a fast-paced, pressure-filled, competitive atmosphere. (See John 16:33.)

3. *Perfectionism.* Having excessively high standards is a great way to set ourselves up for failure and self-rejection. And a perfectionist is hard to live with. Perfectionism usually means insecurity. Those who are secure are flexible and willing to take risks and make positive changes. When a person has unrealistic expectations and doesn't live up to them, he begins to despise himself, which leads to depression. (See 1 John 4:7 and *Making Peace With Your Past*, by this author, for additional information.)

4. *Impatience.* If one is very impatient with others, he is impatient with himself. Not getting things done according to a schedule keeps one's insides in a turmoil. The word "patience" means "forbearance, not hasty or impulsive, steadfast, able to bear." (See Galatians 5:22,23.)

5. *Rigidity.* Inflexibility is closely tied to perfectionism and impatience. Rigid people spend their time prospecting for something to be upset over. Admitting one's error and accepting other people's opinions is a mature and stress-reducing response. Ephesians 4:2 encourages "making allowances because you love one another" (AMP).

6. *Inability* to relax. Many people find it difficult to sit in a chair for 10 minutes and totally relax. Their minds keep running and they push themselves. Their activity is called stress momentum. (See Isaiah 32:17.)

7. *Explosiveness and anger.* If a person's life is characterized by bombs spreading angry shrapnel on others, stress is affecting not only the person but other people as well. (See Proverbs 29:22.)

8. *Lack of humor and little enthusiasm for life.* Those who are filled with self-conceit, self-reproach, and therefore stress are probably depressed as well. (See Philippians 4:13.)

9. *Too much competition.* Comparing oneself with others in terms of what they do and what they have places unneeded pressure on a person. We do not have to let what others do and have affect our own lives. Some competition in certain areas can be fun and enjoyable, but when it is constant it is no fun. (See Psalm 37:3.)

10. *Lack of self-worth.* A low self-concept is the basis for so many difficulties in life. Depression and stress can occur.

Stress Evaluation

1. During the last five years of your life, when have you experienced the greatest amount of stress, and what contributed to this stress?

TIME	CAUSE	Who did you share this with?
Present to 1 year ago		
1-2 years ago		
2-3 years ago		
3-4 years ago		
4-5 years ago		

2. During the last five years of your marriage, which family member has experienced the greatest amount of stress, and what contributed to this stress?

TIME	CAUSE	Who did the person share this with?
Present to 1 year ago		
1-2 years ago		
2-3 years ago		
3-4 years ago		
4-5 years ago		

3. Indicate which if any of these 10 possible causes of stress could cause stress for you.

- An unresolved relationship
- Environment
- Perfectionism
- Impatience
- Rigidity
- Inability to relax
- Explosiveness and anger
- Lack of humor and too little enthusiasm
- Too much competition
- Lack of self-worth

What are the symptoms of stress overload? A number of signals make this easy to detect.

1. Decision making becomes difficult for both major and minor decisions.
2. An excessive amount of daydreaming or fantasizing about "getting away from it all" takes place.
3. The person experiences an increased use of cigarettes or alcohol or an increased use of stimulants and tranquilizers.
4. The person finds that his thoughts trail off while speaking or writing. He says, "What am I saying?" and can't understand why he loses his train of thought.
5. The person does an excessive amount of worrying about all areas of life. It is almost a situation where he takes on everyone else's worries in addition to his own.
6. The person has sudden outbursts of temper and hostility.
7. The person has paranoid ideas and mistrust of friends and family.
8. The person begins to forget appointments, deadlines and dates.
9. The person has frequent spells of brooding and feelings of inadequacy.
10. Reversals in usual behavior occur. People say about the person, "He/she is not quite himself/herself."[1]

Three elements in stress are: the environment, the evaluation of the environment, and finally, the reaction of emotional and physiological arousal. If a person believes negative consequences come from upsetting events in the environment, stress will follow. Emotional and physiological stress will occur when this appraisal is made.

Eliminating Stress

How can we eliminate stress? Here are three ways.

First, we can attempt to alter the environment in order to prevent events that are likely to produce stress. A person could change jobs, move from his neighborhood, or not visit his relatives as often. Unfortunately, most people do not realize that making many additional changes could create even more stress.

The second way of dealing with stress is to work on the symptoms. We can attempt to alter our emotional and physiological response to stress by using medication, tranquilizers, relaxation techniques, meditation or imagery. (See *The Healing of Fears* [Harvest House] and *Making Peace With Your Past* [Revell], by this author, for additional information.)

The third way of handling stress is the best way. This involves altering those beliefs, assumptions and negative ways of thinking, that make us more vulnerable to stress. Our perceptions and evaluations of the world actually can cause stress. Changing our attitudes may be difficult, but it may also be the most expedient way to reduce stress, tension and anxiety.

Here is a diagram of this process and the choices a person has concerning his response to life's difficulties.

Three Levels of the Stress Reaction

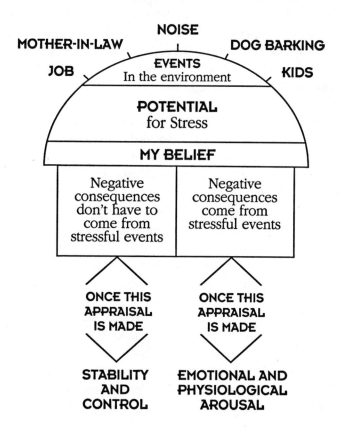

Apply God's Word to Your Life

The solution is to develop a biblical philosophy toward life. How is this done? By discovering and applying the Word of God in a very practical way. Stress comes from the choices we make and from an attitude toward life's situations.

Look at James 1:2,3: "Consider it all joy, my brethren, when you encounter various trials; knowing that the testing [or trying] of your faith produces endurance." The word "consider," or "count" as it is sometimes translated, refers to an internal attitude of the heart or the mind that allows the trials and circumstances of life to affect a person adversely or beneficially. Another way this can be translated is, "Make up your mind to regard adversity as something to welcome or be glad about." We have the power to decide what our attitude will be. We can approach a situation and say, "That's terrible. It's totally upsetting. That's the last thing I want for my life. Why me and why now?" Or we can say, "It's not what I wanted or expected, but it's here. There are going to be difficult times, but how can I make the best of them? How can I learn and how can I grow through this?"

The apostle Paul experienced stress-producing situations. He said:

> Five times I received from the Jews thirty-nine lashes. Three times I was beaten with rods, once I was stoned, three times I was shipwrecked, a night and a day I have spent in the deep. I have been on frequent journeys, in dangers from rivers, dangers from robbers, dangers from my countrymen, dangers from the Gentiles, dangers in the city, dangers in the wilderness, dangers on the sea, dangers among false brethren; I have been in labor and hardship, through many sleepless nights, in hunger and thirst, often without food, in cold and exposure. Apart from such external things, there is the daily pressure upon me of concern for all the churches (2 Cor. 11:24-28).

Paul also had a "thorn in the flesh," and three times he asked God to take it away. But when it persisted, he concluded that it was keeping him humble and enabling him to grow spiritually (see 2 Cor. 12:7-10).

As we look at these and other verses, we get the impression that Paul worked on seeing the positive side of his stressful situations and used them as growing experiences.

We are pressed on every side by troubles, but not crushed and broken. We are perplexed because we don't know why things happen as they do, but we don't give up and quit. We are hunted down, but God never abandons us. We get knocked down, but we get up again and keep going. These bodies of ours are constantly facing death just as Jesus did; so it is clear to all that it is only the living Christ within [who keeps us safe]. Yes, we live under constant danger to our lives because we serve the Lord, but this gives us constant opportunities to show forth the power of Jesus Christ within our dying bodies. Because of our preaching we face death, but it has resulted in eternal life for you (2 Cor. 4:8-12, *TLB*).

Paul was realistic. He knew he could overcome his stresses, but he also realized that other people might have more difficulty with their stress. Stress caused John Mark to give up the ministry, and Demas forsook the faith because of a love for the world. Paul had his struggles with loneliness, as expressed in the last letter he wrote to Timothy.

When a person experiences stress, it can have one of two influences on his relationship with God. It can draw the person closer, or it can cause the person to turn away in bitterness and frustration. Isaiah 43:2 is very realistic about stress: "When you pass through the waters, I will be with you; and through the rivers, they will not overflow you. When you walk through the fire, you will not be scorched, nor will the flame burn you." We are not promised a life free of difficult situations, but we do have the promise that we are not alone when they occur.

Our stability comes from Christ Himself. The Lord is our strength when we counsel a person in stress and crisis, and the Lord is their strength also.

"Now to Him who is able to establish you according to my gospel and the preaching of Jesus Christ, according to the revelation of the mystery which has been kept secret for long ages past" (Rom. 16:25).

"Then he said to them, 'Go, eat of the fat, drink of the sweet, and send portions to him who has nothing prepared; for this day is holy to our Lord. Do not be grieved, for the joy of the Lord is your strength'" (Neh. 8:10).

"And He shall be the stability of your times, a wealth of salvation, wisdom, and knowledge; the fear of the Lord is his treasure" (Isa. 33:6).

The Type-A Personality—A Walking Crisis

More and more we are hearing about the Type-A person. Perhaps you have heard the term used. But do you know that this person holds in his hand the potential for multiple crises? The Type-A person deeply affects the lives of others, often producing family disruption, emotional or physical abuse, stress, a stunting of the development of family members' self-esteem, divorce and untimely death. We talk about the Type-A person, not the Type-A man. The characteristics of this personality are very similar whether male or female.

What is Type-A behavior? It is a continuous struggle. It is an attempt to achieve more and more, or participate in more and more activities, in less and less time. This is often done in the face of opposition, either real or imagined from others. A Type-A personality is dominated by an inner, hidden insecurity of status or hyperaggressiveness, or both.

The insecurity or hyperaggressiveness actually causes the struggle to start. This struggle leads then to a sense of urgency that has been called the hurry-up sickness. And as this person continues his or her inner struggle, the hyperaggressiveness and even the status insecurity manifest themselves in anger. This anger is often reflected in a free-floating hostility and cynicism. You may be dealing with such a person at this time, such as a member of your congregation, a Sunday School teacher, a board member or even another minister.

If the person's inner struggle becomes severe and lasts over a long period of time, it leads to self-destruction.

If this person, who is insecure about his status, confronts situations that are irritating, status threatening or frustrating, he may erupt.

Characteristics of the Type-A Person

What are the specific characteristics of this person? How will you recognize the Type-A man or woman? We can begin by asking ourselves why the Type-A person struggles so to become more involved or to accomplish so much.

Lack of self-esteem. It is not obvious but it is very simple—he suffers from a hidden lack of self-esteem. And his doubts about himself are based upon what he, himself, thinks of himself. He compares himself (inaccurately) with others. His achievements cannot keep up with his unrealistic expectations. He has an inner feeling of guilt that does not go away.

Excessive aggressiveness. The Type-A person is also plagued with excessive aggressiveness. This involves not only a strong competitive desire to win, but also a drive to dominate without regard for the rights and feelings of others. The person can become upset if he does not win at even minor business or social activities. He views everything as a challenge.

Free-floating hostility. The Type-A person experiences free-floating hostility, a sense of lasting, indwelling anger. It increases in frequency to even minor frustrations. The Type-A person is quite clever at hiding this tendency. He finds excuses and reasons for his irritation. But he becomes upset too frequently and well out of proportion to the circumstances. He is overly and outwardly critical and belittles and demeans others.

Because of this anger, it is difficult for the person to attract or accept affection and to give and receive love. He rarely can say that he loves another person.

Sense of urgency. The Type-A person's sense of urgency manifests itself in two ways.

First, he *speeds up his activities.* The way the person, either man or woman, thinks, plans and carries out tasks is accelerated. He speaks faster and forces others to do the same. It is difficult to relax around him. Everything done must be done faster, and the person looks for ways to increase the speed. Shaving and bathing must be done faster. He tries to read faster, write faster, eat faster, drive faster. Any delays or interruptions create irritation. He interrupts others to show them better and faster ways of doing things. Even though he knows better, he punches the elevator several times to speed it up. As he arrives at a street corner, he pushes the button on the signal on each corner, and then whichever light turns green first, he goes that direction.

Second, the Type-A person *engages in polyphasic thinking and performance.* Leisure time does not reduce the tension. He overschedules activities even during recreational time. He attempts to find more time and tries to do two or three things at once. He overextends himself in a multitude of activities and projects, and often some go undone. When doing projects he calls attention to himself and what he does. He will take credit for accomplishments when that credit rightfully belongs to others.

When he eats or talks on the phone, he is reading or shuffling through papers. Two TV's may be on while he is writing memos. The list goes on, and the person is proud of his juggling act!

Self-destruction. The last characteristic for many Type-A's is an unconscious drive to self-destruction. They make major mistakes, and some even mention that they will succumb to the stress they are bringing upon themselves. The Type-A person is five times more likely to have a heart attack than the Type-B person, which we will discuss in a moment.[2]

Results of Type-A Behavior

What are the actual results of Type-A behavior? According to Friedman and Ulmer, Type-A is responsible for "repeated disasters—careers and lives wrecked, whole businesses and large enterprises threatened with ruin."[3]

This type of behavior also causes devastating effects on marital relations and parent-child relationships. All of these become full-blown crises. One of the additional concerns is the physical damage that occurs. Type-A behavior is thought to either initiate or worsen three arterial diseases. These are migraines, high blood pressure and coronary heart disease.[4]

The Type-B Personality

Very little has been said about the Type-B personality. It is important to do so, since the Type-A person lacks some very valuable qualities.

Type-B's do not lead dull and boring lives. They are creative, productive and enjoy life. They do not have the sense of urgency. They are able to accomplish things without the frenzy and rage of the Type-A person. They possess patience and feel secure enough not to have to rush to finish every task on a deadline basis. They delegate authority with the expectation that others will do it differently and within a different time frame. They reflect on life and also on what they like about themselves. They have learned to value and enjoy life and themselves as much or more for what has already been accomplished or experienced as for what may occur in the future.

Type-B personalities differ greatly, but one characteristic is constant: they do not have free-floating hostility. They can handle stress and they have the capacity for empathy. They have a positive sense of self-esteem that is not based upon their accomplishments. They also have an intact personality.

Changing the Type-A's Approach to Life

Is it really possible to change from being a Type-A to a Type-B? The answer is definitely yes. Your ministry is twofold to offering the steps involved in change to both your church members through your teaching and to the person in counseling. Do Type-A's come for counseling? Yes, they do, but often for some other reason. They may come because of some crisis that their approach to life has created. You can assist them in eliminating the cause of this crisis and other potential crises.

Some of the principles for counseling Type-A's that I am going to provide are derived from *Treating Type-A Behavior and Your Heart*, by Meyer Friedman and Diane Ulmer. Their suggestions and research have proven to be very helpful and informative. You may want to read their book for additional information. I would suggest, however, that their low and cautionary opinion of the benefits of exercise need to be reconsidered. Much more extensive study of the value of exercise has been conducted by other researchers, and its use should not be overlooked. I have seen the value of this in many lives, including my own. However, one of their reasons for being overly cautious could be the Type-A's tendency to misuse and overuse exercise, and that concern is justified.

Emphasize Value of Changing

Some of the suggestions offered may seem ridiculous to the counselee, who may discount and resist them. Expect that; accept the person's thinking and response, and continue on with the same approach. You may need to emphasize on occasions the results and consequences of the way this person is leading his life so he can see the need and value of changing. He or she needs to develop new ways of thinking and doing and to discard some old ones.

The first step is to help a person realize that he or she suffers from the disease of urgency. Too many people have come to regard it as a normal way of living. Showing the person the description of this malady can help him identify his own tendencies.

The next step is to help the person discover the causes. In most cases they stem from insecurities and low self-esteem. The main fear is that sooner or later the person will be unable to cope with some task or situation. Because of that, he feels he will lose status and prestige in the eyes of his superiors and peers. He fears he does not have the ability to perform.

Now it is time to help the person identify and replace his beliefs with new ones. Here are some typical beliefs:

"My sense of urgency helps me gain social and economic success." This person actually struggles for success, but it does not come as he wants it to. Any success he has attained has come from something other than the urgency. Have the person review the *failures* of his life, and he will discover that most of them have come from this sense of urgency.

"I can't do anything about my life," and "My insecurity is too deep seated to change." Both of these beliefs are false if the person desires to change and invites Jesus Christ to be the change agent in his life. (See chapter 3 of *Making Peace With Your Past*, by this author.)

A major step toward improvement is to take the time to build an adequate sense of self-esteem. Those who are Type-A's have damaged personalities. They feel that they do not have time for recalling their past, for developing friendships with others and family members. They talk in a way that sounds like a rapid computer void of descriptive adjectives because it takes too much time to use adjectives, metaphors and other figures of speech. Finally, this drive causes the Type-A person to strive for more and more things worth having at the expense of the things worth being.

To help the person repair his personality, ask him to read chapter 2 of *Making Peace With Your Past*, then listen to these tapes by Dr. David Seamands: "Damaged Emotions," "The Healing of the Memories," "My Grace Is Sufficient for You," "The Spirit of a Person," "The Hidden Tormentors," "Is Your God Fit to Love?" and "The Hidden Child in Us All." The tapes and books mentioned are available from Christian Marriage Enrichment, 17821 17th St., Suite 290, Tustin, CA 92680. Be sure you ask the person to sit in a quiet room and listen to the tapes without doing any other task. Nor should he listen while driving.

Help the person learn to express himself in new ways, using emotional words or similes and metaphors. This can be done by reading novels or poetry, observing the style of the writer and how he or she uses descriptive language.

Help the person cultivate relationships. This could involve calling or writing past friends and relatives, or taking his spouse out on a dinner date every week or two weeks—leaving his watch at home and not talking about work or accomplishments. To help men develop friendships, encourage the person to read *Man Without Friends,* by David Smith (Thomas Nelson Publishers).

Create Activities to Facilitate Behavioral Changes

Type the following list of activities, and give a copy to the counselee. Go over them one by one, and ask for a commitment. Do not expect him to try them all at once. Suggest that he choose four or five to begin practicing each week until both he and those around him are able to see a change. Warn him that this may be uncomfortable since he is giving up a way of life that is now comfortable to him, although it is potentially destructive. This list is written to the counselee.

1. Each day, think about the cause for your time urgency. Write down one of the consequences of putting the time pressure on yourself.

2. As part of your new program, read the following book in a leisurely fashion: *When I Relax, I Feel Guilty* by Tim Hansel (David C. Cook).

3. Reduce your tendency to think and talk rapidly by making a conscious effort to listen to others. Become "a ready listener" (Jas. 1:19, *AMP*). Ask questions to encourage others to do the talking. If you have something to say, ask yourself: Who really wants to hear this? Is this the best time to share it?

4. Develop an approach to your work that helps you give priority to those items that need to be done first. Then do only those items for which you have really have time. If you feel you can accomplish five items during the day, do only four.

5. If you begin to feel pressured about completing your tasks, ask yourself these questions: Will completing this task matter three to five years from now? Must it be done now? If so, why? Could someone else do it? If not, why?

6. Try to accomplish only one thing at a time. If you are going to the bathroom, don't brush your teeth at the same time. If you are waiting for someone on the phone, don't attempt to look through the mail or a magazine. Instead, gaze at a restful picture, or do some relaxation exercises. When someone is talking to you, put down the newspaper, magazine or work and give him your full attention.

7. Try to relax without feeling guilty. Give yourself permission to relax and enjoy yourself. Tell yourself it is all right.

8. Reevaluate your need for recognition. Instead of looking for the approval of others, tell yourself in a realistic way: I did a good job, and I can feel all right about it.

9. Begin to look at the Type-A behavior of others. Ask yourself: Do I really care for that person's behavior and the way be or she responds to people? Do I want to be seen in that way?

10. Since you have a tendency to think in numbers such as "how much" and "how many," change the way you evaluate other situations. Express your response in adjectives and not numbers.

11. Begin to read magazines and books that have nothing to do with your vocation. Go to the library and check out novels or books on different topics. Become adventuresome, but don't see how many different books you can read or brag to others about this "accomplishment."

12. Play some soft background music at home or at the office to give a soothing atmosphere.

13. Try to plan your schedule so that you drive or commute when traffic is light. Stay in the slow lane of the highway or freeway. Try to reduce your tendency to drive faster than others or just as fast.

14. Don't evaluate your life in terms of how much you have accomplished or how many material things you have acquired. Recall your past enjoyable experiences for a few minutes each day. Take time to daydream about pleasurable experiences as a child.

15. Make your noon hour a rest time away from work. Go shopping, browse through stores, read or have lunch with a friend. After a meal with a friend, make notes of that person's concerns that he or she mentioned to you. Use this as a prayer guide. Follow up later to see how the person is doing. You may want to call a different person each week. Let them know you have been praying for them and you wanted to know how they are doing.

16. Begin your day 15 minutes early and do something you enjoy. If you tend to skip breakfast or eat standing up, sit down and take your time eating. Look around the house or look outside and fix your interest upon something pleasant you have been overlooking such as flowers in bloom or a beautiful painting.

17. Begin to recognize what your values are. Where did they come from, and how do they fit into the teaching of Scripture? Spend time in the

Scriptures considering what God's plan is for your life. Read Lloyd Ogilvie's book *Discovering God's Will in Your Life* (Harvest House).

18. Each day try to spend a bit of time alone. Whatever you do at this time, do it slowly and in a relaxed manner.

19. Begin to develop some interests and hobbies that are totally different from what you do for a living.

20. Begin to decorate your office or work area with something new each month. Bring in flowers, a plant or a new picture, and take pride in what you do to express yourself.

21. As you play games or engage in sports, whether it be racquetball, skiing or cards, do it for the enjoyment of it and do not make it competitive. Begin to look for the enjoyment of a good run, an outstanding rally, and the good feelings that come with recreation you have been overlooking.

22. If you have a tendency to worry, begin to follow the suggestions given in the book *Afraid No More*, by this author (Tyndale House Publishers).

23. Allow yourself more time than you need for your work. Schedule ahead of time and for longer intervals. If you usually take a half hour for a task, allow 45 minutes. You will see an increase in the quality of your work.

24. Evaluate what you do and why you do it. Dr. Lloyd Ogilvie offers some insights on our motivation and the pressures we create:

> We say, "Look, God, how busy I am!" We equate exhaustion with an effective, full life. Having certain purposes, we redouble our efforts in an identity crisis of meaning. We stack up performance statistics in the hope that we are counting for something in our generation. But for what or for whom?
>
> Many of us become frustrated and beg for time to just be, but do our decisions about our involvement affirm that plea? A Christian is free to stop running away from life in overinvolvement.[5]

In one of Dr. Ogilvie's sermons, he also raised two interesting questions that relate to what we are doing and how we are doing it. "What are you doing with your life that you couldn't do without the *power of God*?" "Are you living life out of your own *adequacy* or out of the abundance of the riches of Christ?" Both questions are worth thinking about.

Have the counselee evaluate all that he does by making a list of all the various activities in which he is involved. Then place each item in the proper column on this chart.

Very Crucial	Very Important	Important	Good

Everything that falls in "Very Crucial" stays in your life. Whatever falls in "Very Important" would probably stay but if necessary could be dropped. Anything that falls in "Important" can either stay or go. And anything listed under "Good" can be dropped from your life. This may be difficult, and you may find it agonizing to drop just one activity. But in time a sense of relief may occur as you consider why you do what you do and what it is doing to you.[6]

25. Each morning and each evening, in a slow, calm, steady voice, read aloud the following poems. Do this for a month, and consider the wisdom of these words.

Slow Me Down, Lord

Slow me down, Lord,
Ease the pounding of my heart by the quieting of my mind.
Steady my hurried pace with a vision of the eternal reach of
time.
Give me, amid the confusion of the day, the calmness of the
everlasting hills.
Break the tensions of my nerves and muscles with the soothing
music of the singing streams that live in my memory.
Teach me the art of taking minute vacations—of slowing down
to look at a flower, to chat with a friend, to pat a dog, to
smile at a child, to read a few lines from a good book.
Slow me down, Lord, and inspire me to send my roots deep
into the soil of life's enduring values, that I may grow toward
my greater destiny.
Remind me each day that the race is not always to the swift;
that there is more to life than increasing its speed.
Let me look forward to the towering oak and know that it grew
great and strong because it grew slowly and well.[7]

I wasted an hour one morning beside a mountain stream,
I seized a cloud from the sky above and fashioned myself a
dream,
In the hush of the early twilight, far from the haunts of men,
I wasted a summer evening, and fashioned my dream again.
Wasted: Perhaps. Folks say so who never have walked with God,
When lanes are purple with lilacs or yellow with goldenrod.
But I have found strength for my labors in that one short
evening hour,
I have found joy and contentment; I have found peace and
power.
My dreaming has left me a treasure, a hope that is strong and
true,

From wasted hours I have built my life and found my faith anew.[8]

These are just some of the suggestions that can help the Type-A person. You may wish to revise the list and adapt it for each person you counsel. Be sure you read the books suggested, which will give you additional ideas. Most of these suggestions have to do with the person's sense of urgency and panicked approach to life.[9]

Evaluate Hostility Level

The next issue to consider is the person's free-floating hostility. This hostility, along with the sense of urgency, are the two main overt characteristics of Type-A behavior.

The first step is helping the person recognize that the hostility is a part of his life. The following nine questions accurately reveal a person's hostility. You may want to ask your congregation or class these questions, either verbally or in writing, and give them an opportunity to evaluate their own lives.

1. Do you become irritated or angry at minor mistakes of friends, family members or acquaintances, or find mistakes hard to overlook?
2. Do you find yourself critically examining a situation for the purpose of finding something that is wrong or that might go wrong?
3. Do you find yourself scowling and unwilling or unable to laugh at things others laugh at?
4. Are you overly proud of your ideals and enjoy telling others about them?
5. Do you believe or say that most people cannot be trusted? Do you believe that everyone else has a selfish motive?
6. Do you regard others with contempt?
7. Do you tend to shift the conversation to the faults or errors of others?
8. Do you regularly swear out loud or in your thoughts?
9. Do you find it difficult to compliment or congratulate others with genuine feelings?[10]

If any of these questions apply, a person has some level of free-floating hostility.

Steps to Overcome Hostility

The other steps involved in helping the person include building his or her level of self-esteem since it is a root cause of anger. Suggest that the person read *When Anger Hits Home*, by Dr. Gary Oliver and this author (Moody Publishers).

Part of the purpose of your ministry with the Type-A person is to move him from being a hostile person to becoming a self-accepting person and one who can reach out in love to others.

Suggest to the person that he identify and challenge the beliefs he holds concerning his hostility. Often a person believes his hostility is necessary, that it cannot be changed and other people deserve it. Once again, here is a list you can duplicate and go over step-by-step with the person. You may want to use all the suggestions or adapt and select specific items.

1. One of the best ways to overcome a negative habit is to make an announcement to significant others in your life of your intentions. Therefore, select those most affected by your hostility, and let them know your intentions. Give these people permission to remind you of your commitment if they see your hostility on the rise. If you feel it beginning to rise, warn them verbally or with some prearranged sign. One man made a miniature flagpole to place on his desk at his office. When he was calm, the flag was green; when he started to become irritated, he changed the flag to yellow; and when he was angry, he promptly hoisted a red flag to warn other people.

2. Go out of your way to recognize the efforts and positive contributions of others and to express your appreciation.

3. In competitive games and fun games, play to lose some of the time. A side benefit of this will be that as you lessen your concentration on winning, you will improve your skills.

4. At first, avoid others who are quick to anger or other Type-A's, since it will take you some time to learn not to react to them.

5. Make a list of the reasons and benefits of eliminating this hostility from your life.

6. Try to identify your trigger point of anger. What irritates you the most? Why? What would happen if you did not become angry?

7. Keep a behavioral diary. Whenever anger occurs, record the following:
   a. the circumstances surrounding the anger- such as who was there, where it occurred, what triggered it, and so on.
   b. the specific ways you acted and the statements you made.
   c. the other person's reactions to your behaviors and statements.

d. the manner in which the issue was eventually resolved.

e. a description of what you will do the next time.

It is important to develop a plan of action for interrupting your anger. This plan should involve immediate action to disengage you from the situation. It should also be a way to face and handle the problem at a later time. Interrupting the conflict is an application of Nehemiah 5:6,7, "I [Nehemiah] was very angry when I had heard their outcry and these words. And I consulted with myself, and contended with the nobles and the rulers" (*NASB*). The Amplified translation states, "I thought it over."

In this diary, keep track of your anger with this chart:

Date Time Intensity of Anger What I Became Angry At How I Responded

1 2 3 4 5

Light Moderate High

8. Read Proverbs 15:1,18; 16:32; 19:11; 29:11; Ephesians 4:26. Write out how you see yourself applying each of these passages to your life. Describe how you will reflect each one in your daily life.

Here is a specific passage of Scripture to use for controlling and replacing anger.

Ephesians 4:31,32

Behavior or attitude to STOP	List the results of this behavior. Give several for each one.
Bitterness (resentfulness, harshness)	
Anger (fury, antagonism, outburst)	
Wrath (indignation,violent anger, boiling up)	
Clamor (brawling)	
Slander (abusive speech)	

Behavior or attitude to BEGIN	What do you think would be the results of doing these three commands? List several for each.
Be kind (goodness of heart)	
Be tenderhearted (compassionate)	
Be forgiving (an action)	

As you counsel a Type-A person, do not become discouraged if change is slow. It will be, and often because the person may be overly concerned with resolving the other problems his behavior has helped to create. But change is possible. One of the most basic and helpful steps to bring about lasting change is helping the person look at his perception of God and come to understand God's qualities and characteristics. Spend time praying with the person. Pray slowly and use guided prayer. Suggest that you each spend several minutes praying silently. It is important that you help him experience this in your counseling office so that it will carry over during the week. Ask for a commitment from the person to pray each day in this manner. Suggest that he pray in a room by himself with no distractions and begin to visualize Christ's being there in the room with him. Suggest that he begin this time by reading, slowly and aloud, a psalm of praise or a psalm dealing with his own personal concerns.

One last thought to consider: Before you or I can help the Type-A person, we need to look carefully at our own lives in light of this chapter. Do we have any of these tendencies, and if so, what steps do we need to take to change? If you have already changed, relate your experience to your counselees. They will appreciate your honesty. And what we ourselves experience can be properly used to minister to others.

Notes

1. Keith W. Sehnert, *Stress/Unstress* (Minneapolis, MN: Augsburg, 1981), pp. 74,75, adapted.
2. Meyer Friedman and Diane Ulmer, *Treating Type-A Behavior and Your Heart* (New York: Knopf, 1984), pp. 36-43, adapted.
3. Friedman and Ulmer, *Treating Type-A Behavior and Your Heart*, p. 62.
4. Ibid., p. 67, adapted.
5. Lloyd Ogilvie, *God's Best for Today* (Eugene, OR: Harvest House, 1981).
6. Dwight L. Carlson, *Run and Not Be Weary* (Eugene, OR: Harvest House Publishers, n.d.), adapted.
7. Orin L. Crain. Source unknown.
8. Author and source unknown.
9. Friedman and Ulmer, *Treating Type-A Behavior and Your Heart*, pp. 166-196, adapted; Rosalind Forbes, *Life Stress* (New York: Doubleday, 1979), pp. 48-51, adapted.
10. Friedman and Ulmer, *Treating Type-A Behavior and Your Heart*, pp. 204,205, adapted.

TRAUMA, AFTER-SHOCK and POST-TRAUMATIC STRESS DISORDER

~~~~~~~~~~~~~~~~

13

Post-Traumatic Stress Disorder (PTSD) has been with us for centuries. We have been made more aware of it since the Vietnam War and we tend to associate it primarily with Vietnam veterans. But you need to be aware that it can happen to anyone—including those called on to help others. That is the main purpose of this chapter.

Post-Traumatic Stress Disorder

PTSD involves a crisis but the concern is the *response* to the crisis more than the event. When a person has a delayed recovery to a crisis and overresponds to a sight, a sound or a smell that reminds him of the original event, he is experiencing trauma. It happens because what occurred was so painful it overwhelmed the person's ability to cope. It also occurs because the person buried his pain rather than let it out so he could work through the experience. He did not face nor release the emotional inner rage that developed in response to the traumatic event.

Robert Hicks, a minister and military chaplain, defines and describes this syndrome in his book *Failure to Scream*. The trauma lasts because the scream of inner rage has been kept submerged. He describes it as follows:

In short, a traumatized person has suffered an extreme blow from life or many blows that have had an accumulative effect over time. Initial reactions reveal some emotional responses of anger, depression, shock, or crying. There may be some behavior and cognitive changes like bargaining with God or denial that anything has happened and a wrestling to find meaning. After six months or more, if the traumatized person has not completed his screaming work (working through the various stages or dramas), then screaming begins to emerge in different forms. There may be recollections of the trauma during sleep or from intruding thoughts. Some may experience flashbacks to such an extent that often smells, certain sights, or associations can trigger an instant replay of the trauma so that one believes the event is happening again. This traumatized person may be plagued by guilt, self-destructive behaviors, or certain startled reactions. She may also appear very numb to life. Things usually enjoyed are found wanting. Hobbies, recreation, and interests are no longer attractive or enjoyable. Avoidance of people may be characteristic.[1]

Why is it so important that we learn about this type of trauma?

We had better learn about screaming because trauma may be the watchword of the future. In one of our after-action meetings following the Delta crash (in Dallas, Texas), Mike Reilly, then director of disaster services for the American Red Cross, said, "Trauma is the vision of the future....From our aging airliner fleets to the decaying of our eastern cities' infrastructures (water and sanitation systems), which are too costly and largely impossible to fix, we had better prepare ourselves for dealing with mass trauma."

This was no doomsday preacher alarming us to the realities of the approaching apocalypse but one who was in the know about what could happen and what seems inevitable on a broad scale. In 1989 *USA Today* reported, "In the 108-year history of keeping such records, the year 1989 was the worst for disasters. From tornadoes, hurricanes, and earthquakes, more deaths were the result of these than at any other time in history."[2]

Even the workplace is not safe. One researcher notes that 10,500 people die every year because of unsafe work environments.[3]

Add to these numbers the AIDS epidemic, violent crimes, divorces, wars, and traumas of unemployment and poverty, and it is no wonder that self-help books sell so well. It is no wonder that the counseling field has so many therapists. We are a traumatized society. We are screaming on the inside. Some are beginning to scream on the outside as well.[4]

We live in a day and age where more and more trauma is occurring and we hear about it immediately through the various media. This past year (1992) we experienced the continuing pattern of earthquakes in Southern California. But what was perhaps the most traumatic event of all, which will take us years to overcome, was the April 1992 riots in Los Angeles. For 7 nights, we in Long Beach lived under a curfew and buildings were burned less than 3 miles from where we live. We average at least 5 to 10 gang killings every week in Southern California. Trauma? It is everywhere.

Aftershock of a Crisis

Dr. Andrew Scaby, a psychiatrist, has coined the word "aftershock" to describe any significant delayed response to a crisis. The word is borrowed from geology and describes the rebound tremor that comes on the heels of the earthquake. Often the aftershock can create the worst damage because of the weakened structures from the initial shock.[5]

Vietnam War

The problem of aftershock came to the forefront during and after the Vietnam War. The aftereffects seen in the lives of the veterans is shocking. Approximately 25 percent of those who were involved in heavy combat have been involved in a criminal offense since coming back from Vietnam. Out of the 500,000 aftershock-afflicted veterans, it is estimated that 150,000 have such trauma they will never lead normal lives without therapy or medication.[6]

We lost 58,000 men and women during the Vietnam War but it has been estimated that around 150,000 have committed suicide since the war. What caused this? Can anything be learned from this experience? Hopefully, yes.

In World War II, the average age of the soldier was 23. In Korea, it was 24 but in Vietnam it was only 18. The young soldiers were less knowledgeable about life, their identity and emotional development was still in process and they were less able to handle the horrors of war. One young man from my church went to Vietnam as a young medic and the first day there a soldier in his unit committed suicide by putting a gun to his head. This was the young medic's first case!

The Vietnam War had no consistency. The intensity of combat varied from year to year as did the attitude of the troops and the political mood in our country toward the war. Our troops had to fight a guerrilla war with no real battle lines drawn in a strange type of environment and culture. Many of our men and women were killed by what is referred to as "friendly fire," not by the enemy.

One of the worst features of the Vietnam War was the rotation system, which shattered moral support, friendships, a sense of security and destroyed group support. A serviceman had a 12-month tour of duty and a battalion had a constant coming and going of soldiers. A soldier just got comfortable with those fighting around him and learned to trust them; the next day they were gone and so was his support—he felt isolated. Back in the United States very little support was evident and an abundance of hostility was directed toward involvement in the war. This was often taken out on the returning servicemen and these conditions led to a tragic aftermath of the war. Robert Hicks describes it well:

> As we look back on the Vietnam era and how we treated our soldiers, one thing has become certain. We blew it! We put new recruits into already cohesive units. When the tour of duty was over, we sent him or her home alone! Even the wounded were moved to the rear immediately, never to see their buddies again. Soldiers woke up in rear hospitals without legs or arms or badly mutilated, no longer in their uniforms but in hospital gowns stripped of identity, dignity, and continuity with the only other guys who knew what had happened. It's no wonder that our veterans have not done well.[7]

Instead of becoming warriors, these young soldiers had to develop new identities. They were trained to fight but now had to learn how to relate to others in a new way. In a way, they and others in similar traumas become emotional ice cubes. They may look like they are relating to others and are loving them, but inside is a numbness.

Disasters and Violence

It is not just war that can create aftershock. Any type of violent situation, community disaster or personal crisis carries the potential for aftershock.

In 1983, 20 of the 50 firemen in South Australia who were caught and almost killed in a huge bushfire developed PTSD. Unfortunately, only one of them sought any help. Four years later, 12 of the firemen were still struggling with aftershock symptoms.

Of the 99 victims of the Mount Saint Helens' volcanic eruption several years ago, 87 experienced at least one episode of PTSD.[8]

The failure to scream after a crisis is seen in those who have been abused, children of divorce, survivors of the holocaust, those displaced from their homeland and those involved in natural disasters. Those who work with people involved in traumatic events, such as paramedics, police officers, hospice staff, medical personnel, crisis chaplains, ministers and therapists, are also affected. The newest trauma is the AIDS epidemic.

Anytime a catastrophe involves children, serious long-term effects can be expected, especially among the rescue workers and helpers. The most traumatic kind of disaster is violence involving multiple murders. Technological disasters, such as plane crashes, seem to be more traumatic than natural disasters such as tornadoes, hurricanes or earthquakes. When a disaster occurs around a major holiday it becomes linked to that holiday and the next year the holiday is spoiled by the association with the disaster.

Those who have researched the effects of trauma have discovered a difference between so-called natural events versus technological events. Those involved in a technological disaster, such as a plane crash, tend to suffer longer and experience more rage because they are able to question why it happened and they have someone to blame. But they also experience tremendous turmoil and frustration when they do not discover any clear-cut answers. It is more difficult to be angry at God for a tornado or earthquake.[9]

Six Characteristics of a Traumatic Event

What makes an event a trauma? Basically, six characteristics are prominent. Some events have all six characteristics and some have as few as one. The following elements of a crisis contain some overlap.

1. *Expected compared with unexpected news.* When an event is known in advance, you can handle it better but the surprise is what throws you.

2. *A sudden shock.* A sudden shock may not be a negative event, it could also be positive, such as winning or suddenly inheriting a million dollars. Either way your life is disrupted.

3. *Personal history.* This affects the intensity of what happens. Any unresolved issues from the past will come alive and intensify the present situation.

4. *Unfairness.* This permeates life and is part of an event becoming traumatic. Too many unfair events happen around us. It is unfair when you are honest in business and your partners take your company away from you. It is unfair to die of AIDS because of a blood transfusion. It is unfair when your daughter is raped. It is unfair when your husband divorces you after you put him through eight years of medical school...and the list goes on.

5. *Powerlessness.* How do you stop the two major hurricanes that devastated parts of our country in 1992? How could you stop Mount Saint Helens from blowing its top and spewing volcanic ash halfway around our country? You can't!

6. *Loss of control.* You can tell a tornado or hurricane is coming but you cannot stop it. When a situation is out of control, four questions will help determine the possibility of PTSD occurring.

They are:

Was your life in any danger? If so, for how long? (The longer, the worse it is.)

Did many others die? If so were there any friends or loved ones? (The more there were, the more traumatic it is.)

Were you exposed to the trauma for a long period of time? (The longer, the worse it is.)

How well organized were the helpers and rescue units after the disaster occurred? This would include someone to help you talk through your experiences. (The more, the better.)

The final element is blame. Especially, self-blame for that breeds guilt, and coupled with the other elements, can produce aftershock.[10]

A trauma needs to be faced emotionally but various stages of acceptance will also occur. They are the same stages of acceptance identified for a dying person, which were given in detail in chapter 7 (The Crisis of Death). To review them, they are denial, anger, bargaining, depression, acceptance and hope. The problems arise when a person does not go through these stages or becomes stuck. That is when aftershock sets in.

Five Levels of Anxiety

The level of anxiety you experience either before, during or after a traumatic event affects your possibility of experiencing aftershocks. The higher the anxiety level, the more likely you are to perceive an event as traumatic and this increases your chances of experiencing aftershock. In his book *Post-Traumatic Stress Disorder*, Dr. C. B. Scrignar identifies five levels of anxiety that can indicate the potential for developing aftershock following a trauma.

Level five: panic. This is the highest level of anxiety. A person sees nothing but gloom and pessimism and has sudden panic attacks and intense thoughts that he or she is going crazy.

Level four: severe anxiety. It includes trembling or shaking, hot flashes, dizziness or fainting and other physical sensations.

Level three: moderate anxiety. This includes stomach disorders or trouble breathing.

Level two: mild anxiety. Symptoms include feeling edgy, tense or nervous.

Level one: calm anxiety. This contains no symptoms.[11]

Aftershock Emotions

Keep one word in mind when you think about trauma and aftershock: "emotions." Emotions are the outlet for the reactions to trauma; they always exist but sometimes they are frozen. At some point in time emotions will thaw and if they have built up, an unchecked flood can occur. Whatever the cause, or the event, everyone experiences five aftershock emotions.

Fear

Fear of the trauma repeating. If someone you loved died, perhaps it can happen again to another person you love.

There may be fear of the victim's similarity to you. If someone you know has been a victim of a crime, you can be, too.

You could be afraid of aggressive loss of control. Anger can be very threatening, especially when you feel an inability to control yourself and to express your anger.

Worry

This can occur because of the failure to prevent whatever occurred. You could not stop the trauma and you are feeling ashamed and useless.

Rage

Rage is felt toward anyone you feel was responsible. We all like to blame someone, even if it is totally irrational.

The rage is also directed at anyone who was fortunate enough not to be involved in the event. The feeling of unfairness at what the victimized person is experiencing and others are not, tends to plague the person and feed his rage.

Guilt

But then guilt sets in and often it is about the rage. Your mind tells you that others are not to blame, or it is good that they are not experiencing the trauma, but your feelings say otherwise. You also have guilt about feeling responsible for what happened, though logic says something else. And often the guilt arises because you survived when others did not. You have a mixture of elation and delight about surviving, which is tainted with guilt.

This tendency to feel blame and experience guilt is characteristic of the victims in a tragedy as well as those called upon to help and rescue them. When United Flight 232 crashed into the cornfields at the Sioux City, Iowa, airport, the fire fighters were there and ready. Their initial responsibility was to put out the fire. But when they arrived they were confronted with injured and screaming people. They had to determine what to do first, put out the fire so those inside the plane would have a chance, or help the survivors. A number of the fire fighters struggled for weeks with the question, "Did I make the right decision? Did I do the right thing? Did I do enough?" A chaplain who was there said,

> A fire fighter is feeling guilty because the new tanker truck would not work properly. After having it malfunction in the field, he drove it back to the shop where it worked perfectly. He drove it back to the field where it again malfunctioned....He is pouring down coffee and says he can see the nightmares coming....Other fire fighters reassure him that it was indeed the equipment's fault and not his.[12]

Sadness

The final aftershock emotion is sadness. It is usually present in any loss and carries with it a series of regrets.

How can you know if those you are helping are undergoing the effects of trauma? How can you tell if you as a helper are experiencing the effects of trauma?

The early signs of aftershock are varied. The criteria for determining if it is occurring is based on having at least two of the following:

1. Sleep disturbances, which often include sleeplessness. And unfortunately the lack of sleep increases the tendency toward anxiety during the day.
2. Jumpiness, increased irritability or exaggerated startle response.
3. Nightmares. Sometimes dreaming again and again about a situation is an attempt to correct what was done or to gain control over it. Unfortunately, every time it is dreamed about it keeps the situation alive.
4. Numbness is a form of denial. It is a desensitization to what has happened as a means of dealing with the intense trauma.
5. Guilt about surviving the tragedy when others did not or about not having done enough to help.

6. Mental confusion, including difficulty concentrating and poor memory.
7. Avoidance of any activities that remind the person of what happened. When they are confronted with a situation that reminds them of the event, there is an intensification of the symptoms.
8. Impulsive and erratic behavior.[13]

The longer the symptoms persist, the more intense they become. In time, the person's problems shift from the original trauma to these intensified symptoms. They can expand into other problems including depression, phobias, panic attacks, sexual dysfunction, hallucinations and flashbacks. Vietnam veterans especially experience drug and alcohol abuse, antisocial behaviors, mental disorientation and breakdown, and suicide.

Assisting Potential PTSD Candidates

Aside from the techniques discussed earlier in this book and the suggestions on reducing stress in one's life, what can be done to assist the potential candidate for PTSD or the person already exhibiting the symptoms? Sometimes if the case is severe enough you may need to recommend a complete physical checkup, and the doctor may recommend medication. In some cases, treatment in a hospital setting may be warranted.

For those of us involved in helping troubled people and those in trauma, we must have an outlet for our own feelings or we will experience aftershock. What can we do to help ourselves so we do not end up in aftershock as a result of attempting to help others?

My son-in-law, Bill, is a fireman and is an open, sensitive, caring person. Both my daughter and I wondered how he would handle his first DOA (dead on arrival) child. In his second year as a fireman, Bill's fire station responded to a call and when they arrived, he discovered a 13-year-old boy swaying from a rope in the garage. The 13-year-old had taken his own life after an argument with his mother. Bill had to cut him down. Fortunately, when Bill came home he unloaded his feelings right away. In these cases, someone needs to be available to debrief the helpers.

More recently, Bill's fire station was called to an accident on the freeway. They had to use the jaws of life to open the top of the car after another car had crushed it by landing on top. When they peeled back the top, they discovered the parents and three children all sitting there dead with their necks broken. On the way back to the station, they joked and laughed to enable them to handle what they were feeling.

When the firemen arrived at their station, the Battalion Chief had already arranged for a professional therapist to be there for counseling. But each of the firemen said they were all right and could handle it. The counselor did not push himself on them but left his card with them in case they wanted to talk. On their own, each of them did call the counselor to talk; it was safer than unloading in front of the others.

Sometimes people do not open up and they carry the images and devastation by themselves in order to appear strong or because it is too painful to face what they experienced. None of us should have to carry our pain alone. It does not work and it becomes too heavy. The Lone Ranger approach does not work if you are in the helping profession. Robert Hicks describes an incident that happened in Washington, D.C., years ago and was also the subject of a television movie:

When the Air Florida flight crashed into the Potomac River after leaving National Airport, most of the passengers were immediately submerged in the dark, icy-cold waters. Very few passengers escaped the rapid descent into the depths of the Potomac. Within hours the navy Seals were on the scene, doing their well-rehearsed diving routine. Their task was to bring up the bodies of the passengers still trapped in the coffin of the jetliner. Navy Seals are thought of in the military establishment as the finest, the toughest, and the best trained of the special forces. But in the dark hours and early morning of the next day chaplains were placed in tents on the banks of the river. The tough Seals would take turns coming up from their dives and unloading on the chaplains about what they were seeing and experiencing. One of the navy Sprint team members shared what was happening with the divers: "In the darkness of the river and not being able to see more than one foot in front of your face, suddenly there would be a body right in front of you. It was freaky, eerie, bodies, faces, hands appearing out of nowhere." These tough, well-trained special elite of the navy were freaking out. As well trained as they were, they were still human, with wives, sons, and daughters of their own. They needed a human touch.

When they came up, the chaplains put their arms around them, offered them coffee, and got them to talk about what they had seen. In the midst of the traumas these divers needed to feel human again. They needed to talk. They needed to be comforted. The touch was both physical and verbal, but the healing was at a psychological level.[14]

Helping the Helpers

Fortunately, in each major trauma we learn more and more how we need to help the helpers. In December 1988, a Pan American airplane was blown apart by a bomb over Lockerbie, Scotland, and 259 passengers and crew members were killed. Because the crash was caused by a bomb, human body parts and personal belongings were scattered over an 850-square-mile area. Rescue workers were searching for remains 9 months later.

Many of the rescue workers suffered aftershock from the trauma. They kept dreaming that they were unable to find any bodies as they searched. As the study of this disaster and rescue efforts continued, it was concluded that each rescue team should be given a very specific area to search, having clear boundaries. In doing this, they would have a "sense of closure" and feel they were thorough and had done their task completely. It sounded like a minimal step and yet it was very important.[15]

Although you may never be called upon to deal with a disaster of this magnitude, you will have situations in which you wonder, *Did I do enough? What else could I have done?* It could happen when the woman you were counseling to help her put her marriage back together decides to divorce. It could happen when that depressed man takes his life. It could happen when that young girl you were helping runs away and turns to prostitution. The more traumatic the event the more potential for you as a helper to be traumatized.

Traumatic stress is an equal opportunity that can strike any of us at any time. In our own training as counselors and helpers, we have often been taught to take proper steps to help, but not necessarily how to feel or deal with the feelings we experience in helping others. We learn to departmentalize, to be the professional at work and to feel elsewhere. That is a myth. You and I have feelings wherever we are. Have you ever cried in a session as you attempt to help someone? I have. Have you cried and dumped your feelings after a difficult crisis situation or session? I have. To survive, we must.

Helping Males

Dealing with feelings is not easy if you are a male victim or a male helper. Men do not like to admit they have a problem they cannot handle. They do not want to ask for help. They need to feel in control at all times and when they do not, it is a major stressor. This is why so many men resist going for therapy.

And men have to contend with our cultural expectations, which is a source of additional stress and pressure. A man is expected to be in control, not lose it. He is expected to be confident and assertive, not be afraid, hesitant, anxious, cry, insecure or sad.

A man is supposed to be sufficient and know what he is doing, be rational and analytical, not passive, needy, dependent, hesitant, or express a need for support or comfort. Men are well aware of these expectations and put forth energy to live up to them. They try to guard against what they must not be in the eyes of society.

I have talked with fathers who wanted to tell others they could not cope with what was happening to them anymore. But their resources were being depleted as they were guarding against sharing their true feelings. I have talked with men who wanted to tell others they were afraid; but they resisted doing so. I have talked with others who sat in my office telling me they could not feel during their loss. They just handled it and moved ahead in life unaware of the abundance of silent pain and hurt screaming to be released. Numbness had set in and the cries were not heard. Instead the pain began coming out in symptoms similar to PTSD.

Sometimes in counseling a man I will keep talking and pushing about what happened and how painful it must have been, how empty he must have felt, how much he must have wanted to cry, become angry or yell. And in many cases, after 10 to 15 minutes of encouraging the man to feel, the feelings that had been buried for months or years come rushing to the surface to be released. Often, it is the first time someone has encouraged him to feel rather than reinforce his nonexpression using a comment such as, "You're doing so well. It's good to see you be strong and rely upon the Lord to keep you going." What a misperception of what strength is and what God expects from us.

Listen to the words of several men who talked about their response to a significant crisis in their lives and why women handle it better:

"She got over the death of our daughter much faster than I did. I think it was because she spent so much time talking about it with her friends. I didn't feel like it was something I could talk to anybody about. I still don't. Women are much better with each other over things like that than men are. I didn't know how to handle it, and it was obvious that my friends didn't either. In fact, I think it made them uncomfortable just to be around me, knowing that I was upset. To be truthful, things haven't been the same between my friends and me ever since."

"The difference is that women talk their way through things and men think their way through things. Talking is something you do with somebody. Thinking is not. It stands to reason that women are going to spend more time with others when they have something important to deal with. Men, thinking alone, never really get at what is troubling them because they're not talking, not explaining, not asking questions, not using someone else to figure out their own feelings. Of course, they can't do that unless they are going to fully share all of what they are thinking. Men just don't do that with their friends."

"Women lighten their load by sharing the weight. We men tend to think it's the manly thing to do to carry all the weight ourselves. That's why men get what I call 'emotional hernias.' We need to learn from women to share the load."[16]

Experiencing Personal Help

I, too, have had to learn to open the door to my feelings and it has helped in handling my own traumas as well as handling the deep hurts of others.

Years ago, after we were told about the severity of our son's retardation by the medical staff where he underwent evaluation, I did not cry over it for months. I still had a sense of disbelief, which can happen in any major crisis. One evening about 10 months later my wife and I were watching a television program called "Then Came Bronson," in which the main character traveled around the country on a motorcycle. In this episode we were watching, Bronson worked at a ranch for autistic children who could not speak. He worked with this one child day after day and week after week. By the end of the program the child spoke one word.

It was as though a key had unlocked the vault door holding back all my grief. As I felt the flood of tears coming, I quickly left the room (the old message was intact—do not cry in front of anyone), went to the kitchen and wept by myself. Fortunately, my wife, Joyce, came in and held me so we could grieve together.

Debrief Others

Many men postpone their grief but at some point in time they need their turn to grieve, regardless of the loss. Perhaps the best word to use is "debrief." As counselors, we need to debrief others and help them identify their thoughts and their feelings for recovery and healing to occur. And it is the same for you and me.

Experience Worship

Often a tragedy in people's lives becomes the point in time around which their entire lives revolve. They divide their lives into two distinct time periods—what happened before and what happened since then. This has been especially true for Vietnam veterans. Hospital chaplains have discovered a unique way in helping these veterans recover. They create a special worship service to help the participants begin anew. At this service, there is a time of confession, forgiveness and a recommitment of their lives to the Lord. They are encouraged to begin seeing their lives starting again from this point in time rather than the time of the tragedy. This worship experience has been a turning point for many. Worship is a wonderful time for grieving, cleansing and restoration.

Worship provides us with the deep resources we need to draw upon when everything else in the world is falling apart. I have seen this in the lives of counselees and have experienced this in my own life.

Recommended Resources:

Walsh, Froma, and McGoldrich, Monica. (Editors) *Living Beyond Loss.* New York: W. W. Norton and Co., 1991. (See especially chapter 10, "Mourning in Different Cultures.")

Wright, H. Norman. *Recovering From the Losses of Life.* Tarrytown, NY: Fleming H. Revell, 1991.

Wright, H. Norman. *Recovering From the Losses of Life*—Curriculum. Tarrytown, NY: Fleming H. Revell, 1991.

Counseling Resources:

Dershimer, Richard A. *Counseling the Bereaved.* New York: Pergamon Press, 1990.

Janosik, Ellen H. *Crisis Counseling—A Contemporary Approach.* Monterey, CA: Wadsworth Health Sciences Division, 1984.

Slarker, Karl A. *Crisis Intervention.* Boston, MA: Allyn and Bacon Inc., 1984.

Wolfelt, Alan D., Ph.D. *Death and Grief—A Guide for Clergy.* Muncie, IN: Accelerated Development Inc., 1988.

Notes

1. Robert Hicks, *Failure to Scream* (Nashville, TN: Thomas Nelson Publishers, 1993), p. 10.
2. "Disasters of '89 Worst in 15 years," *USA Today,* 17 November 1989.
3. "Experts cite 10,500 deaths every year," *USA Today,* 5 September 1991.
4. Robert Hicks, *Failure to Scream,* p. 11.
5. Andrew E. Scaby, *Aftershock* (New York: Villard Books, 1989), p. XIV, adapted.
6. Ibid., p. 78, adapted.
7. Robert Hicks, *Failure to Scream* (Nashville, TN: Thomas Nelson Publishers, 1993), pp. 83,84.
8. Andrew E. Scaby, *Aftershock,* p. 85, adapted.
9. *Los Angeles Times,* "Nightmares That Never End" Monday, December 18, 1989. Metro Section 2B, adapted.

10. Andrew E. Scaby, *Aftershock*, pp. 17-20, adapted.
11. C. B. Scrignar, *Post-Traumatic Stress Disorder* (New Orleans, LA: Bruno Press, 1988), p. 27, adapted.
12. After-action report by Chaplain 1st Lt. Gregory Clapper, Iowa's Air National Guard, 186th Tactical Fighter Group, Sioux City Gateway Airport, 19 July 1989.
13. Andrew E. Scaby, *Aftershock*, p. 49, adapted.
    Diagnostic and Statistical Manual of Mental Disorders, 3rd ed. (Washington, DC: American Psychiatric Association, 1985), p. 238, adapted.
14. Robert Hicks, *Failure to Scream*, pp. 80,81. Ronnie Janoff-Bulman, "The Aftermath of Victimization: Rebuilding Shattered Assumptions," in Charles R. Figley, Ed., *Trauma and Its Wake*, (New York: Brunner-Mazel, 1986), p. 19.
15. *Los Angeles Times*, Monday, December 18, 1989. Metro Section, p. 32, adapted.
16. Michael E. McGill, Ph.D, *The McGill Report on Male Intimacy* (New York: HarperCollins, 1985), p. 176.

CONCLUSION:
USING SCRIPTURE and PRAYER, and MAKING REFERRALS

~~~~~~~~~~~~~~~~~~~~

As you minister to people in all types of crisis situations, you will find this is a tremendous opportunity to lead them to Christ, to help believers become aware of the strengthening power and comfort of the Word of God, and to assist them in the practical application of the Scriptures to their lives. The Word of God can be used in a healthy way to give insight and strength. Or it can be merely tacked on to the person's problem or used to increase guilt and distress.

Sensitivity to Holy Spirit's Leading

It is vital that you be sensitive to the leading of the Holy Spirit concerning when to bring in Scripture and what Scriptures to discuss. Be sure you do not shortcut the person's expression of feelings or grief by bringing in a verse too soon. Sometimes, because of our own anxiety or lack of knowing what to say to some of their angry questions, we rattle off verses indicating, "God is in charge" or "Everything will work out according to His will" or "There is a purpose in your suffering."

Two questions to ask the counselee are: "What passages of Scripture have been of help to you during this time?" "Which passage do you feel would help you right now?" As you discuss a passage with him you might ask, "How do you feel this passage can assist you at this time? Let's talk about what it means to you and how you see it as being useful."

Discovering God's Omnipresence

One of the questions you might hear during a time of crisis is: Where is God in all of this? That is an excellent question. Where is He? He is present just as He was before the problem occurred. If you are asked that question, respond with a question of your own "Where is God for you right now? I hear you questioning where He is, and that is an honest question. We feel abandoned. In fact, you may feel that if God were around this wouldn't have happened." Some counselees may really mean what they say in their question, whereas others are just venting their anger. Let them express their questioning, and do not be threatened by it. You may have asked the same question at times. At the proper time you can respond to the question.

This question raises an important issue, God's omnipresence. This concept is important for you as the counselor as well as for the counselee. You need to realize that during the most painful and difficult counseling sessions, God is there with you as well. And as the counselee is guided and directed to discover and define his difficulty, God is present, working in the person's life.

A person discovers God's omnipresence not by envisioning that God is everywhere, but by recognizing that He *is* there already. This can be dealt with through two means—through the counseling session and through assignments between sessions. The Scriptures dealing with this concept are Joshua 1:9; Psalms 16:11; 23:4; 73:28; 121:1-8; 139:7-12; Matthew 28:20 and Hebrews 13:5.

Understanding God's Omnipresence

The following list contains specific ways to help a counselee understand the meaning of God's omnipresence in his life. The Scriptures can be interchanged in some of the methods. A few of these assignments accomplish the same aim only in a different way, so you need to select the way of dealing with the concept that will be most comfortable for the counselee.

1. Memorize the last part of Joshua 1:9: "For the Lord your God is with you wherever you go." Then concentrate on being more conscious of God's presence by selecting something you always have with you. For example, it could be a watch, a ring, tie pin or a neck chain. Then each time you are conscious of that item, say the verse and know that God is there with you.

2a. Read Psalms 16:11; 23:4; 73:28; 121:1-8; Matthew 28:20; Joshua 1:9 and Hebrews 13:5, and identify the characteristic of God that these verses describe.

 b. Select one passage and memorize it.

 c. Write a paragraph describing what your life would be like during the next week if you were to be more aware of this attribute of God.

3a. Choose a second passage and follow the instructions for 2a and b.

 b. Choose a third passage and follow the instructions for 2a and b.

 c. Write one of these verses on a card, and put it in a prominent place where you spend a lot of time (by the kitchen sink, on your bulletin board, on your desk, on the refrigerator and so on).

4a. Read Psalm 139:7-12 and rephrase it.

 b. List at least 15 different places where you will be this week and write a paragraph explaining how this passage would apply to your life in those situations.

5. Describe your life tomorrow if you were to be consciously aware of God's presence every hour of the day.[1]

Hope in Affliction

The following Bible study on hope in the midst of affliction is from Waylon Ward's excellent book *The Bible in Counseling* (Moody). The best time to use such a study is with an individual person or a group when they are not going through a crisis in order to prepare them for the times when they will experience some of life's problems. It could also be used when the person has worked through some of the stages of the crisis and is open to and capable of seeing his difficulty from the perspective of Scripture.

Read 2 Corinthians 4:7-18 from two or three different translations or paraphrases. Recommended are the *New International Version, The Living Bible, the New American Standard Bible,* and *The Amplified Bible.* After you have read the passage, complete the following questions.

1. What is the "treasure" (v. 7)?

2. What did Paul mean by "jars of clay" (v. 7)?

3. What is the reason that this "treasure" is in "jars of clay" (v. 7)?

4. In verses 8 and 9, Paul listed several feelings of affliction he had experienced or was experiencing. List these experiences.

5. Do any of Paul's experiences compare to the experiences you are having or have had?   Which ones?

6. Paul compared his experiences of affliction with what most people would consider the end result of each affliction. Four phrases show that Paul was greatly afflicted but that he still had hope. List these four phrases below (vv. 8,9).

a. _____ but not _____
b. _____ but not _____
c. _____ but not _____
d. _____ but not _____

7. Paul said we always carry around in our body the _____ of Jesus so that the _____ of Jesus may also be revealed in our _____ (v. 10).

8. Verse 11 says basically the same thing as verse 10. Read these two verses and relate them to 2 Corinthians 12:8-10. Is there a similar message? What would you say this message is to you?

9. What was Paul's hope in the midst of his affliction (2 Cor. 4:13,14)?

10. In verse 16, Paul pointed out that our outer body is _____ away but that we are being renewed _____ day by day.

11. Paul compared our affliction with our hope in verse 17. Write this comparison in your own words.

12. Paul's conclusion was that we should not _____ but we should _____. Because what is seen is _____ _____, but what is unseen is_____ _____ (v. 18).

13. Rewrite Paul's conclusion in your own words.

14. What do you choose to focus your attention on? Are you going to focus on the seen or the unseen?

15. Write a prayer to God expressing what your hope is, in light of your affliction, and telling Him of your commitment to focus on the internal and eternal working in your life.[2]

Help from Scripture

Many Scriptures can be used as you minister to others. Here is a practical list of verses I find helpful. Be sure you take the time to read each verse in several versions and keep it available. The verses are listed for you topically.

Comfort

Psalm 46:7	Psalm 103:17	Romans 8:38,39
Numbers 14:9	Deuteronomy 31:6	Psalm 27:10
Psalm 73:23	Matthew 28:20	John 6:37-39
Isaiah 41:17	Psalm 94:14	

Peace

Romans 5:1,2	Exodus 33:14	Psalm 85:8
Psalm 119:165	Isaiah 26:3	Isaiah 57:2
Isaiah 32:17	Matthew 11:29	Ephesians 2:14
Colossians 3:15	John 14:27	Numbers 6:24-26

Fear

Hebrews 13:6	Deuteronomy 7:21	1 Chronicles 16:25,26
Jeremiah 15:20	Isaiah 41:10	Proverbs 16:7
Isaiah 35:4	2 Corinthians 1:10	Philippians 4:9;
Nehemiah 4:14	Psalm 28:7	Deuteronomy 1:17
Joel 3:16	Psalm 4:8	Psalm 56:3

Anxiety

Matthew 11:28	John 16:33	Genesis 28:15
Job 34:12	Psalm 20:7	Psalm 50:15
Psalm 55:22	Psalm 86:7	Isaiah 41:13
Proverbs 3:5,6	Isaiah 40:11	Psalm 68:19

For Those Who Feel Weak

Psalm 142:3	Psalm 147:6	Isaiah 57:15
Habakkuk 3:19	1 Chronicles 16:11	Psalm 37:10,11
Psalm 72:13	Psalm 55:18	Psalm 62:11
Ephesians 3:16	2 Corinthians 12:9	Jeremiah 10:6

Despair

Haggai 2:4	James 1:12	Ezekiel 34:16
Isaiah 40:29	Isaiah 51:6	Daniel 2:23

2 Thessalonians 3:3	Hebrews 10:35	Jeremiah 32:17
Ephesians 1:18	Psalm 46:1	Psalm 119:116
Psalm 100:5		

Grief

Isaiah 43:2	Psalm 116:15	Revelation 21:3,4
Psalm 71:20,21	Psalm 119:28	Psalm 119:76
Psalm 119:50	2 Corinthians 1:3,4	2 Thessalonians 2:16,17

Times of Trouble

Psalm 50:15	John 16:33	Psalm 121:5-8
Psalm 9:12	Psalm 37:39,40	Psalm 34:7
Psalm 46:1	Psalm 138:7	

Feeling Desperate and Depressed

Zephaniah 3:17	John 10:10	Psalm 126:5
Psalm 30:5	Psalm 34:18	Psalm 40:1,2
Psalm 42:11		

Prayer

Prayer is a very important part of counseling. There will be times when you pray during the session and times when you pray during the week for the counselee. Sometime during the counseling, it might be helpful to attempt to discover the person's pattern of prayer and what he or she usually prays about. Many Christians have not been taught the meaning and purpose of prayer. Teach your congregation the importance of prayer, and help them experience a meaningful and consistent prayer life. It will be a tremendous resource during the crisis time of life.

Ask the counselee, "How can I pray for you at this time?" and "How can I pray for you during this next week?" Be sure you let the person know at the next session that you were praying for him. Many counselees have told me that the only thing that kept them functioning and even alive was the knowledge that they knew one person was praying for them.

Determine Needs

Do not feel you should open every counseling session with prayer. The needs of the person you are helping should determine your prayer ministry.

Ask yourself the question and ask God, "Is prayer a resource that is applicable at this time with this person?" Praying for or leading people into prayer when they are reluctant is not helpful.

During times of stress and crisis, you will be able to discover the person's concept of God. Often his or her prayer pattern prior to or during this time will give you this information. The use of prayer can raise many questions about God. Who is this God that we call on in prayer? What is God's responsibility during life's problems and distresses? What kind of power does God have to relieve a person of distress? Some people find help in accepting their troubles as the will of God. Others refuse to accept this perspective. The book of Job raises many questions that people still ask today. God is involved in every crisis and stress situation. He does care.

Prayer Is Not Magic

Some people feel prayer is a form of magic. They feel that by praying they will influence God to lift the problem and reverse the process. As one person said, "I don't know about prayer and God. When I was sick the last time, I prayed and got better. But this time I prayed and I haven't gotten any better. Where is God?" This is a limited view of prayer and God. Prayer is not just a way to reverse difficulty but a means of giving meaning to what is occurring in our lives.

Some in their prayers will raise the question "Why, God? Why?" This is not so much a question as it is a protest. It is a normal part of working toward acceptance and greater faith in the midst of adversity. Telling a person he should not question at this time, or pointing to another person who never expressed any questions and had such "outstanding faith and trust in God" creates guilt and is damaging. Each of us progresses through the Christian life at a different rate. Faith is easier for some than for others. Protesting to God and raising questions of Him is one form of prayer. Unfortunately, we may not have included that in our definition of prayer. It is helpful to let the person know that his protest is prayer.

Help Counselee Express Feelings

You may find some people who do not want to pray because they say they are bitter and angry toward God. Ask them to imagine God sitting in another chair in the room and telling Him how they feel. As the person does this, you can tell him that what he just expressed was prayer. And God does want him to discuss all his feelings with Him.

As you pray for the person, be careful what you ask God to do. It is important that we ask God for His comfort, His strength, His support, His insight and also that we thank Him for what is going to occur in the future even though we do not know what is going to happen.

I like what Lloyd Ogilvie says in his book *God's Will in Your Life*:

When we are in a tight spot, not knowing what to do, we need to praise God for the very thing which is causing our tension or pressure....Consistent praise over a period of time conditions us to receive what the Lord has been waiting patiently to reveal to us or release for us.

Prayer is not overcoming God's reluctance to guide us; it puts our wills in a condition to receive what He wills for us. It changes our moods and gives us keen desires.[3]

But reaching this attitude and belief is a process, and it cannot be forced upon the person to whom you minister. Through the process of counseling, looking into the Word and praying, you can help the counselee progress. Consider your own beliefs and practice of prayer. Many helpful and practical books aid us and others in this process. One especially good book is *When God Has Put You on Hold* by Bill Austin (Tyndale).

Making Referrals

Many of those who come to you will benefit from your counsel. But some will need to be referred to another professional with more expertise because of the severity of their difficulties. Some of the best counsel you can give is to make a referral. It is a sign of inner strength and security to be able to refer without condemning yourself for your lack of knowledge. Some in ministry feel very possessive and have an inflated perspective of their capability. Knowledge and acceptance of one's ability and spiritual gifts is essential.

Paul said:

Do nothing from factional motives—through contentiousness, strife, selfishness or for unworthy ends—or prompted by conceit and empty arrogance. Instead, in the true spirit of humility (lowliness of mind) let each regard the other as better than and superior to himself—thinking more highly of one another than you do of yourselves.

Let each of you esteem and look upon and be concerned for not [merely] his own interests, but also each for the interests of others (Phil. 2:3,4, *AMP*).

I make referrals to other professional counselors, ministers, lawyers, medical specialists, financial specialists or whoever has the necessary expertise. It is unreasonable to expect every counselor to be able to help in every situation. Our training, experience, and personality are all variables that affect what happens in counseling.

Know When to Refer

How do you know when to refer? One of the most common reasons is that the person in crisis needs specialized assistance that a minister is not able to give. This does not necessarily mean the counselee's need or problem is severe or radical, but it is one that you are not able to handle. Do not convey to the person that his problem is very serious, for this can increase the stress and crisis. Let him know a different specialization is needed.

Another reason for referral is when there may be indications of a potentially serious risk that is beyond your training or expertise. Whenever the counselee's well being is at stake, ask yourself the question: Do I have the time and capability to assist this person? This may be where referral to a professional therapist such as a psychologist, psychiatrist or marriage and family therapist is necessary.

Another reason for a referral is when a counselee prefers a different approach from the one you have to offer. However, this does not happen often with immediate crisis counseling.

If the crisis situation that prompted the person to seek counsel begins to lessen but there is indication that longer-term counseling for the problems is needed, referral may be necessary. Most ministers have not been trained for long-term treatment, nor do they have the time for all those who come in with a crisis.

Finding a Referral

How do you find a referral? You can get personal recommendations from other ministers and from Christian doctors and lawyers. Local seminaries, Christian colleges and private Christian schools also are able to provide referrals. Many communities have Christian business and professional directories that list only therapists who profess to be Christians.

Referrals to Christian therapists may also be obtained from CAPS, P.O. Box 890279, Temecula, CA 92589 (714) 695-2277; Focus on the Family, Colorado Springs, CO 80995; Rosemead Graduate School of Psychology, 13800 Biola Ave., La Mirada, CA 90639; Fuller Theological Seminary and Graduate School of Psychology, 135 N. Oakland Ave., Pasadena, CA 91101; American Association of Christian Counselors, 2421 W. Pratt Ave., Suite 1398, Chicago, IL 60645.

It is perfectly all right to call a therapist or meet the person for purposes of gaining more information concerning his or her approach and beliefs.

Should you always refer someone to a Christian therapist? I agree with Dr. Keith Olson's criteria for selecting a therapist, which are listed in a descending order of desirability: (1) Good therapists who are Christians; (2) Good therapists who are not Christians.[4]

Steps Involved in Making a Referral

What are the steps involved in actually making the referral?

Do your homework. First of all, be sure you have done your homework by gathering all the information the person will need. Location, hours, type of counseling, services offered and financial policies are concerns for the counselee.

The way you broach the subject and handle this discussion will be very important for the referral to be successful. It is easy for the person in counseling to feel either that his problem is so severe and radical that you must refer, or that you do not like him or want to help him, which makes him feel rejected. Your care and sensitivity need to come through here. A casual, relaxed approach is much better than leaning forward with a serious expression of deep concern. A statement such as, "I appreciate all that you have shared with me since it helps me know how much I'll be able to assist you, because I want to help you the best way possible. I think I can help you the most at this time by putting you in contact with a professional counselor who works with these issues and situations far more than I do, and has more training and expertise than I do. How do you feel about this possibility?"

The person may accept this very readily or may seem hesitant and puzzled. He may say, "You don't want to help me" or "You don't want to see me any more."

"No," you reply, "I *do* want to help you and may continue to see you from time to time. But I want you to have the finest help available, and that is why I'm making this recommendation."

The counselee may reply by saying, "But I've shared so much with you and it's difficult for me to share, and now you want me to talk with a stranger."

"I realize that it's a bit scary to begin this process again," you assure the person, "but it took courage for you to come see me and share as openly as you have. I feel you still have this courage and capability to begin with someone who is better equipped than I am. What could I do to make this transfer easier for you?"

Help counselee make personal choice. The counselee then has the choice of accepting or rejecting your suggestion of referral. The person needs to make his own decision. If the person has a serious difficulty—has deep depression, is suicidal, has a physical difficulty, or has been abused—an immediate referral is needed. You may have to be gently insistent by asking the person to go along with your decision and trust your judgment. In a nonemergency situation, ask the person to consider your suggestion and let you know. Be sure you let him know he does not have to accept the referral or the person(s) you are suggesting just to please you. You may want to suggest two or three names if possible.

When the person makes the commitment, then help him with the steps necessary. This can involve having the person make the call from your office, giving direction verbally reinforcing the decision, praying with him about the process or even going with him the first time.

You may want to see the person or call him following his first visit with the new source of help. Let him know you will continue to pray for him and you are interested in his continued growth.

Notes

1. Adapted from a paper by Betty Chase.
2. Waylon Ward, *The Bible in Counseling* (Chicago: Moody, 1977), pp. 111,112.
3. Lloyd Ogilvie, *Discovering God's Will in Your Life* (Eugene, OR: Harvest House, 1982), pp. 136,164.
4. Keith Olson, *Counseling Teenagers* (Denver, CO: Group Books, 1984), p. 239.

APPENDIX 1
CONFIDENTIALITY
and PRIVILEGED
COMMUNICATION

~~~~~~~~~~~~~~~~~~~~~~~~~~~

Laws concerning confidentiality and privileged information vary from state to state for ministers, and even for professional counselors. Most of the time what is revealed to you is privileged information and is held in confidence. But there are a few exceptions. It is important that you check with a lawyer or state agency to determine the laws for your state and when you must inform the authorities because of a difficulty. In some states, some of the courts have determined that if a person intends to take harmful, dangerous or criminal action against another human being, or against himself, it is the counselor's duty to warn appropriate people of such intentions. Those needing a warning may include the following:

1. The person or the family of the person who is likely to suffer the results of harmful behavior;
2. The family of the client who intends to harm himself or someone else;
3. Associates or friends of those threatened or making threats;
4. Law enforcement officials.

   Your state laws may also require notification of law enforcement or public health agencies in situations where indications of suicide, child abuse or sexual abuse are present.

The state of California has very specific laws concerning child abuse and sexual abuse. These laws apply to many who are involved with children including teachers, principals, day-care workers, foster parents, medical doctors, dentists, psychologists, marriage and family therapists, religious practitioners and many others. (Religious practitioner means those ministers recognized by their denomination, organization or religion.)

The law states that any of these people who, in their professional capacity or within the scope of their employment, reasonably suspect that a child has been the victim of abuse shall report the known or suspected instance to a child protective agency immediately or as soon as is practically possible by telephone. He or she shall then prepare and send a written report within 36 hours of receiving the information concerning the incident. And no person who makes such a report shall be civilly or criminally liable for any report required by the stated laws. If a person fails to report an instance of child abuse, as specified by law, he or she will be guilty of a misdemeanor.

Ask an authority or lawyer to go over your state laws with you to explain them and their interpretation.

Recommended Resources:

Levicoff, Steve. *Christian Counseling and the Law.* Chicago, IL: Moody Press, 1991.

Ohlselager, Mosg. *Law for the Christian Counselor.* Dallas, TX: WORD, Inc., 1992.

APPENDIX 2
CRISIS ASSESSMENT SUMMARY

Adapted from: Karl Slaikeu and Ruth Striegel-Moore (1982)

~~~~~~~~~~~~~~~~~~

Name:_____Age:_____Sex:_____

Marital Status:_____Occupation:_____

Name of
Counselor:_____Date:_____

Directions

This questionnaire may be used either as a guide for structuring a crisis intake interview or as a summary sheet to record information gathered from the client, family member, referral source and others. When used as an interview guide, it is important to take a flexible approach, allowing the client to determine the sequence of his/her report as much as possible and to reorder questions in accordance with the client's readiness to discuss various aspects of the crisis.

I. Precipitating Events

    A. What event brought on the crisis?

B. When and where did this event occur?

C. Who else besides the counselee was involved?

D. What similar events have occurred before in the counselee's life?

E. How were these events handled?

II. Presenting Problem
A. What is the counselee's description of the problem(s) at this time?

B. Does this differ from concerns of family members or others?

C. What does the counselee want from you?

III. Crisis BASIC Functioning
Examine the impact of the crisis event on each of the five modalities.

Behavioral functioning: How has the crisis event affected the counselee's behavior? For each of the following areas, indicate the impact of the crisis event:

No impact	Change did occur	Specify
☐	☐	work:
☐	☐	exercise:
☐	☐	use of leisure time:
☐	☐	eating habits:
☐	☐	smoking:
☐	☐	drinking habits:
☐	☐	use of drugs:
☐	☐	sleep:
☐	☐	spiritual life:
☐	☐	control of feelings (e.g., outburst of temper, frequent crying, etc.):

No	Yes	
☐	☐	Indications of aggressive and/or self-destructive behavior:
☐	☐	Are there any specific behaviors or habits that the counselee wants to change?
☐	☐	The client wants to learn a new behavior: The client wants to do *more* often: The client wants to do *less* often: The client wants to stop completely:

List 3 of the client's favorite activities:

1._____

_____

_____

2._____

_____

_____

3._____

_____

On the average, how much time does/did the client spend performing these activities?

Now   Prior to crisis event

1._____hrs./week   1._____hrs./week

2._____hrs./week   2._____hrs./week

3._____hrs./week   3._____hrs./week

Affective functioning: Examine the feelings that are most characteristic of the client at this time in her/his life. (Check as many as apply.)

excited	☐	overwhelmed	☐	anxious	☐
angry	☐	tense	☐	energetic	☐
lonely	☐	cheerful	☐	guilty	☐
happy	☐	restless	☐	comfortable	☐
sad	☐	afraid	☐	bored	☐

numbed ☐   jealous   ☐   exhausted   ☐
relaxed ☐   contented   ☐   other   ☐

What are the situations in which the counselee feels most upset?

What are the situations in which the counselee feels most relaxed?

What situations/events/experiences might make the counselee function better?

What are the situations in which the counselee would be most likely to lose control over his/her emotions?

What feelings would the counselee like to experience more often?

What feelings would the counselee like to experience less often?

Which feelings were characteristic of the counselee before the crisis event?

Evaluate the overall level of physical tension experienced by this client:

☐ ☐ ☐ ☐ ☐   ☐ ☐
completely relaxed   extremely tense

Is the client now taking medication?
    ☐ No.
    ☐ Yes. List drugs prescribed: _____

_____

_____

Other aspects of client's physical health prior to the crisis that were not discussed above:

Interpersonal relationships. The following concerns important aspects of the counselee's relationships with other people.

Does the counselee have close family ties?
    ☐ No.
    ☐ Yes. Specify:

Does the counselee have close friends?
    ☐ No.
    ☐ Yes. Specify

Is the counselee a member in a social organization (church, social club, etc.)?
    ☐ No.
    ☐ Yes. Specify:

Who is currently the most important person in the counselee's life?

What is the impact of the crisis event on the counselee's social relationships (spouse, children, friends, etc.)?

Is the counselee open to accepting help from family or friends?
    ☐ Yes.
    ☐ No. Why not?

Who in the counselee's life might hinder successful crisis resolution?

Describe the counselee's interpersonal style during the time of crisis.
    ☐ withdrawn   ☐ aggressive
    ☐ dependent   ☐ assertive
    ☐ affiliative   ☐ independent
    ☐ rejecting   ☐ other:

Overall, the client describes his/her interpersonal relationships as:

	Satisfying	Acceptable	Conflict-laden
parents	☐	☐	☐
siblings	☐	☐	☐
spouse	☐	☐	☐
children	☐	☐	☐
coworkers	☐	☐	☐
friends	☐	☐	☐
neighbors	☐	☐	☐

Was the quality of any of these relationships different before the crisis event occurred?

    ☐ No.

    ☐ Yes. Specify:

Cognitive functioning: The next set of questions examines how the client perceives and interprets the crisis event.

False	True	
☐	☐	The crisis event threatens the attainment of a highly valued life goal. Specify:
☐	☐	The counselee verbalizes many "I should have" statements. Specify:
☐	☐	The counselee ruminates excessively over the crisis event and/or its consequences. Specify:
☐	☐	The counselee feels responsible for the occurrence of the crisis event.
☐	☐	"It's all my fault..."
☐	☐	"It is not completely my fault, but I contributed to it."
☐	☐	"I am really confused. Maybe it was my fault."
☐	☐	Since the crisis event, the counselee is experiencing nightmares. Specify:

☐   ☐   Since the crisis event, the counselee has
recurring destructive fantasies.

☐   ☐   self-destructive

☐   ☐   homicidal

☐   ☐   abusive toward spouse

☐   ☐   abusive toward child

☐   ☐   other:

☐   ☐   As a result of the crisis event, the counselee
has fearful thought/images about the future.
Specify:

Examine the counselee's self-talk patterns. What self-statements are reported?

Indicate the presence of any of the following:
☐ catastrophizing   ☐ delusions
☐ irrational self-talk   ☐ rationalization
☐ hallucinations   ☐ paranoid ideation

Has the crisis event touched off "unfinished business" (unsuccessfully resolved previous crisis, repressed conflicts, etc.)? Explain.

How has the crisis affected the client's self-image?

Describe any recurring day and night dreams.

What was the counselee's mental picture of life before the crisis?

Other relevant observations:

Appendix 2 may be photocopied for your use.

APPENDIX 3
A CASE STUDY

~~~~~~~~~~~~~~~~~~~~~~~~~~~

To illustrate the process of crisis counseling, I am including a case study I found in another resource. Reading through the situation and the analysis may help you with the process and progression of crisis counseling.

Precipitating Event

Jim wondered about the knock at the door. Who would be out at this time—11:30 p.m.—on a cold December night? Having just finished a busy day in his law practice (interviews with clients, four hours in court, three hours in meetings with staff and other attorneys), he was ready to turn in for the night.

Jim opened the door to find one of his law clerks, Frank, asking if he could come in to talk. As they walked toward the living room, Frank began: "I'm sorry to barge in on you like this, but I've got trouble. It looks like Jean and I are going to get a divorce."

Choking back tears, Frank spoke rapidly about what had happened earlier that evening. Frank's wife, Jean, had said she "wanted to tell him something." After a little coaxing, she confessed that for the last four months she had been having an affair with a man who was a good friend of Frank's.

Not believing his ears, Frank reacted at first with a shocked and dazed look, and then with a series of questions, some of which Jean could not or would not answer. Struggling to keep feelings of hurt from becoming too apparent, Frank finally broke off the conversation and said he was leaving. He then grabbed his jacket, walked quickly out of the apartment and drove away. After driving around for about 30 minutes, Frank showed up on Jim's doorstep.

Frank's first words came out in a torrent, and to hear him tell it, everything, including his marriage, was over. Barely stopping to sip the tea Jim had offered him, he told of loving his wife, not wanting to lose her, but feeling it was inevitable that he would. After all, she was supposedly "in love" with this other man.

Frank and Jean had been married slightly more than three years. They had moved to this community two years ago so Frank could attend law school. Jean had been the primary breadwinner in her job as a high-school math teacher. They had dated each other for about four years in college prior to being married at graduation. They grew up in the same small rural southern community, and attended the state university for their undergraduate degrees. Though each had dated other people in high school, neither had any serious romantic involvement prior to marriage. Both came from devout Roman Catholic backgrounds, though neither had attended church regularly for the past year or so. For the most part, the marriage had undergone few stresses and strains up to this point.

Frank and Jean knew each other quite well before marriage so they had many things in common (e.g., interest in music, jogging, etc.) and felt comfortable with one another. The main concern over the past year for Frank had been Jean's unexpected flirtatiousness with other men at parties. At first it did not bother him, though as it became more obvious, it led to frequent quarrels after social events. At no point, however, did he have any concern that Jean might go any further than talk.

Jim's reaction to Frank's story was to listen sympathetically, interrupting every now and then to paraphrase, or play back what he was hearing.

"I can see how upsetting all of this is for you."

"So you're feeling that Jean has really betrayed you by this."

"You also seem to feel that now that she had this affair, you will never be able to stay together."

Jim listened to what Frank was saying and used Frank's own words whenever possible in reflecting back *what had happened* and *how Frank felt about it.* Frank felt tremendous emotional pain, which he experienced as hurt, feeling as though he was wounded. He felt Jean had betrayed him. He was upset because she had lied to him. He also seemed to be turning much of this crisis back on himself, suggesting he was "no good" because he had been rejected for another man. He saw the whole matter as a reflection on his manhood.

Jim encouraged Frank to talk concretely about how things had been going prior to this news. Frank said he thought their relationship had been a good one. To be sure, Jean's flirtations had bothered him some. Moreover, the two had sometimes thought they might have married too young, allowing for little experience with other people before getting married. Nevertheless, the affair was a complete surprise to Frank.

Frank made few distinctions between what happened in the past, his current situation (that very evening), and the future (beginning with tomorrow, and extending into the next several months and years). Instead, he was combining all of these categories together, and talking painfully of how his whole world was collapsing on him right now. In this case, his "whole world" referred to his marriage, his self-image, his career (I'll never be able to study for the exam I have in two days, and I might fail it"), and the rest of his life (talking surely as if he could never trust another woman again). His self-statements were critical:

"What's wrong with me? Why wasn't I good enough for her?"

"It's all my fault!"

Jim continued to listen, offering empathetic and understanding responses, all in an attempt to offer support and hopefully thereby ease some of the emotional stress of that evening.

Immediate Problems

After about 30 minutes of this kind of talk, Jim directed the conversation toward the immediate difficulties confronting Frank:

Where to spend the night—to go home or not.

What to say to Jean the next time he saw her—if not tonight, then tomorrow.

What to do about the exam he needed to take on Friday—two days away—how to prepare for it when he was so emotionally upset.

Issues to Address Later

Other matters would certainly need to be dealt with at some time, but were out of reach that night. Frank would need to talk to Jean to find out about what the affair actually meant to her. What were the implications for their relationship? Was divorce really the only option? Might they not work through this crisis, learn from it, make adjustments in their marriage because of it, and stay together after all?

Emphasis on Immediate Concerns

Jim's approach was to say straight out to Frank: "Let's see what you need to deal with right now, tonight, and what can wait until morning."

Jim then confronted Frank with the idea that although divorce was certainly a possibility, it was not something he needed to decide on that night. Jim then asked Frank what he would like to do about the most immediate needs he had identified, (i.e., where to stay, how to deal with Jean, and the pending exam).

Possible Solutions

Jim's aim was to get Frank to generate as many acceptable solutions as possible, and, if these were found wanting, for Jim to offer some of his own. In his distraught state, Frank had not separated the issues in this way. He also had no solutions to any of these difficulties. He thought he might simply drive around" and then sleep in the car. He was afraid to confront Jean, not knowing what to say to her, and afraid that he would break down and cry in her presence, giving her yet another reflection against his manhood. The exam increased his panic further. It was a major exam in constitutional law, given on one day only, with very little chance of makeup. Besides, if he were to ask for a makeup he would have to admit to his marital difficulties to a very stern professor.

Focus

Jim continued to work toward condensing the problems into smaller pieces, examining possible avenues for each. He told Frank that the entire problem could not be solved right then, so they would need to take the pieces that needed the most attention and deal with them first. Where to spend the night was the easiest issue to solve. Jim assertively told Frank that driving around was not a good idea and he should stay at Jim's that night, sleeping on the couch. After a little resistance, Frank accepted this idea.

Advice

Dealing with Jean presented a more difficult problem. Frank's chief concern seemed to be that he did not know what to say to her and that he might break down, so Jim took it upon himself to offer a few ideas of his own at this point. He said, first of all, that breaking down was a rather human reaction to this crisis, and that Frank should be careful about passing judgment on his manhood based on something like this. In a friendly, joking manner, he criticized Frank for assuming he had to take a John Wayne approach to the problem (i.e., show no emotion for fear it would be a sign of weakness). Jim suggested that both Frank and Jean see a marriage counselor soon, as soon as tomorrow, and talk in the presence of a third party.

Confronting Obstacles

As they discussed options, such as the student counseling center on campus, the mere mention of a counselor raised other problems for Frank. Would it be confidential? Would seeing a shrink be on his record, possibly something he might have to mention in his application for the state bar? The application had recently come in the mail. Frank had noted there was a question something like: "Have you ever been treated for a nervous or mental disorder"? Frank certainly felt that at the time he was having a nervous and mental disorder, as if he were cracking up. He did not want to have to tell anybody about it, surely not the state bar.

Jim and Frank talked about the issue for several minutes, moving toward an agreement: this would be marriage counseling, and not something he would need to list on his bar application. No one was having his head shrunk by a psychiatrist or anyone else. This would be short-term counseling for working through a crisis. Jim was certain that the records at the student counseling center were confidential. In any case, a decision did not need to be made right then; it could wait until morning. Frank could call the counseling center and ask these questions before setting up an appointment.

They talked about the upcoming exam as well. Frank's chief concern was that he could not concentrate enough to study. Again, Jim reminded him that he would not be able to concentrate tonight, and that he should not try to study. If he needed to ask for an extension, he should ask for one. He would not have to tell the professor all of the circumstances. Again, he could see how he felt in the morning. Though he did not feel like studying now, he might well be able to put in a couple of hours tomorrow afternoon.

The conversation proceeded and Jim helped Frank work toward acceptable solutions to each of the immediate concerns. At times, Frank tried to inject issues about what happened in the past, or about the future (e.g., "I wonder how many times she slept with him," "How long does it take to get a divorce?"). When this happened, Jim recognized that this was a concern (e.g., "I know you must wonder about that"), but reminded Frank that he had time to find out about these things. Nothing could or needed to be decided on right now. The strategy was to articulate that there were concerns but that they did not need to be dealt with now. When they talked again, they would see when, how and whether these concerns would be addressed.

Contract for Action

After an hour-and-a-half talk, Jim convinced Frank that it was time to get some rest. They had agreed that Frank would sleep there that evening and call Jean in the morning to ask if she would consent to their talking with a marriage counselor that afternoon. Next they had agreed that Frank would call the student counseling center to ask for an appointment, and at the same time ask questions about confidentiality. Finally, Frank would put the whole exam question on a shelf until later in the afternoon, after classes, at which time he would try to put in one or two hours of studying. He would call Jim later that afternoon to let him know how things worked out.

Follow-up
Almost as an afterthought for both of them, they realized that Jean might

wonder where Frank was, and whether he would be coming home. Though Frank was reluctant to talk to her right then, he agreed to call and tell her that he had come over to Jim's for a talk, that he would stay there that evening, and that he would call her in the morning. Frank made the brief call, and Jim gave him a blanket and pillow for sleeping on the couch. The two then retired for the evening.

Comment

This case demonstrates how any person can minister during the initial stages of a crisis.

Jim's main response was to listen, and to reflect back what he was hearing about Franks' situation. He responded to the facts (what happened) and his feelings of how he was reacting to it. Jim avoided the usual error of taking sides in the marital dispute: he was careful not to share his own judgment of Jean. Any judgments he offered were about how Frank might cope with his most pressing concerns facing him at that moment.

Dimensions of the Problem

Frank exhibited classic crisis behavior: disorganization, confusion and worrying about everything all at once. This affair shattered Frank's expectations about marriage and the potential for its survival. His panic grew, in part, from his catastrophizing ("this one affair means all we had in the past and might have had together in the future is lost") and over interpreting ("her sleeping with this man must be a reflection on me and my inadequacies"). This is typical. How this crisis affects Frank's values, expectancies and self-image will need to be faced in some way or another as he works through the crisis. If he continues in short-term crisis therapy, this will be at the heart of the working through process of the crisis.

The significance of the affair to each spouse will need to be explored. It is possible it could be examined as a developmental problem in Frank and Jean's marriage, and a discussion might lead to a reexamination of a whole range of issues. As a result, all aspects of their marriage including their sex life to the way they talk to one another, express affection or divide household chores may be addressed. But during the first part of helping the person in crisis you do not give this much attention. It is important to pick up on these cues for use in subsequent sessions.

Though Jim probably understood little of all that was involved in Frank's specific crisis reaction, he used healthy and positive principles of helping. He assisted Frank in sorting through what needed attention right away and what could wait until the next day. He also helped him to take the first steps toward problem solving. As there was no talk of Frank physically hurting himself or anyone else, he did not have to take steps to reduce lethality.

Possible Solutions

The way Frank began the conversation, "It looks like we will be getting a divorce," is very common for a person in crisis. They often begin by identifying one solution or a seemingly inevitable outcome to their crisis. This may be one possible solution to the problem, but the options should not be limited for either the person in crisis or the helper. The better approach is to recognize the solution, state it in words as a possibility, something that may in fact happen (such as divorce), but to generate other alternatives as well. The goal is to keep the person from moving toward simple solutions for complex problems. Jim accomplished this by encouraging Frank to put the divorce issue on hold for now and deal with the most pressing concerns first.

Jim also had to deal with several obstacles to the solutions generated, for example, what seeing a shrink might mean to Frank's career. Throughout, Jim's tactic was to work toward generating possible alternatives. This involved rechecking the various alternatives with Frank to see how acceptable they really were and whether he would be able to carry them out.

Concrete Action

As Jim found himself giving Frank advice on certain aspects of the crisis (not driving around that night, not assuming that divorce was inevitable, not assuming that his own manhood was necessarily in question simply because Jean had an affair), he was actively involved in the decision-making process.

It is important to note that, in each case, the advice given was limited; its purpose was to help Frank calm down, gain time so issues could be examined more calmly, and keep options open.

Frank will need to make his own decisions on several other aspects of this crisis (such as whether he will stay in the relationship with Jean or not).

For now, because Frank's own upset state seemed to be standing in the way of several immediate decisions, Jim gave advice on what to do. Jim attempted to dissuade Frank from making any decisions about the future right then, or drawing any major conclusions about his own self-worth. He was encouraged to wait until he had a chance for marital counseling. All of the advice given by Jim then, was aimed at specific objectives, such as managing the immediate situation, and taking initial steps toward problem solving.

Follow-up

Jim and Frank's agreement to talk to one another over the phone the next afternoon was a very important step. It would also be beneficial for either Jim or Frank to make notes on what Frank would do so he would be able to remember. Too often when the person in crisis walks out the door, they forget what they were going to do. The agreement showed continued interest in Frank's problem, and it built in a check-up system to see if something else might be needed the next day.

At the end of this late night conversation, the three objectives of initial helping procedures had been achieved.

1. Jim provided support for Frank, through listening and talking. He offered further physical assistance in the form of a place to spend the night. Although he could not take away the hurt Frank felt that night, he provided an atmosphere within which he could express his feelings and share them with another person who cared. Frank will need to live with his hurt for a while before its eventual effect on his life is clear. That evening, however, he was provided support from a friend.

2. Lethality was low in this case, which eliminated the need for strong directive action.

3. Linkage to a helping resource was accomplished through the student counseling center referral. Marital counseling seemed the best approach to take to help the couple.[1]

Note

1. Karl A. Slaikeu, *Crisis Intervention: A Handbook for Practice and Research* (Boston, MA: Allyn and Bacon, Inc., 1984), pp. 105-110, adapted.